War, Armed Forces and Society

The politics of
manpower, 1914–18

Keith Grieves

The politics of manpower, 1914–18

Manchester University Press

Copyright © Keith Grieves 1988

Published by Manchester University Press
Oxford Road, Manchester M13 9PL, UK

British Library cataloguing in publication data
Grieves, Keith
   The politics of manpower. 1914–18.—
   (War, armed forces and society).
   1. Great Britain —Armed Forces—
   Recruiting, enlistment, etc.—World
   war, 1914–1918
   I. Title II. Series
   355.2′23′0941   VB325.G7

ISBN 0 7190 2253 3 *hardback*

**Printed and bound in Great Britain
by Billing & Sons Limited, Worcester.**

Contents

Acknowledgements

In the writing of this book I have benefited greatly from the expertise and kindness of many people. During my three years of research at the University of Manchester my supervisor, Mr Alex Robertson, gave freely of his time. I have continued to be deeply grateful for his advice during these past two years of recasting my ideas in book form. I also wish to acknowledge the continuing encouragement I have received in pursuit of the study of manpower from Dr David French and Dr Chris Wrigley. Their work on aspects of the First World War were formative influences on the development of my work. Of course responsibility for errors of fact or judgement is entirely mine. I have cause to record my appreciation of two lively forums, namely, the discussion groups chaired by Dr Michael Rose and others in the Department of History at Manchester and the military history seminar chaired by Mr Brian Bond at the Institute of Historical Research.

For permission to use quotations from copyright material I am grateful to Lord Addison, the British Library of Political and Economic Science (Beveridge mss. and V. Markham mss.), Mr A. J. P. Taylor and the Trustees of the Beaverbrook Foundation and the House of Lords Record Office (Bonar Law mss., Lloyd George mss., F. Stevenson mss. and Pringle mss.), *Spectator* (St. L. Strachey mss.), the University of Birmingham (A. Chamberlain and N. Chamberlain mss.), the Trustees of the Liddell Hart Centre for Military Archives, King's College and Lord Robertson (Clive mss., Kiggell mss., Robertson mss. and Murray–Robertson mss.), Lord Derby, Lady Patricia Kingsbury (French mss.), Lord Haig and the Trustees of the National Library of Scotland, the Master and Fellows of Churchill College, Cambridge (Hankey mss.), Mrs Crispin Gascoigne (Harcourt mss.), the University of Sheffield (Hewins mss.), Lord Long, the Warden and Fellows of New

College, Oxford (Milner mss.), the University of Manchester (C. P. Scott mss.), *The Daily Telegraph*, *The Guardian* and *The Times*. I am also indebted to Mr Julian Amery, Lord Bonham Carter (Asquith mss.), Lord Buckmaster, Lord Croft, Lord Fisher, Lord Geddes, Mr Milton Gendel (Montagu mss.), Lord Ravensdale (Curzon mss.), Mrs Primrose Reynolds (H. Wilson mss.), and C & T Publications Limited (Churchill mss.) for permission to use material of which they own the copyright. Crown copyright material is reproduced by kind permission of the Controller of Her Majesty's Stationery Office and the Cabinet Office. To anyone whose copyright I have unwittingly infringed I offer my sincere apologies. The jacket photograph is reproduced by permission of the Trustees of the Imperial War Museum.

Some of the ideas in Chapters 7 and 8 were first discussed in less detailed form in the *Journal of Strategic Studies*, vol. 9 (1986), pp. 79–95. I am grateful to the editors and publishers for permission to reprint this material. The research on which this book is based was made possible by a grant award from the Social Science Research Council and a Harry Pickles studentship at the University of Manchester.

In the process of completing this book I have appreciated the work of Mrs Penny Cooper, who typed the final manuscript, and Mr Ray Offord of Manchester University Press, who has guided this project to fruition. Finally, I have received immense support from my parents, Robert and Dorothy Grieves, at all stages of the path towards publication. This book is dedicated to them.

                                                                Keith Grieves

Introduction

The study of the manpower problems which faced the British government in the First World War has been dominated by memoirs and theses which have polarised the military, industrial and labour perspectives of the debate by adopting one specific angle of enquiry. Soon after the war the Ministry of Munitions was identified as the main determining authority in the utilisation of industrial manpower.[1] At the same time the flood of military memoirs presented the argument that successive governments failed to provide sufficient supplies of drafts to maintain the British armies in France.[2] For example, some senior officers wrote books as part of their search for a retrospective vindication of their military careers. Such volumes tended to depend on the development of an effective attack on the government's control and distribution of manpower in relation to the Allied offensives on the Western Front.[3] The 'Maurice case' had already publicised this viewpoint and it was represented as the sole area of interest in the whole issue of manpower.[4] Consequently, the theme of manpower provision was either approached from the study of one specific component of the war effort or it was neglected altogether in volumes which considered the condition of British society during the war years.[5]

Consequently, historians have not provided an overall examination of the British government's response to the increasing shortage of manpower as the key factor in the conduct of the nation's war effort. In the recriminations between politicians and general officers the study of successive government's attempts to secure a coherent framework for the survey of manpower needs and the allocation of labour to priority areas of the war effort was lost from view, in favour of emphasising the clash of personalities. The problem of narrow perspectives on this issue is virtually non-existent in the historiography of the Second World War. The Civil Series of official histories included a volume on *Manpower* which adopted a wide perspective of the issue.[6] However the term 'manpower', which was, initially, hyphenated, was invented during the 1914–18 war. Humbert Wolfe, Director-General of Labour Regulation, defined the term as the development of policies which would enable men and women to do the work of one and a quarter or even one and a half persons, and, while increasing everybody's productivity, to ensure that such work was directly beneficial to Britain's conduct of the war.[7] Its widespread use in official memoranda indicated the concern which politicians felt for the social consequences of an industrialised war which required the mobilisation of the civilian population.

The British government's gradual development of interest in manpower was necessitated largely as a consequence of the 'continental commitment' which required the concentration of men and resources on the Western Front.[8] The manpower problem arose and became increasingly severe because, more than any previous war, the conflict of 1914–18 took many forms. Traditional elements of warfare were joined by new developments, particularly of scale, as a result of technological change. Firstly, land battles led to an unprecedented demand for munitions which required the retention of men on vital war production. Secondly, sea engagements included an unrestricted submarine offensive which had an impact on manpower planning for merchant shipbuilding and the home food programme. Thirdly, the war in the air required the creation of an aircraft industry. The purpose of this book is to examine these conflicting aspects of the British war effort in terms of how the government made decisions which led to the allocation of manpower for various forms of war work. It will be argued that the issue of manpower has been too long ignored as a central theme of the 1914–18 war, and in studying it historians could assess more precisely the effectiveness of the British government's management of the war effort. In a war characterised by attrition, manpower supply became the most important aspect of strategic policy, and the domestic as well as the military implications of this form of warfare will be considered in this study. Hitherto, studies of manpower which remained in civilian life during the First World War have been considered only in relation to the expansion of essential war output and the growth of the labour movement. Similarly, manpower conscripted for military service has been examined, predominantly, within the context of Allied operations on the Western Front. Consequently, the perspective offered by this book is an overall consideration of the manpower problem as a crucial dimension of civil–military relations in Britain in the First World War. The substance of antipathy between the War Cabinet and the General Staff, namely manpower, is assessed, rather than placing undue emphasis on the personality clash between Lloyd George, as Prime Minister, and Field-Marshal Sir William Robertson, as Chief of Imperial General Staff.

In Britain the main dilemma which faced the Government in the years 1916–18 was to what extent, and for how long, could manpower be provided in order to maintain the armies in the field, vital war production and the export trade in the prolonged war of military and economic 'attrition' against Germany? Central to this problem of strategic policy was the capacity of the Government to make rapid and effective responses to the manpower requirements of the various components of the war effort. In order to achieve an equitable balance of manpower provision for military and industrial purposes the Asquith and Lloyd George Governments appointed central administrative authorities. These 'co-ordinating' offices were empowered to survey the available field of manpower and make recommendations on the allocation of labour. In this respect at least the element of continuity between the premierships of Asquith and Lloyd George was considerable.

It is the purpose of this book to examine the political and administrative innovations which were initiated in response to the competing military and industrial demands for manpower. In particular, the constitution and work of the Man-Power Distribution Board, National Service Department and the Ministry of National Service will be evaluated in the context of the specific problems of labour supply which these authorities faced during their existence. The ministerial careers of Neville Chamberlain, as Director-General of National Service, and Sir Auckland Geddes, as Minister of National Service, will be assessed. It is hoped that their remarkable periods of office in the First World War will be rescued from the shadow of later political events, as far as Chamberlain was concerned, and from unwarranted oblivion, in the case of Geddes. Neville Chamberlain's unhappy first experience of government office in 1917 was referred to in David Dilks's biography of *Neville Chamberlain*, but the significance of the National Service campaign has remained uncertain.[9] Sir Auckland, later Lord, Geddes methodically destroyed his private papers and his unusual memoir is unhelpful to students of his political career. Only fifty pages referred to his own work and few letters were mentioned.[10] During the war Chamberlain and Geddes inhabited that 'curious and rather neglected world where politics and administration intersect'.[11] Consequently, the origin and implementation of the British government's manpower plans will be examined on two levels. Firstly, to consider the range of political, industrial and military expertise which was available to the wartime governments in the formulation of their response to the shortage of men, usually of military age. It should be emphasised that the problem of manpower existed in direct relation to the range of tasks which befell the military and naval services and the essential war industries. Secondly, to provide an administrative history of the Ministry of National Service and its predecessors in the context of political and military expectations of departments which, at different times, were the nearest approximation to the ideal of a single central authority on manpower. This book contributes to the interest in wartime administration and the 'pattern of interdepartmental competition' which was identified in John Turner's work on the higher direction of the war.[12] It also benefits from the work of Rodney Lowe on the Ministry of Labour, as there were many intersections between that department and the theme and implementation of National Service.[13]

This study of the manpower problem will seek to substantially modify two assumptions which have dominated studies on the First World War, namely the notions of 'total war' and 'discontinuity'. The term 'total war' has been used to describe the impact of compulsory military service in 1916 and the Munitions of War Act of 1915.[14] With evidence of general compulsion, a 'total war' effort has been located yet it is frequently overlooked that a commensurate total war organisation was not available until 1918. Until then the allocation of requisite levels of manpower was not integrated with prevailing strategic plans. A total war effort should include the ability to make effective use of mobilised resources and the existence of a co-ordinating manpower authority which did not arise until the last year of the war.

The other assumption which should be overturned is the identification of 'discontinuity' in the political crisis of December 1916 and the interpretation of the premierships of Asquith and Lloyd George as fundamentally dissimilar.[15] The received view continues to be that the Asquithian images of 'Wait and See', 'Business and Usual' and Cobdenism were banished by the rise to power of a dynamic war leader. Lloyd George's creation of new ministries and a small War Cabinet, it is argued, brought remarkable changes to the British war effort and government policy-making. In historiographical terms this viewpoint was developed in Lloyd George's *War Memoirs* and further embellished in Lord Beaverbrook's writings.[16] The study of manpower reveals the extent of continuity between the governments of Asquith and Lloyd George. In August 1916 Asquith created the Man-Power Distribution Board which concluded that volunteer industrial enlistment should be adopted. Along with universal national service this recommendation was appropriated by Lloyd George as the best means of quickly placing the supply of manpower on a secure basis.

Lloyd George had promised in his policy statement on 19 December 1916 that a dramatic improvement would occur in manpower management. This declaration was central to his image as the epitome of an improved war effort. Other studies have not indicated the yawning gulf which existed early in Lloyd George's premiership between the promise of the efficient distribution of manpower and the reality of mismanagement, dispersed political control and weak administrative structures. *Ad hoc* responses which drew much on the experience of Asquith's government, but did not improve upon it, continued. Instead of arguing that the conduct of the war in the years 1917–18 was entirely unlike 1915–16 this study argues that an improvement in the control and utilisation of manpower – such a basic prerequisite for ultimate victory – only occurred in the last twelve months of the war. *

The framework of this book developed by relating strategic policy to the fabric of national life. Consequently, this book will not only assess the politics and administration of manpower but how the issue, lying at the centre of the war effort, affected the course of military operations, the priority areas of essential war production, the incidence of social discontent and relations with Britain's allies. Most of all, its broad perspective should clarify the Government's response to the increasing shortage of manpower and highlight its changing attitude to competing military and industrial demands for scarce labour as the war remorselessly wore on.

* This was DLG's own conclusion at p. 211 *War Memoirs* Vol I

Notes

1 *History of the Ministry of Munitions*, London, 1922, VI, Man-Power and Dilution; C. Addison, *Politics From Within, 1911–18*, London, 1924.

2 W. Robertson, *Soldiers and Statesmen 1914–1918*, London, 1926; C. F. N. Macready, *Annals of an Active Life*, London, 1924.

3 For example, see J. Charteris, *At G.H.Q.*, London, 1931, entries for 16 December 1917, p. 274 and 27 March 1918, p. 294; H. Gough, *Soldiering On*, London, 1954, pp. 148–157.

4 N. Maurice (ed.), *The Maurice Case*, London, 1972.

5 L. Woodward, *Great Britain and the War of 1914–18*, London, 1967.

6 H. M. D. Parker, *Manpower*, London, 1957, Preface.

7 H. Wolfe, *Labour Supply and Regulation*, London, 1923, p. 1.

8 M. Howard, *The Continental Commitment*, London, 1974, pp. 54–9; D. French, *British Economic and Strategic Planning 1905–1915*, London, 1982, pp. 124–7.

9 D. Dilks, *Neville Chamberlain*, I, Cambridge, 1984, pp. 199–250.

10 A. C. Geddes, *The Forging of a Family*, London, 1952.

11 J. Turner, *Lloyd George's Secretariat*, Cambridge, 1980, p. 1.

12 *Ibid*, pp. 2, 8, 40–2.

13 R. Lowe, 'The Ministry of Labour, 1916–19; a "Still, Small Voice"?' in K. Burk (ed.), *War and the State*, London, 1982, pp. 57–83.

14 M. Ferro, *The Great War 1914–1918*, London, 1973, pp. 120–1; J. Stevenson, *British Society, 1914–45*, Harmondsworth, 1984, p. 46.

15 See A. J. P. Taylor, *English History 1914–45*, London, 1970, p. 109; S. Pollard, *The Development of the British Economy 1914–50*, London, 1960, p. 42.

16 D. Lloyd George, *War Memoirs*, London, 1933–6, II, pp. 1033–7; Lord Beaverbrook, *Men and Power 1917, 1918*, London, 1959, pp. 38–9; see also T. Jones, *Lloyd George*, London, 1951.

1
Building the continental commitment
August 1914–July 1915

In the first twelve months of the First World War Britain's contribution to the Allied war effort was perceived to depend on the effectiveness of its land commitment. On the outbreak of war on 4 August 1914 the enlargement of the British Army for the purpose of maintaining an expeditionary force in defence of France and Belgium depended entirely on the large scale recruitment of men through the voluntary principle. The British 'genius' for improvisation and the remarkable enthusiasm for enlistment among all classes would facilitate the creation of New Armies which would symbolise a nation – voluntarily – in arms determined to eradicate 'Prussian militarism'. Initially, no manpower problem existed because recruitment for the army was entirely unrestricted. Consequently, the importance of retaining skilled men in industry for vital war work was completely ignored. This outlook created a formidable problem which would only belatedly be resolved at a late stage in the war. How could the competing demands for manpower be adequately met and how might clear priorities for manpower allocation be established in times of labour shortage?

Although Lord Kitchener as Secretary of State for War appreciated that a long war of, perhaps, three years duration required unprecedented levels of recruitment, he failed to acknowledge the wider ramifications of the outbreak of war on civilian employment patterns. The most well-known recruitment poster of the war reflected the War Office's viewpoint that all other claims on manpower should be subordinate to the needs of the military war effort. Alfred Leete's poster featured Kitchener's unwavering finger pointing at the public. It first appeared in September 1914 and its significance lay in the instruction 'Join Your Country's Army!' It

was a view of the war effort which accorded with the firm
pronouncements of the Adjutant-General's department of the War
Office. Its circulation and impact was far greater than the generalised message which was conveyed later, in 1915, by Sir Robert
Baden-Powell's poster 'Are *You* in this?' In the scene a nurse,
soldier, sailor, boy scout and munition workers were depicted
labouring for the common cause while a well-dressed onlooker
gazed, hands in pockets, at a united effort from which he felt
excluded and worthless. Class unity was one message yet the
government was unprepared for the other point which the poster
conveyed, namely, that a close interrelationship existed between
economic activity on the home front and the enlargement of the
British forces at war.[1] Such an obvious link would not be discussed
in detail until nearly one year later when declining recruitment
figures led to the start of the debate on the effective utilisation of
manpower.

Asquith's non-party appointment of Lord Kitchener as Secretary of
State for War on 5 August 1914 had the dramatic and desired
effect of depoliticising the issue of military recruitment. Not only
the House of Commons, but also the Cabinet, were unable to
scrutinise the raising and organisation of the New Armies.
Attempts to do so by individual ministers were met by threats of
resignation from Kitchener, which would have damaged the very
process on which information was sought. Kitchener appealed for
batches of 100,000 volunteers on three occasions in August and
September 1914, and authorisation for an increase in the size of the
army in stages of 500,000 men was obtained by Kitchener on 7
August and 9 September. On 12 November a further increase of
one million men was authorised. Throughout this time Kitchener
was usually unwilling to disclose his view on the eventual size of the
armies required for the 'continental commitment.' On several
occasions later in the autumn of 1914 he indicated that his aim was
the creation of a seventy division force, or 1,200,000 men, but the
proposed strength of the British armies in France was not
considered by Cabinet Committee until August 1915. In the first
year of the war clear plans for the regulated increase in the size of
the army did not exist and the effectiveness of this considerable
undertaking depended largely on a process of improvised decision-
making at departmental level.

At the outset the main source of opposition to the creation of New Armies came from the General Headquarters of the British Expeditionary force. Taught to believe in the sanctity of 'limited liability' and suffering acutely from 'short-war delusion', staff officers in the field argued strongly that reserve armies were unnecessary because the outcome of the war would be decided by a grand decisive battle in the opening weeks of hostilities.[2] They argued that Kitchener's 'gigantic experiment'[3] was irrelevant because military victory would be secured by ensuring that the maximum force available was rapidly deployed at the decisive point.[4] Lieutenant-General Sir Douglas Haig, commanding First Army Corps, pithily observed, 'New formations will be no use for two years.'[5] On 15 September 1914 Brigadier-General Henry Wilson, Sub-Chief of General Staff in France, at characteristically greater length, declared,

Can't the b—— fools at home realise that we are fighting ag[ains]t a perfectly glorious army led by real generals & soldiers, & that nothing but the best is of any use whatever. K[itchener]'s shadow armies, for shadow campaigns at unknown dates are becoming a positive danger, as they rob us of good officers & men.[6]

The miscalculation which these comments embodied was recognised by Kitchener as an erroneous interpretation of the strategic task facing Britain, and reinforced his determination to secure full control of the raising of the New Armies. This brief controversy contributed to his instinctive belief that centralisation was the best policy to adopt during the rapid increase in the size of the army.

With the exception of his brief visits to Australia and New Zealand in 1910[7] Kitchener had no experience of the organisation of citizen forces and was aware that legal obstacles existed to the employment of the 'Town Clerk's Army' abroad.[8] In identifying the need for a national army, raised largely in the atmosphere of confidence which Kitchener engendered, the utilisation of the County Associations which administered the Territorial Force was avoided. Briefly Lord Midleton, Secretary of State for War in the years 1900–1903, chaired a committee which co-ordinated the assistance which County Associations provided regarding equipment and accommodation, but this support was curtailed by Kitchener on 11 September 1914.[9] The irony of the problem of raising and organising new recruits, as with other national initiatives during the war, was that the credibility of the task actually depended on the 'just' method of voluntary effort. Consequently, local autonomy and dependence on regional magnates, municipalities and voluntary agencies were more significant sources of recruitment supply than the War Office in the first six months of the war. As the problems of restricted training facilities, limited barrack accommodation and increased billeting became more acute in October 1914, greater reliance was placed on the search for local solutions to chaotic conditions which existed on a national scale.[10]

The blend of voluntary effort and local enthusiasm was particularly pronounced in the formation of 'pals' or 'comrades' battalions in large towns and cities by Mayors, Corporations and territorial dignitaries on the understanding that their maintenance would subsequently be taken over by the War Office. Lord Derby raised three 'pals' battalions for the King's Liverpool Regiment within one week of recruiting commencing through this system on 31 August 1914.[11] Derby had recruited most units of the 89th Brigade which consequently remained in the grounds of his house at Knowsley, Prescot. Although Derby's role as Chairman of the West Lancashire Territorial Association had been circumscribed by Kitchener's approach to the raising of new units for the New Armies, Derby had effectively taken the initiative in large parts of Lancashire by becoming the county's recruiting officer *par excellence*. War Office policy or not, Lord Derby's historic association with the north-west had turned it into his fiefdom as far as recruiting activity was concerned. Elsewhere recruiting work was on a smaller scale, but the relationship with the Adjutant-General's department of the War Office was similar. In two weeks in September 1914 a battalion of one thousand men was recruited from the small valley towns and villages of East Lancashire on the initiative of the Mayor of Accrington. The battalion remained in its home area without khaki uniform or much equipment until the 'Accrington Pals' left for its first training camp in February 1915. 'Pals' could be middle-class too and Mrs Cunliffe-Owen raised a Sportsman's battalion for the Royal Fusiliers in London for which the social qualifications were riding, shooting or walking.[12] Inevitably, some sponsors enjoyed an element of discretion in the appointment of officers which was a social cost Kitchener had to pay for the benefits which were derived from the emphasis given to the local affiliation of the recruit.[13] This problem was one factor which led Kitchener to oppose the establishment of the Welsh Army Corps. His disagreement with Lloyd George on this issue on 28

October 1914 provided the occasion of the first effective criticism of the Secretary of State for War at Cabinet level.[14] In total the recruiting campaign under the 'pals' system raised 172 battalions, including ten in Newcastle and eight in Manchester.[15] By taking on the full administrative burden of raising battalions, local authorities and territorial magnates made a substantial contribution to the development of the fourth and fifth New Armies and indicated still further Kitchener's much weakened powers of control in the face of high recruiting returns.

Underpinning the voluntary recruiting campaign was the propagandist work of the Parliamentary Recruiting Committee. The joint chairmen of the Committee were the Whips of the political parties. At the preliminary meeting on 27 August 1914 at Westminster it declared that the services of MPs should be used so 'that the grave issues of the War should be fully comprehended by the people, and thereby to give a powerful impetus to recruiting'.[16] To that end it made use of technological innovation by acquiring three vans and a cinematograph exhibition. Guidelines were issued by the Committee to political agents on arranging public meetings, but the effect of too many continued to be wasted by the excessive time given for votes of thanks to visiting speakers. By securing the sympathy and help of peers, MPs and candidates, political agents in the constituencies were informed that a high degree of 'local autonomy' could be obtained. They were encouraged to work in conjunction with the needs of the recruiting agencies. Although the Parliamentary Recruiting Committee deferred to the uncertain objectives of the War Office, its proceedings revealed the sense of frustration and gulf in communication which existed between the central authorities and the variety of local recruiting initiatives. 1,068,000 men enlisted by the end of November 1914, but the discrepancy between 30,000 recruits per day in early September and 15,000 recruits per week in mid-October worried the War Office deeply. In part this problem arose because the overall needs of the army remained unclear and such plans as existed were consequently nebulous.

As a result at national level a 'stop-go' approach had arisen due to the lack of available supplies and equipment for the recruits. Kitchener was keenly aware than any slight restriction would have a disproportionate effect on recruiting and cause a serious decline, which had actually occurred by mid-October. Kitchener noted, 'I have held up my finger, and the men are flocking to me in thousands; how can I hold up my hand, and tell them to go back.'[17] One device which provided a notable disincentive to recruiting was the fluctuating minimum height requirement for enlistment. From 5'4" it was raised to 5'6" on 11 September but lowered to 5'3" in November 1914 and to 5'2" in July 1915. Maximum age limits also varied between thirty-five and forty years during the same time. In September 1914 the scheme of deferred enlistment had a far more disastrous impact on weekly recruiting figures. In order to reduce pressure on the over-strained regimental depots recruits, having declared their intention to serve, were required to remain at home until they were called up. Under this scheme recruits were paid sixpence per day but as many men had left their work to enlist the initial level of payment led to cases of acute hardship. Confusion arose because the system received minimal publicity and subsequently Asquith raised the daily payment to three shillings. This administrative procedure failed to regulate the flow of recruits and led to criticism of the Recruiting Department of the War Office for two reasons. Firstly, it was insensitive to the social and economic costs of recruitment for the married industrial wage-earner, which was a reputation which persisted into 1917. Secondly, the impression that fit men of military age were no longer needed reinforced the movement towards a more localised form of recruitment. The rate of expansion of the 'privately-organised' units was difficult to control and duplication of effort occurred in the provision of accommodation and equipment.

In drawing the problem of a downward trend in enlistment to the attention of the Parliamentary Recruiting Committee, the Recruiting Department sought its support as 'the idea had got abroad that no more men were wanted and that it was important to disabuse the public on this point'.[18] Major Gosset, representative of the Recruiting Department, explained on 26 October 1914 that the weekly recruiting level needed to be at 40,000 men instead of 16,000, because a further 500,000 men were required for the army within three months. To meet this requirement the War Office encouraged and approved the 'Householder's Return' canvassing scheme. It was designed to obtain information from men, aged nineteen to thirty-five years, concerning their occupation, height, marital status and number of children. This plan formed the basis of the first 'inquisitorial' scheme which employed 'battalions' of voluntary workers who were to reappear, under varying guises, throughout the rest of the war.[19] In some localities during November and December 1914 the scheme was implemented by house to house calls, which was regarded as a questionable procedure by several members of the Committee on the grounds that privacy was infringed. In comparison few qualms arose over the registration procedures which attended the worsening manpower problem in the course of the following three years. The administrative efficiency of the 'Householder's Return' varied enormously. It fell short of the desired outcome, which was to be able to conclude whether recruiting in each constituency was satisfactory in relation to the size of population.[20]

The returns did little to quell the political debate which surrounded the relative performance of rural and urban areas on recruiting. In March 1915 the Parliamentary Recruiting Committee was dismayed to note that the result of the 'Householder's Return' had still not been disclosed and that it remained 'in the dark' on the further number of men required for the army.[21] With a greater sense of realism the Committee turned its attention to the preparation of new posters which explained the revised scale of Separation Allowances. By June 1915 the Parliamentary Recruiting Committee essentially lacked the guidance and direction it had received, initially, from the War Office. Furthermore, its strength, which lay in publicity activities, was being dissipated through involvement in the Post Office's National Thrift Campaign.[22] For the members of the Committee and 'raisers' of new battalions at large the uncertain political commitment to their work was diminishing public confidence in their voluntary work. The image of Kitchener on thousands of recruiting posters depicted a symbolic 'centraliser' rather than one in actuality. The credibility of the voluntary recruiting effort, with which Kitchener was so closely associated, was being damaged by the undisguised dissatisfaction at the War Office's inability to identify clear objectives, particularly with regard to manpower targets.

In May 1915 Lord Derby asked a pertinent question. To what extent could voluntary enlistment and a localised recruiting machinery maintain the size of the existing British armies in France? He wrote,

I really do not know how we are going to find men any longer for drafts. I hear our West Lancashire Division have had awful losses. Dick Cavendish as you know is wounded & back in London. He is going on all right, but if what

I hear is true, his battalion hardly exists. It went out 1,000 strong & there are only 140 on parade & I hear the St Helens & Warrington Battalions have got most fearfully knocked about. We have come to the end of our tether for voluntary enlistment of that I feel perfectly certain. We shall go on taking enough to keep the force that is now in the field fairly well supplied with drafts but when they get the rest of the 1st army & the 2nd, 3rd & 4th out, I am sure voluntary enlistment will not provide enough men.[23]

By May 1915 and the formation of Asquith's Coalition government this viewpoint was shared by many leading Unionist politicians. However, their paths to the compulsionist position could be quite dissimilar and Walter Long's route was particularly idiosyncratic. As early as December 1914 he had stated,

The Gov[ernment] ought to go in for Conscription based on population & number already join[sic] to Colours: they are drawing the life blood of our Agricultural districts & leaving the streets of some of our towns full as ever of stalwart loafers.[24]

Long's recruiting experience lay in the villages of Wiltshire. His correspondence early in 1915 with fellow Wiltshire landowner and senior Unionist Lord Lansdowne revealed more than anything else his concern for the fragility of rural society in war. Consequently, he misjudged the impact of war as early as 1914 on industrial areas and failed to recognise that the reserves of manpower which were being drawn on most heavily were in northern and midland industrial towns. The abandonment of the territorial basis for new divisions disguised this trend, however many 'Service' battalions were being raised for the Wiltshire Regiment and however many tenant farmers were enlisting in the yeomanry. At an early stage Long had argued that 'stalwart town loafers' should be compelled to join the army 'as they contribute a minimum to the national output'.[25]

   In mistakenly attempting to differentiate between the relative merits of the contribution of town and village to the war effort, Long had arrived at a critique of the problems caused by indiscriminate recruiting. By May 1915 he was the foremost Unionist advocate of a system of compulsion which would allocate fit and unfit men to tasks for which they were best suited in the interests of the nation's war effort. Few Liberal ministers were ready for the thorough revision of the relationship between the state at war and the individual which Long urged, and Asquith continued to impress upon Kitchener the debilitating effect which compulsion would have on national unity and the government's conduct of the war.[26] For Long compulsion, possibly followed by martial law, would serve the need of expressing a commitment to a more organised war effort which he could not find in the existing government. He saw the introduction of compulsion as a cipher for 'firm' government. During the reconstruction of the government in which he became President of the Local Government Board, Long told Asquith,

The real criticism upon the Admin[istratio]n is to be found in the phrase: 'We want to be led; we want to be governed.' In other words, it is time for an autocracy, not for constitut[iona]l government of the ordinary kind, and this finds expression in the adoption of Compulsion.[27]

Long marshalled opposition to the continuation of the voluntary principle as an example of Asquith's 'wait and see' policy because he regarded the system as wasteful on grounds of financial cost and lost production. The high cost of separation allowances suggested that insufficient numbers of single men were enlisting. Also, labour shortages in munition works had led to an elementary form of 'badging' for vital workers which was administered by the employer according to the scale of the firm's war work and was open to abuse. Long's condemnation of the War Office was too frequently unsubstantiated but in August 1915 he accurately concluded,

I don't believe that K[itchener] realises how his Officers work the Recruiting. There is no doubt that every attempt is made to force men; there is no doubt that no regard whatever is paid to any consideration other than that of joining the Army; and the result is that the present system is the most extravagant that we could possibly have.[28]

This viewpoint was amplified and embellished in the *Daily Mail* conscription campaign during August 1915 with results which initially damaged the cause of compulsion. By this stage H. A. Gwynne, editor of the *Morning Post*, was arguing that the adoption of compulsion would demonstrate to France that Britain was determined to play a full part in the war effort, which might otherwise be regarded as inadequate. It would also show to Germany that Britain would wage war until 'permanent security' was obtained.[29]

In the absence of clear support from Kitchener, Unionist politicians found it difficult to demand the immediate introduction of conscription. Long believed that Kitchener felt that parliamentary debates on the issue would lead to a bill so modified that the injustices of the voluntary system would persist in the new procedure.[30] Kitchener was also known to have argued with decreasing conviction that 'it was impossible to graft any form of compulsion upon a volunteer army in the midst of a great war'.[31] However, the essence of his position was that Kitchener was not opposed to the conscription of fit men for the army, but favoured its delay.[32] The New Armies had been raised haphazardly and, consequently, uncertainty about the size of the army had prevailed. In the context of unlimited growth, recruitment to the army had been presented in the form of an urgent priority. Conscription in the first year of the war was politically impracticable and although no real alternative to the voluntary system of recruiting existed, the cost of this approach had been economic dislocation.

Kitchener was becoming aware that in preserving the priority of unlimited recruiting which met the initial military manpower targets, the demand for goods and services necessary for the continental-scale force could not be met by an economy managed on 'business-as-usual' lines.[33] The number of men who enlisted up to the end of July 1915 was 2,008,912 and very little thought had been given to the impact of such a large withdrawal of labour on the economy.[34] Kitchener had sought to uphold unity of effort and his fears concentrated on the contentious nature of two factors relating to the introduction of compulsory service. Firstly, many conscriptionists, such as Long, desired the complete 'direction of labour' in wartime. The trade union movement was implacably opposed to the introduction of conscription in the workplace. Its 'perils' were highlighted in many labour pamphlets including the Independent Labour Party's 'Manifesto against Conscription'.[35] Secondly, Kitchener feared that the introduction of conscription and the establishment of tribunal machinery would provide the occasion for a re-evaluation of the war effort and an assessment of the relative significance of its components.

Even though the Recruiting Department's administration of the enlistment machinery had been far from effective, Kitchener's appeal had succeeded in conveying the message that every fit man of military age should be in uniform. In seeking to turn British society into a nation-in-arms, uncertainty about the eventual size of the army had been a positive asset.[36] Kitchener therefore felt that in resolving this dilemma and introducing conscription the military component of the war effort might be damaged. Conscription would introduce the more equitable distribution of scarce resources which the creation of the New Armies had largely ignored. If a concerted attempt was made to balance the economic and military needs of the nation, Kitchener was concerned that the recruitment of increased numbers of men might prove to be as difficult under a system of conscription as before. Traditional Liberal anxieties about the financing of the war effort, the survival of the export trade and the condition of domestic industry had been raised by the Board of Trade early in 1915 and Kitchener wanted to be certain that the need for compulsion existed before this difficult step was taken.[37] During the autumn months of 1915 he was persuaded that compulsion should be introduced. The declining effectiveness of the voluntary system had rendered it no longer able to replace the high wastage rates on the Western Front and, in particular, the level of casualties which had resulted from the Loos offensive. One year after the war had started a manpower problem had arisen whose dimensions would grow incessantly and whose worsening political and administrative implications would remain with the government throughout the course of the war.

Notes

1 J. Darrocott and B. Loftus, *First World War Posters*, London, 1972, pp. 13, 37, 63.
2 Ferro, *The Great War*, pp. 28–30.
3 G. H. Cassar, *Kitchener, Architect of Victory*, London, 1977, p. 202.
4 V. W. Germains, *The Kitchener Armies*, London, 1930, p. 23.
5 Kiggell mss. I/38, Haig to Kiggell, 4 October 1914.
6 Kiggell mss. III/1, Wilson to Kiggell, 15 September 1914.
7 P. Magnus, *Kitchener. Portrait of an Imperialist*, Harmondsworth, 1968, pp. 293–4.
8 Lord Grey, *Twenty-five Years, 1892–1916*, London, 1925, II, p. 68.
9 Midleton mss. PRO 30/67/25, Letter of dismissal, unsigned, 11 September 1914; Earl of Midleton, *Records and Reactions 1856–1939*, London, 1939, p. 286.
10 P. Simkins, 'Kitchener and the expansion of the army', in I. Beckett and J. Gooch (eds.), *Politicians and Defence. Studies in the formulation of British Defence policy, 1845–1970*, Manchester, 1981, p. 101.
11 Kitchener mss. PRO 30/57/73, Printed pamphlet 'Locally Raised Units'. The entry for the 'raiser' Lord Derby listed eighteen infantry and artillery units, all of which were recruited in Lancashire; Germains, *The Kitchener Armies*, pp. 74–5.
12 *Ibid* pp. 76–7; C. Hughes, 'The New Armies' in I. F. W. Beckett and K. Simpson (eds.), *A Nation in Arms*, Manchester, 1985, p. 106.
13 Kitchener mss. PRO 30/57/73 WS/15, Derby to Kitchener, 29 November 1914; C. Hughes, 'The New Armies', p. 115.
14 E. David, *Inside Asquith's Cabinet. From the Diaries of Charles Hobhouse*, London, 1977, diary entry for 28 October 1914, pp. 203–4.
15 Germains, *The Kitchener Armies*, p. 148.

16   Minutes of the Preliminary meeting of the Parliamentary Recruiting
     Committee (PRC), Add. mss. 54192, 27 August 1914.
17   Quoted in Cassar, *Kitchener*, p. 206.
18   Minutes of the General Purposes Committee (GPC) of the PRC, Add.
     mss. 54192, 21 October 1914.
19   This viewpoint which expressed suspicion at the potential threat to
     individual privacy was expressed by Sir Arthur Steel-Maitland,
     chairman of the Unionist organisation.
20   Of the 4,400,000 householders canvassed, the assumption being that
     they were male, 225,000 promised to enlist. See R. Douglas, 'Volun-
     tary enlistment in the First World War and the work of the Parlia-
     mentary Recruiting Committee', *Journal of Modern History*, XLII,
     1970, pp. 571–3.
21   Minutes of the GPC of the PRC, Add. mss. 54192, 5 March 1915. For
     wider complaints see Lord Lansdowne's attack on secrecy on
     recruiting activities in January 1915, quoted in Lord Newton, *Lord
     Lansdowne*, London, 1929, p. 444.
22   Minutes of the GPC of the PRC, Add. mss. 54192, 25 June 1915.
23   Derby mss. 920DER(17) 33, Derby to Lieutenant-General Sir Henry
     Mackinnon, 15 May 1915, unsigned copy. See also Kitchener mss.
     PRO 30/57/59 WI/32, Esher to Kitchener, 20 March 1915.
24   Gwynne mss. 20, Long to Gwynne, n.d. Gwynne's reply to this letter
     was dated 1 January 1915.
25   Long mss. Add. mss. 62419, Long to Colonel Repington, 1 January
     1915, copy.
26   For example Sir Edward Grey, Foreign Secretary, aligned himself
     with the 'civilian party' in the government. K. Robbins, *Sir Edward
     Grey. A Biography of Lord Grey of Fallodon*, London, 1971, pp.
     321–2.
27   Long mss. Add. mss. 62404, Long to Asquith, 22 May 1915, copy.
28   Long mss. Add. mss. 62403, Long to Lansdowne, 5 August 1915,
     unsigned copy.
29   Gwynne mss. 14, Gwynne to Asquith, 26 July 1915, copy.
30   Viscount Long, *Memories*, London, 1923, pp. 225–6.
31   Newton, *Lord Lansdowne*, p. 447.
32   Cassar, *Kitchener*, p. 445; Magnus, *Kitchener*, p. 334.
33   French, *British Economic and Strategic Planning*, pp. 98–118.
34   PRO CAB 25/95, Enlistments for the Regular Army and Territorial
     Force August 1914 – November 1918. See Appendix 5.
35   See also G. D. H. Cole, *Labour in War Time*, London, 1915.
36   This theme is pursued in Ian Beckett's 'The nation in arms, 1914–18'
     in Beckett and Simpson (eds.), *A Nation in Arms*, pp. 1–35.
37   French, *British Economic and Strategic Planning*, pp. 156–9.

2
Voluntary recruiting and the impact of compulsion
August 1915 – July 1916

In August 1915 the degree of disharmony which existed in the Coalition government on the issue of adopting compulsory powers to achieve an efficient distribution of manpower led Asquith to establish an inquiry into the organisation of recruiting. It was primarily concerned with the eventual size of the army and the capacity of the voluntary recruiting system to maintain the British armies in France. Lord Crewe, Lord President of the Council, was given the difficult task of chairing the War Policy Cabinet Committee which Asquith hoped would facilitate a reconciliation of the divergent attitudes to compulsion which existed in the Cabinet. David Lloyd George, as Minister of Munitions, proposed 'that every man and woman was bound to render the services that the State required of them, and which in the opinion of the State they could best render'.[1] His evidence emphasised the importance of retaining skilled men in the munitions industry but accepted the military requirement of regular drafts of fit men. To meet these twin demands Lloyd George forced the pace of debate by drawing upon his interpretation of the French war effort. His thinking had been heavily influenced by the socialist Albert Thomas who directed the Sous-Secrétariat d'État de l'Artillerie and became the first Minister of Munitions in France when that department gained its independence from the War Ministry in December 1916.[2] Lloyd George believed that a general form of compulsion across military and economic activity existed in France whereby 'you can take 10,000 men away from the trenches and put them into Creussot's [sic] yards'.[3] In fact due to the extremely ruthless mobilisation of all reserve forces, individual employers in the French armaments industry, which required skilled labour, only had access to

rearward army depots for men and did not offset production losses
through universal military service until 1917. Lloyd George used
this confused but unquestioned view of the French war effort to
urge a form of 'National Organisation' which would transcend the
competing military and civil demands for manpower in Britain.

Unionist members of the War Policy Cabinet Committee took
Lloyd George's intervention as their cue, and resisted Crewe's
attempt to conciliate the military and industrial spheres of the war
effort. In his evidence Reginald McKenna, the Liberal Chancellor of
the Exchequer, had contended that Britain could not afford to
recruit and equip an army of more than fifty divisions.[4] A Supplementary Report signed by Austen Chamberlain, Lord Curzon, Lord
Selborne and the Liberal Winston Churchill, which overshadowed
Crewe's general statement, concluded that it would be possible to
arm, supply and maintain an army of seventy divisions in 1916 and
fulfil all other obligations to the Allies, provided that compulsory
military service was introduced and a proper system of selection of
men for military service was established.[5] Consequently, the
signatories of the Supplementary Report, who all supported Kitchener's demand for seventy divisions, also advocated 'National
Organisation'. They acknowledged that this level of military
commitment to the Allied war effort could only be maintained in
1916 by conscription and the development of effective administrative machinery.

The close identification of the demand for a large army with the
call for an effective organisation of manpower for military purposes
encountered immediate opposition from A. J. Balfour, First Lord of
the Admiralty. He questioned the figure of seventy divisions which
the French government had been led to expect would be the
eventual scale of the British military commitment on the Western
Front. From the Admiralty's perspective and after a reading of
naval history since the Spanish Armada, he was critical of the new
found readiness with which Britain judged its contribution to the
Allied war effort solely in terms of armed men. He noted, 'In truth,
we are making in this war the same kinds of contribution to the
cause of our Allies as we have in all our great wars since the days of
Queen Elizabeth, namely: ships, money and soldiers.'[6] Balfour
emphasised that the factors had been noted in their order of
importance and, consequently, the army was third in his scale of
priorities. In direct opposition to Lloyd George's wide-ranging

proposals for the control of labour in wartime, Balfour earnestly desired to avoid the situation whereby the government would assume responsibility for deciding what task each man ought to do for the state.

Clearly viewpoints accorded more closely with ministerial responsibility than with party label. The tension within the Cabinet on this central issue was generally exacerbated by the dependence on statistical information of different departmental origin. Most of the discussions which took place in the summer of 1915 between the Board of Trade and the War Office on the future of the export trade and the size of the army were rendered meaningless by the use of separate data. This problem was overcome by the National Register which was implemented by Walter Long as President of the Local Government Board.[7] With hindsight this canvass of all men between the ages of nineteen and forty-one years who remained in civilian life has been identified as the first step towards compulsory military service. However, there was an urgent need to place all debates on a sound statistical basis, which became possible in September 1915 as the results of the National Register were made available to the relevant departments. So great were Kitchener's misgivings that he initially argued that this examination of the nation's manpower had delayed the recruitment of more men for the army. He cited his recent military conversation with Marshal Joffre who had stated that 'he did not know where to turn to supply the men he requred, and that they were not available in France'.[8] However, when the provisional figures of the National Register were made available, the War Office was clearly encouraged in its efforts to recruit as many men as it could for the military operations planned for 1916 in the face of continued opposition from Walter Runciman, President of the Board of Trade.

The Report of the Registrar-General's Committee estimated that the number of men still available for military service in England and Wales was 1,413,000, after allowing for men reserved for the essential war, domestic and export industries.[9] The Committee advised that this figure should be regarded as an upper recruitable limit, though, inevitably, the War Office viewed the figure as exactly the number of men that the army should be allowed to recruit in 1916. In a short memorandum Walter Long indicated that the number of men available in Scotland, on the same basis, was 150,000.[10] He further noted that by raising the age limit for military service from forty-one to forty-five, dispensing with the luxury trades and encouraging large numbers of women to replace male labour, the number of men available for recruiting in England and Wales could be raised to 1,500,000.[11] Consequently, the Registrar-General's figures had swiftly become the basis on which Kitchener requested a weekly recruiting level of 35,000 men up to 31 December 1915 to maintain a vast field army of 1,400,000 men, whereas for the seven weeks ending 14 August 1915 the average number of men enlisting each week was only 19,000 under the voluntary system.[12] Due to this exaggerated requirement for fit men of military age, Lord Derby's scheme of attestation, in a final effort to improve the weekly recruiting figures through voluntarism, came under immediate pressure from the General Staff in France. On 5 October 1915 Derby was appointed Director of Recruiting to initiate a 'group' or 'Derby scheme' which was designed to secure pledges from single and married men, between the ages of eighteen and forty one years, that they would join the army when they were called on to do so. This would occur in two groups, each sub-divided into twenty-three age classes, so that the younger single men were called up first and no married men were required to join the army until all single men had enlisted.[13] This scheme was based on the information gleaned from the National Register. The casualty levels incurred by the British armies in France during the Loos offensive of 25 September to 8 October led to both Kitchener and Asquith acquiescing in a scheme which put a limit on the future existence of the voluntary recruiting system. Although 650,000 of 1,000,000 unmarried men who were 'available' for military service failed to register, almost 1,200,000 men had either enlisted or attested by 24 December 1915.[14] Consequently, Kitchener agreed with Unionists that the large unattested number of unmarried men would have to be compelled to enlist, for which government legislation would be necessary.

In fact the end of the voluntary system did not occur because an insufficient proportion of single men refused to attest. It failed simply because the demand for 35,000 recruits per week was a grossly inflated target which any system in an industrial society after sixteen months of war was unable to meet. Walter Runciman had correctly insisted that the upper recruiting limit of 1,400,000, following the National Register, would not be feasible in practice because twenty per cent of the industrial male population of military age had already enlisted. He had therefore argued that in order to maintain essential trades and exports the number of men available for recruiting should be reduced to 1,200,000.[15] In the short-term the different interpretation of statistical information from the National Register between the War Office and the Board of Trade was not resolved. Furthermore, this controversy highlighted the absence of any effective co-ordination of the demands of major departments for manpower from the remaining, non-essential, labour in civil industries. Differences of opinion on the role of the state in relation to the organisation of manpower continued to indicate the existence of a schism within the Coalition government. If A. J. Balfour was concerned that the many practical difficulties of military conscription, such as indiscriminate enlistment, would dislocate the war effort, Walter Long was just as firmly convinced that voluntary recruiting impaired the government's ability to organise the available labour to prosecute the war effort effectively.

Lieutenant-General Sir William Robertson, Chief of Imperial General Staff, shared Long's view that the necessity for co-ordinating the work of departments which employed labour on a large scale was as important as legislation to conscript men for the army or redirect men from the luxury trades to essential industry. He wrote to the newly-appointed commander of the British armies in France, General Sir Douglas Haig, on the last day of 1915,

There has been no co-ordination of the different departments. I have been working up to 70 Divisions. L[loyd] George has ordered material for 100 Divisions. The Chancellor of the Exchequer did not till yesterday know either of these things. Now he says the money will not run to it and I do not think it will.[16]

Robertson told Haig that the uncertain military outlook and the inability of the government to decide what force they could maintain had ensured that no intelligent plan had been formulated for using the available manpower in the first eighteen months of the war. By January 1916 the War Office demand for the size of the army to be increased and the forecast by the Board of Trade on the number of men that could be spared for military service, without the severe dislocation of trade and industry, had not been reconciled. In fact Robertson put further pressure on the Government in arguing that the military operations in 1916 would mark the critical stage of the war. As one of very many to propound this theme Robertson was an influential figure. He noted that 'it is therefore encumbent on us to fulfil the expectations of our Allies and put all our forces in the field with the object of inflicting serious reverses on Germany by the vigour of our operations'.[17] In order to emphasise the argument that Britain's military involvement on the Western Front should now be substantially increased the Secretary of State for War drew a comparison with the French war effort. It was a statistical exercise which was repeated at regular intervals throughout the rest of the war and was a simplification of the meaning of the allied war effort which was to no country's advantage. Kitchener noted that France maintained 108 divisions with a population of 39,500,00 and on that analogy Britain should maintain 131 divisions in the field.[18] He made no allowance for the manpower which was required for the Royal Navy and the merchant fleet, and it was remarkable that this comparison of the military war efforts of Britain and France continued to be drawn by Lord Kitchener in 1916. He feared that the thirteen divisions which were being formed in Britain would not take their place in the field because their units would be absorbed into the fifty-four divisions already overseas. Kitchener concluded that it was unacceptable to reduce the force of sixty seven divisions or cut Britain's financial assistance to the Allies. In effect Kitchener told the Treasury that neither option need be taken because the fiscal situation could be relieved by making savings in other areas of expenditure, such as local government.

Although military conscription for single men had been conceded, firm adjudication was needed to resolve the continuing differences between the War Office and the Board of Trade on the utilisation of manpower. In January 1916 a Cabinet Committee on the Co-ordination of Military and Financial Effort was established comprising Asquith, Austen Chamberlain, who was Secretary of State for India, and Reginald McKenna. It heard evidence and received written statements from the departments concerned most directly in the war effort as employers of labour. The Board of Trade calculated that 1,250,000 men could be spared from trade for military service in 1916, which reflected the impact of the National Register's figures on the department, for at the time of the War Policy Cabinet Committee its estimate was no higher than 800,000. The papers which Walter Runciman submitted to the Committee during January 1916 reflected the acute concern of his department about the intention of the War Office to request the withdrawal of 250,000 men per month from industry for service in the army.[19] Runciman agreed that the Committee was correct to assume that the withdrawal of labour from industry on such a large scale would not result in a 'terrible industrial crash', but he warned the Committee about the potential impact and deleterious effect on national finance, the solvency of individual traders and the reaction of the labour movement. The Board of Trade indicated that it should direct the 'calling up' of men for the forces by exercising supervision over the sources from which men were to be taken each month. Runciman foresaw a tremendous risk in the accelerated pace of 'calling up', which could only be attempted 'provided we can watch the pressure gauge week by week and immediately slide down to a slower rate of enlistment no matter what be the number of divisions in the Army if grave industrial dangers heave in sight'.[20] On this basis the Board of Trade recommended a general scheme which, under its supervision, would balance the claims of the various industries to retain labour. It would instruct local Tribunals and Recruiting Advisory Committees to adhere to national guidelines established by the Board of Trade. However, the War Office was suspicious of any action that would impair the freedom of action of the local Recruiting Officers, particularly by a scheme administered by a civil department.

Runciman's recommendations on the co-ordination of the military and financial war effort were received by Robertson with deep misgivings. He was particularly hostile to ministers who sought to maintain pre-war trading relations, where feasible, or who had a record of political opposition to conscription. Robertson observed that the

attitude of some ministers is rather to find out what is the smallest amount of money and smallest amount of men with which we may hope, some day, to win the war, or rather not to lose it, whereas the proper attitude is to see what is the greatest number of men we can put into the field in the shortest possible period of time.[21]

In presenting his evidence to the Cabinet Committee Robertson's two uncompromising objectives were that none of the existing divisions should be scrapped, and the offensives planned in conjunction with the French armies should not be delayed. He was deeply suspicious of the presence of Asquith and McKenna on the Committee and he found the compromise formula which the Cabinet Committee produced on 4 February 1916 most unsatisfactory.

The main problem which the Committee had considered was the future of the thirteen Territorial divisions in Britain which were under strength but intended for France. To bring the divisions up to strength or not to, symbolised the gulf which existed between the proponents of a dominantly military or financial war effort. The Committee examined the feasibility of a sixty-two division scheme by which the fifty-four divisions in, or about to be sent to, France would be joined by eight of the thirteen Territorial divisions when they had been brought up to full strength and provided with reserves. The remaining five Territorial divisions, whose existence had been consistently overlooked by Kitchener, would be used for Home defence. The Committee calculated that the number of men that would be required to complete and maintain a field force of sixty-two Divisions for the period January to September 1916 was 1,366,000.[22] Again this new number of men required for military service was set at an unrealistic level in view of the condition and organisation of manufacturing activity in Britain. The Cabinet Committee on the Co-ordination of the Military and Financial Effort acknowledged the Board of Trade's conclusion that 1,275,000 men could not be spared from industry, 'without considerable dislocation of trade and reduction of exports'.[23] Furthermore, the Report noted that it was questionable whether the administrative innovations introduced during the 'Derby scheme', namely the tribunal system and the revised medical boards, would be able to operate rapidly enough to release even 100,000 men per month from industry. To have suggested any diminution in the size of the field force and reduced the scheme from sixty-two divisions to fifty-four divisions, which was much nearer the level of military commitment that was acceptable to the Treasury, would have been rejected by the War Office, which was ever mindful of French expectations with regard to Britain's commitment to the Western Front as the main theatre of war. Consequently, in theory, the sanctity of the sixty-two division scheme was preserved but, in practice, the Cabinet Committee accepted that it would be undermined by the improbability of the timetabled arrangements being carried out according to schedule. The army was extremely unlikely to recruit sufficient men in time for the sixty-two division scheme to be at full strength in France in June 1916. Munitions production would be maintained and the strain on the available labour in industry substantially reduced.

The pattern of recruitment in the first quarter of 1916 accorded closely with the conclusions which had been reached at Cabinet level in January. Lord Lansdowne joined the Cabinet Committee on the Co-ordination of Military and Financial Effort and it produced a Second Report in April 1916. As expected the Territorial divisions which had remained in Britain in January had not crossed the Channel as early as Haig wished. The timetable for the reinforcement of the British armies in France had been disrupted because the recruiting level was far lower than even the Cabinet Committee had expected. Despite the introduction of compulsory military service for single men in January 1916, on the evidence of three months' recruiting it was anticipated that 545,000 men would be secured for the army in the months January to June 1916 compared to the original demand for 967,000 men.[24] In July 1916 there were sixty British divisions in France, of which nineteen had arrived since the beginning of the year.[25] The plans for the rapid enlargement of the British armies in France had not been obstructed by civil departments. The factors which most strikingly explained the failure of the War Office to recruit the men it required were, firstly, the absence of a general plan of co-ordination and, secondly, the newly established tribunal system which conducted local investigations of industrial labour without sufficient advice and supervision from the Coalition government.

During this initial phase of military conscription Asquith's War Committee, or Cabinet, did not assume any direct control over the utilisation of the nation's manpower, which remained divided between the Admiralty, Board of Trade, Home Office, Ministry of Munitions and the War Office. An early attempt to co-ordinate the military and industrial demands for men by a manpower committee chaired by Lord Lansdowne dissolved in February 1916, when an attempt to reconstitute it on a permanent advisory basis collapsed.[26] In addition, the tribunal system, which considered applications for exemption from military service, was adversely compared to similar administrative machinery in France. Lord Esher erroneously claimed that in France the replacement of male with female labour in agriculture had been conducted under the auspices of tribunals which responded more directly than in Britain to the needs of the War Ministry.[27] Meanwhile Derby continued to criticise members of the War Committee who opposed the more stringent investigation of industry to provide more men for military service.[28] Despite compulsory military service, albeit in gradual stages, no progress had been secured towards the creation of an effective central authority to distribute manpower in relation to the requirements of sections of the war effort. The army was still being enlarged and the War Office still believed that all fit men of military age should be enlisted into the army.

During the campaigns of 1916 the British military involvement on the Western Front constituted the sole reason for the legislative measures taken on the issue of manpower and, as such, were in stark contrast to the complex patterns of demand for labour which increasingly threatened the dominant position of the War Office. In March 1916 Robertson noted that the number of infantry abroad was 78,000 men below establishment. He complained to the similarly-minded Duke of Connaught that employers and the Ministry of Munitions were failing to release men for military service. He wrote on 5 April 1916, 'We are in great trouble at present because we cannot get the number of men we want. I am giving the Government no peace on the subject and intend to give them none. But they are very difficult people to deal with.'[29] For example, the intake of men during March 1916 barely replaced 'normal wastage' in France and certainly had not increased the available reserves.[30]

However, the fault for the deteriorating recruiting situation lay with the War Office. It had accepted the calculations on casualties which had been projected by the General Staff of the British armies in France. A maximum 'wastage level' of nine per cent per month was forecast for the period April to September 1916, but the General Staff had already imposed on the Cabinet Committee in January 1916 an unacceptably high level of 'wastage' of 123,000 per month. As a result of this figure only in May and June 1916 did the monthly supply of recruits from all sources rise above the recognised 'wastage level'. Yet the total number of men that enlisted during the year was as high as 1,138,070 by December 1916. The War Office remained dissatisfied with the recruiting returns throughout 1916, whereas it should have expressed some satisfaction that over one million men joined the army in the first full year of compulsory military service despite the many administrative problems. Privately, the Chief of the General Staff in France, Lieutenant-General Sir Launcelot Kiggell, had admitted the impact of a higher than expected level of casualties on the reinforcement of the British armies in France. In March 1916 he wrote to the army commanders that 'the numbers coming out as drafts have increased appreciably since Macready has been home, but, unfortunately, so has the wastage, so that the net gain is not great'.[31] Sir Nevil Macready returned from France and became Adjutant-General at the War Office on 20 February 1916. Robertson thought highly of Macready's expertise on manpower management in France[32] and as early as March 1916 the new Adjutant-General had written to Kitchener, now with much reduced powers, 'urging the formation of one central authority, who alone would be responsible for the distribution of national man-power'.[33] This theme was developed by Macready in his first few months as Adjutant-General, while Robertson attended to the delicate task of urging the War Committee to reconsider the military manpower position.

Robertson was under considerable pressure from Haig to impress on the War Committee the adverse effect of a reduced infantry establishment on the military plans for the Western Front. The characteristically Asquithian forum for this debate was the Cabinet Committee on the Size of the Army which held its only meeting on 18 April 1916. Unlike the Cabinet Committee on the Co-ordination of Military and Financial Effort it was attended by all the senior members of the government and advised by Robertson and Macready. This meeting was more significant for the content of the main contributions to the discussion, than for the conclusions which were reached. The anxiety expressed by military participants reflected the problem of consolidating the military war effort at a specified level and the meeting was also remarkable for the minimum amount of collaboration which appeared to exist between 'labour-employing' departments. Robertson informed the meeting that the sixty-two division scheme had collapsed and that fifty-seven divisions were now abroad and ten divisions were in Britain. Lloyd George's forceful assessment that Britain should place the maximum force available in the field dominated the proceedings. He did not argue that military victory could be won in 1916, but that German reserves on the Western Front should be reduced through offensive activity which would enable the Russian army to achieve success in 1917 and create the conditions for an Allied advance into Germany.[34] In his memoirs Lloyd George developed the theme that Russia was 'tottering' during 1916, which did not accord with the great reliance he actually placed on the capacity of the Russian armies to take the initiative on the Eastern Front in the spring of 1917.[35] Lloyd George therefore supported

the War Office's call for the compulsory enlistment of married men
of military age which marked the major outcome of this Cabinet
Committee. When introduced in May 1916 this development
represented a further step towards the form of 'national organisation' desired by the military authorities, despite Arthur Henderson's contention, as the sole Labour member of the government,
that the rapid mobilisation of the French war effort had only been
possible with British money, coal and steel.

However, the Cabinet Committee on the Size of the Army was
shocked to learn that the total number of men in khaki in Britain
was 1,327,000 which included a Home Army of 350,000.[36]
Balfour observed that the size of the force allocated to Home
Defence was far too large and Henderson maintained that men
must be returned to their civil occupations, particularly if munitions production could be increased.[37] Kitchener stated that, 'If a
number of young men were seen walking about in plain clothes it
was a visible contradiction to the policy of the Army Council to
obtain the services of every man.'[38] This view was more appropriate to the circumstances of raising the New Armies. It reflected
the continuing determination of the War Office to supervise
manpower supply on the assumption that the war on the Western
Front was the sole factor which would determine success or failure
in the conflict against Germany. Following the astonishing revel-
ation about the size of the home forces, tentative, and abortive,
enquiries were made by civil departments about the distribution of
general service men in France. Information was not readily available on this subject in 1916 and the government had little knowledge of the extent to which military administration and supply
services in the British armies in France were extravagantly manned.
The only pressure on the General Staff at General Headquarters
(GHQ) to reallocate personnel in France during the first half of
1916 came from the War Office in March. Robertson requested
Kiggell to reduce the number of category 'A', or general service,
men in work on the lines of communication, which could be
undertaken by garrison battalions.[39] Kiggell replied that Haig
wished to avoid dismantling divisional and specialist units, such as
medical and transport services, which, he argued, were unlikely to
provide a significant source of supply of drafts for the infantry.[40]
The Chief of Staff in France believed that the remedy, namely of
increased recruitment, lay with the government. In so doing he

reflected military high command's perception that the army's demand for men was the only substantial claim on the nation's manpower supply.

In July 1916 Macready wrote a review which expressed alarm at the competitive element of the manpower situation as civil industries sought to retain skilled labour in essential war work.[41] The Admiralty, Home Office and Ministry of Munitions were all criticised for retaining fit men of military age in the shipbuilding, coal mining and munitions industries. From a narrow perspective Macready noted that the new gun and aeroplane programmes would reduce still further the supply of recruits for the infantry. He also argued that the expansion of the Royal Artillery and the Royal Flying Corps should not be allowed to affect the recruitment of one million men in the period July 1916 to June 1917. The Adjutant-General put forward the view that sufficient labour for the military and industrial requirements could be found provided that a four-point plan was implemented. These four factors reappeared in various guises throughout the rest of the war.

Firstly, he urged that foreign labour should be used to release men in industry for military service. This idea was a constant feature of the manpower problem, but only occurred on a limited scale in the raising of labour units for work in rearward areas on the Western Front. Secondly, Macready suggested that the Home Army should return men to civil industry who were unfit for service in France or for garrison duties. The size of the army in Britain posed a continuing dilemma for the War Office because it suggested that reinforcements for France could be found from within the Home Army. At the same time, as Kitchener had persistently argued, to release men for industry would reduce the impact of the appeal for more men to enlist in the army. This dilemma was partially overcome by the inefficient utilisation of men from the Home Army for agricultural and transport purposes in the last two years of the war. Macready's third point was that a definite decision should be reached on which trades were to be 'sacrificed', so that all men of military age could be withdrawn from them. This recommendation was not acted upon until 1917 and 1918 when Schedules of Protected Occupations were continually revised to raise the minimum age levels of skilled men in selected industries. Linked to this notion was the fourth point which urged that exemptions granted by tribunals and employers should be progressively withdrawn from men under thirty years of age.

Macready's series of demands illustrated the extent to which the War Office sought to reinforce its case for the concentration of all suitable manpower on the Western Front. The Adjutant-General's suggestion of methods by which enlistment could be increased indicated the extent of the government's abnegation of powers to supervise the provision of labour in favour of the authority of the War Office. In his criticism of departments who protected or 'badged' their skilled workers, Macready drew attention to the complete lack of administrative machinery to distribute the available manpower supply or establish clear priorities areas in the war effort in relation to the prevailing strategic situation. He viewed the programme for increased gun output with suspicion as the realisation dawned that additional labour would be required in coal and iron-ore mining, pig-iron, optical glass and motor transport production rather than in the provision of more divisions for service in France. By August 1916 the clash of interests in the distribution of manpower between the military authorities and the munitions industry had become too acute for either side to ignore.

Stephen Tallents, Director of Badges and Exemptions at the Ministry of Munitions, noted 'The story of my year with the Ministry was a tale of a struggle against the War Office to secure an initial immunity from conscription for men who held badges.'[42] In particular, the most contentious issues which had arisen between the two departments were the military requirement for skilled engineers and the release of men from the army for civil industries. In July 1916 the Ministry of Munitions and the War Office had made an agreement whereby the munitions industry would make up any deficit which might occur in the preliminary military demand for artificers for the technical corps of the army, despite the fact that 25,000 more skilled men were required for essential war production. The Ministry of Munitions firmly believed that

There appears to be very little doubt but that the War Office could get all the men they want if they combed the Armies thoroughly and systematically; and I think that they ought to help themselves before coming down on us for men, and before refusing to give us specified men that we have asked for as long ago as three months.[43]

When Lord Kitchener died in July 1916, Lloyd George became Secretary of State for War and he was succeeded by Edwin Montagu as Minister of Munitions. Montagu informed Lloyd George that pig-iron production had fallen in the first two weeks of August 1916 and the munitions industry required thousands of men for its existing and renovated blast furnaces, coke ovens and steel works. He concluded, testily, 'The matter is really most serious, and I do wish that the A[djutant] G[eneral]'s Department would indicate a more practical realisation of the state of affairs.'[44]

Conversely, the Adjutant-General's department was irritated by the enquiries about the release of men from the army who were required for skilled work in essential war industries. It had been suggested to the Director of Recruiting, Brigadier-General Auckland Geddes, that men suitable for blast furnace works who were being called up might be returned to industry.[45] However, the Army Council directed Geddes that men fit for general service should be taken into the army. In addition to the continuing problem of recruitment from munition works Christopher Addison, Parliamentary Secretary at the Ministry of Munitions, had a further cause for dispute with the War Office. On 7 June he had reached an agreement with the Adjutant-General that 2,200 skilled men should be returned to their firms. By 22 August the men had still not been released by the army. Macready retorted, 'I do not think that either you or the people who bombard you [with enquiries], have any conception of the amount of time it takes in most cases to trace, and after tracing, to push through the release of the men for munition work.'[46] Most plans to release men from the army during the First World War were severely hampered by the fact that the Adjutant-General's department at the War Office, having obtained men for service in France, did not exercise any control over the placement and utilisation of men on the Western Front. Throughout the war the General Staff of the British armies in France rarely agreed to the return of men to civilian life in Britain, unless Haig came under very heavy pressure from the government. Macready's department did not maintain records on men in France. Consequently, he could only inform Addison that men were slowly being released from the Home Army. In fact, as Stephen Tallents concluded, the War Office and Ministry of Munitions continued to 'act more or less independently and largely without knowledge of each others needs'.[47]

While attempting to meet the requirements of an army of 1,400,000 men in France, Macready did not accord a high priority to the return of selected men to civilian life and vital war work. He had already considered the practicality of demanding the creation of a Board which would supervise the distribution of manpower. However, it was the necessity to replace the first of almost 500,000 British casualties suffered in the campaign of attrition on the Somme which led the War Office to seek some form of co-ordination machinery for the allocation of labour. The Somme offensive had immense manpower implications which were difficult for the War Office to comprehend in the first two weeks of the advance in July 1916. It had failed along most of the fifteen mile British front to penetrate the German defence system and losses were appallingly heavy because the advances had taken the tactical form of 'dense and rigid "wave" formations'.[48] At GHQ the heavy casualty figures rumoured in Britain were denied. Kiggell informed army commanders that exaggerated reports of casualties should be corrected. He wrote disingenuously,

the actual truth is our casualties for the month of July were, roughly, 120,000 over and above the ordinary trench warfare casualties in the preceding month, which may be taken as somewhere about the monthly average previously.[49]

His term 'ordinary trench warfare casualties' was a reference to the base 'wastage' level which had been adjusted to 75,000 men per month.

Robertson did not regularly receive a strategic appreciation of military operations on the Western Front from Haig or Kiggell. When news from France was not deliberately vague or non-existent, it was over-confident and misleading. The Fourth Army was the most heavily engaged army in the Somme offensive. Its commander, General Sir Henry Rawlinson, mistakenly reported that the German army's two main lines of defence had been captured. He further noted, 'The spirit of the troops is excellent, we have ample reserves behind us, and munitions, though not too plentiful, are, I think, sufficient to enable us to accomplish this task.'[50] This statement was most pertinent as far as the Ministry of Munitions was concerned, in view of the Recruiting Department's repeated attempts to strip the essential war industries of labour. These reports reflected the prevalent 'break-through' mentality which stemmed from Haig's original objective for the Somme offensive.[51] However, the Adjutant-General and the Army Council foresaw that this form of military commitment, if extended throughout the summer, would deplete the available reserves and create a severe military manpower shortage in 1917. Unable and unwilling to question the scale of British operations in France, Macready appreciated that action needed to be taken to re-establish the military priority over all industrial demands for labour.

The assumptions upon which the summer campaign had been planned were completely upset by the disastrous casualty levels of the British forces during the months July to September 1916. In March 1916 a General Staff paper proposed that 'provided Germany can be made to suffer approximate equal loss, it is in the interest of the Entente Powers to force the fighting on the main fronts to the fullest possible extent'.[52] This plan was based on the calculation that, provided an average 'permanent wastage rate' of 150,000 men per month was inflicted on the German army, it would be unable to hold its existing front lines for longer than nine or ten months. The Somme offensive was therefore planned on the assumption that by the end of the campaign the level of monthly 'wastage' inflicted on the German army would force it to make a partial withdrawal. The 'break-through' would then be secured after a more fluid operational situation had arisen. The two crucial mistakes were to overestimate Germany's average permanent loss at 150,000 infantry per month, and to severely underestimate the number of German reserves which could be drawn upon to defend the existing front lines. At the same time GHQ did not clearly inform the government that inflicting heavy casualties on the German army in a static context would similarly necessitate severe British casualties. This correlation had been experienced during the Loos offensive in the autumn of 1915 and actually took a heightened form once the French army had reduced its commitment to the Somme offensive after the Battle of Verdun. The War Committee remained remarkably unaware of the military advantage of holding well fortified positions against attack, and of the fact that to inflict a given 'wastage' on German forces entailed accepting an even heavier 'wastage' in the Allied armies.

The problem of manpower was not only renewed but emphasised dramatically by the demand for reinforcements for the British armies in France after the opening of the Somme offensive.[53] Robertson had for a long time been critical of the lack of government supervision over manpower supply. Instead of identifying the real problems associated with British tactical doctrine on the Western Front, Robertson took refuge in statements which suggested that the nation was not yet committed to the implications of trench warfare, without providing sufficient evidence for his conclusions. He informed Lord Nunburnholm, President of the East Riding Territorial Association, that 'most other

countries have organised their manhood while we have no organization of this kind I am sorry to say. In Germany for example every
man, woman and child is allotted its proper place'.[54] By late July
the Badge Committee, which comprised representatives of the War
Office, Ministry of Munitions and the Reserved Occupations
Committee, had reported that it was unable to settle points of
difference over the utilisation of skilled labour.[55] Each question
which arose at the Badge Committee was approached from a
predominantly departmental viewpoint by the representatives.
Lloyd George chaired the Cabinet Committee which supervised the
Badge Committee, and Brigadier-General Auckland Geddes
complained that the representatives did not receive clear guidance
from the government on the relative urgency of the programmes of
the Admiralty, Ministry of Munitions and War Office. Minor
differences were tackled by the Badge Committee, but it was unable
to adjudicate on questions which involved policy-making. Without
the existence of general principles formulated at Cabinet level,
interdepartmental questions which impinged on manpower utilisation continued to remain unresolved.

The problems of the Director of Recruiting at the Badge Committee were relayed to Macready who urgently wanted an arrangement
which would re-establish the pre-eminence of the military demand
for men. On 31 July 1916 he took the initiative and urged the
establishment of 'a Board which will be able to determine the
relative importance of competing demands, and which possesses
powers of final and absolute decision as to the allocation of men
available'.[56] Macready's call for the establishment of a Man-Power
Distribution Board marked the culmination of periodic attempts to
investigate and co-ordinate the military and industrial use of
manpower which the War Office had viewed with impatience and
dissatisfaction. The Army Council argued that it was quite unable
to make the most appropriate use of personnel unless a more
regular supply of recruits was found under the legislative authority
of the Military Service Acts. It had therefore concluded that the
best means of subordinating the requirements of industry to the
provision of men for France would be to urge the establishment of a
committee which would be sympathetic to the interests of the army,
but not administered by the War Office. In an effort to retain its
direct supervision over munition work and free the industry from
military interference, the Ministry of Munitions had agreed that a

permanent tribunal should be established. Whereas the War Office emphasised that the Board 'should regulate the number of men retained in civil life', [57] in favour of the military demand for more men for France, Addison recommended that it should determine all inter-departmental differences relating to the allocation of manpower. Lord Derby, Under-Secretary of State for War, consulted Addison in the preparation of a draft proposal which was accepted by the War Committee on 22 August 1916.

The establishment of the Man-Power Distribution Board marked an important stage in the history of manpower planning in the First World War. Its primary function was 'to determine all questions arising between Government Departments, relating to the allocation or economic utilisation of Man Power'.[58] The more effective organisation of the war effort in its broadest sense was promoted and secured by the Ministry of Munitions in the draft proposals. The Man-Power Distribution Board was not to be provided with an elaborate system of Inspection Boards which would seek out men from industry and commerce for the army. Instead, all important demands for men by departments were to be referred to the Board, who would have the power to call for any evidence it required. Its decisions were to be final unless a department appealed to the War Committee. The departments which were most directly involved in the manpower issue were distrustful of each other's motives in supporting the Board's formation and this ambivalence was reflected in the close attention which was given to the composition of the Man-Power Distribution Board. The inter-departmental relations of the Admiralty, Board of Trade, Ministry of Munitions and the War Office remained competitive. However, the departments were agreed, if only to strengthen their own individual claims in relation to the provision of manpower, that the innovation of a central authority should be supported in the absence of any government policy on the distribution of the labour supply.

Notes

1 PRO CAB 37/132/28, Report of Proceedings at Meeting of the War Policy Cabinet Committee on 18 August 1915.
2 G. Hardach, *The First World War 1914–1918*, London, 1977, pp. 89–91.
3 PRO CAB 37/132/28 *op. cit.*
4 PRO CAB 37/133/9, Report of Proceedings at Meeting of the War Policy Cabinet Committee on 23 August 1915.
5 PRO CAB 37/134/7, Supplementary Report, 7 September 1915.

6   PRO CAB 37/134/25, Efficiency in War and Compulsion, Balfour, 19
    September 1915. McKenna agreed fully with this assessment as late as
    February 1916. See T. Wilson (ed.), *The Political Diaries of C. P. Scott
    1911–1928*, London, 1970, p. 182.
7   Long, *Memories*, p. 221.
8   PRO CAB 37/135/26, On making available the resources of man-
    power, Kitchener, 12 October 1915.
9   Beveridge mss. Collection on Food Control, Coll. Misc. 92, vol. I, Men
    Available for Military Service in England and Wales, Estimate made
    by Registrar-General's Committee, 6 October 1915. See Appendix 1.
10 PRO CAB 37/134/32, National Register, Long, 29 September 1915.
11 PRO CAB 37/135/3, National Register and Recruiting, Long, 5
    October 1915.
12 PRO CAB 37/135/22, Asquith to King George V, 12 October 1915;
    PRO CAB 37/134/9, Report of the War Policy Cabinet Committee, 7
    September 1915.
13 Derby mss. 920DER(17) 26/2(ii), Memorandum (Circular letter),
    Derby to Mayors, Lord Mayors and Chairmen of County Councils, 16
    October 1915.
14 Cassar, *Kitchener*, p. 451.
15 Beveridge mss. Collection on Food Control, Coll. Misc. 92, vol. I,
    Extent of the Field Available for Recruiting, The President's criticism
    of the figures of 1,400,000, Runciman, 5 October 1915.
16 Robertson mss. I/22/4, Robertson to Haig, 31 December 1915, signed
    copy.
17 *Loc. cit.*
18 Kitchener mss. PRO 30/57/73 WS/43, Note by the Secretary of State
    for War on the Military and Financial Situation, Kitchener, January
    1916.
19 Beveridge mss. Collection on Food Control, Coll. Misc. 92, vol. I,
    Memorandum by President about 15.1.16., Runciman, 18 January
    1916.
20 *Loc. cit.*
21 Robertson mss. I/12/30, Robertson to Colonel Wigram, 12 January
    1916, signed copy.
22 PRO CAB 27/4, Report of the Cabinet Committee on the Co-
    ordination of Military and Financial Effort, 4 February 1916.
23 *Loc. cit.*
24 PRO CAB 27/4, Second Report of the Cabinet Committee on the
    Co-ordination of Military and Financial Effort, 13 April 1916.
25 V. Bonham Carter, *The Life and Times of Field-Marshal Sir William
    Robertson*, London, 1963, p. 170.
26 Derby mss. 920DER(17) 26/2(i), Mallet to Derby, 25 February 1916.
27 Kitchener mss. PRO 30/57/59 WI/108, Esher to Colonel Fitzgerald, 19
    March 1916. See also J-J Becker, *The Great War and the French
    People*, Leamington Spa, 1985, pp. 125–7.
28 Derby mss. 920DER(17) 26/5, Derby to Northcliffe, 23 February
    1916, signed copy.

29 Robertson mss. I/35/12, Robertson to Connaught, 5 April 1916, signed copy.
30 Robertson mss. I/11/2, Memorandum by the Chief of the Imperial General Staff regarding the supply of personnel, Robertson, 21 March 1916; Milner mss. dep. 144, Recruits from all sources 1 January to 30 November 1916, inclusive, Director of Recruiting [A. Geddes], 4 December 1916.
31 Kiggell mss. V/11, Kiggell to Allenby, 16 March 1916, signed copy.
32 Robertson mss. I/32/7, Robertson to Murray, 24 February 1916, signed copy.
33 Macready, *Annals of an Active Life*, I, p. 238.
34 PRO CAB 27/3, Minutes of Proceedings of the Cabinet Committee on the Size of the Army, 18 April 1916.
35 Lloyd George, *War Memoirs*, II, pp. 531, 846.
36 PRO CAB 27/3, *op. cit.*
37 Lord Riddell, *War Diary 1914–1918*, London, 1933, entry for 24 April 1916, p. 177.
38 PRO CAB 27/3, *op. cit.*
39 Robertson mss. I/35/62, Robertson to Kiggell, 19 March 1916, signed copy.
40 Kiggell mss. V/14, Kiggell to Robertson, 24 March 1916, signed copy.
41 PRO WO 62/28, Minute to Chief of the Imperial General Staff, Macready, 21 July 1916.
42 S. Tallents, *Man and Boy*, London, 1943, p. 226.
43 Addison mss. Box 46, To consider Military requirements of artificers, Covering note for meeting on 2 August 1916, n. d.
44 Addison mss. Box 22, Montagu to Lloyd George, 17 August 1916.
45 Addison mss. Box 46, Minute to Addison, C. F. Rey, 2 August 1916.
46 Addison mss. Box 22, Macready to Addison, 24 August 1916.
47 Addison mss. Box 46, Minute to Addison, Tallents, 2 August 1916.
48 B. H. Liddell Hart, *History of the First World War*, London, 1972, p. 208.
49 Kiggell mss. V/31, Kiggell to Plumer, 6 August 1916, signed copy.
50 Derby mss, 920DER(17) 27/4, Memorandum, Rawlinson, 18 July 1916.
51 P. Guinn, *British Strategy and Politics 1914 to 1918*, Oxford, 1965, pp. 135–9.
52 Kitchener mss. PRO 30/57/74 WS/74, A Note on the resources in men, of the Allies and of the enemy, and their effect on the duration of the War, General Staff, 31 March 1916.
53 See Woodward, *Great Britain and the War of 1914–1918*, p. 469.
54 Robertson mss. I/35/95, Robertson to Lord Nunburnholm, 4 February 1916, signed copy.
55 Addison mss. Box 46, Minutes of Cabinet Committee, 2 August 1916.
56 PRO WO 162/28, Proposed Establishment of a Man-Power Distribution Board, Macready, 31 July 1916. A copy of this paper can also be found in IWM MPDB 77/66/1.
57 Addison mss. Box 46, Minutes of Cabinet Committee, 2 August 1916.
58 Beveridge mss. IV. 12, Extract from the Proceedings of a Meeting of the War Committee, held on 22 August 1916, Man-Power Distribution Board. See also Addison mss. Box 46, Final draft, Addison, 10 August 1916.

3

The Man-Power Distribution Board: an Asquithian response
August – November 1916

The strong demand which Macready had made for the establishment of a Man-Power Distribution Board was forcefully supported
by Lloyd George. As Secretary of State for War he impressed the
need for reform on the Cabinet Conference on exemptions. This
Conference was chaired by Walter Long and consisted of twenty
ministers and senior civil servants. The Conference met to discuss
the claims of each department on the available supply of manpower, but frequently failed to obtain evidence and advice on the
implications of its assessments.[1] Lloyd George was further
impressed with the Director of Recruiting's suggestion that the
number of men retained in civil life should be regulated by a board
of three members. Auckland Geddes argued that it should comprise
a chairman and two members, one with experience in engineering
works and the other with experience in business finance. On 5
August the War Committee decided that the powers and constitution of the proposed Board should be examined by a special
committee which was chaired by Lord Derby. During the course of
the war he had become closely identified with the search for
solutions to national controversies, from the recruitment of men for
the army during the final voluntary campaign to the recurrent
military involvement in the economic use of manpower in the
munitions industries. Derby left much of the work of drafting the
terms of reference to Christopher Addison, whose final draft was
accepted by the War Committee on 22 August. Addison's terms
excluded the establishment of local Inspection Committees, which
had the weakening effect of ensuring that the proposed Board
would not be able to supervise any reallocation of labour that it
might recommend. In this respect Addison aimed to make certain

that the Board's intervention in the munitions industry would ultimately depend on working agreements being reached on the proposed movement of labour with the Ministry of Munitions. The War Office had originally urged that the number of men retained in munition factories and mines should be closely monitored.

With continuing disagreement on the precise functions of the Man-Power Distribution Board, much importance was attached by the War Office and the Ministry of Munitions to ensuring that the composition of the Board would be favourably disposed towards their department's viewpoint. The Ministry of Munitions was aware that the work of its Labour Supply department was at risk if the Board was too sympathetic to the reinforcement of the British armies in France. The War Office was known to favour the Board structure as a more efficient machinery on the regulation of exemptions than the Cabinet Conference, which had been identified by munition officials as being weighted too heavily in favour of the military war effort. Stephen Tallents warned the munitions ministers on 1 August,

it is important to secure that the Cabinet Committee [Conference] which has hitherto shown an extreme bias in favour of the requirements of the Army as against all others, does not exercise its executive powers at tomorrow's meeting in the appointment of a Board which will represent the Army at the expense of the other Departments.[2]

On 22 August 1916 Asquith urged Austen Chamberlain to accept the chairmanship of the Man-Power Distribution Board. The Prime Minister acknowledged Chamberlain's preoccupations as Secretary of State for India, but stated that 'it is of the greatest importance that this body should have at its head a Cabinet Minister' and he was 'best fitted' for the task.[3] Austen Chamberlain was a firm supporter of military conscription as early as May 1915 and, as a senior Unionist, his appointment was designed to forestall the development of cabal politics on the distribution of manpower, as had occured on the introduction of compulsory military service.[4] Asquith's invitation to Chamberlain was immediately accepted and on 23 August Lord Midleton was asked to become Vice-Chairman of the Board.[5] Both Chamberlain and Midleton had worked together on the *ad hoc* Coal Committee. Apart from Asquith's wish to involve Unionist politicians more closely in the practical difficulties of co-ordinating this aspect of the war effort, their appointments were also explained by the strong pressure which Lord Curzon and Walter Long had exerted on this matter in the War Committee. The Chairman and Vice-Chairman of the Board were closely associated with the 'military interest' and curiously Curzon had written to Midleton on 21 August to hope that he would be willing to serve on the 'Man-Power Committee'.[6] Robertson was 'very pleased' that Midleton had agreed to serve on the Board.[7] As Midleton had no particular expertise on the organisation of engineering works or finance it soon became apparent that his appointment had fundamentally altered the size and balance of the Board.

Lord Derby gave Sir Maurice Hankey, Secretary to the War Committee, a list of proposed members of the Man-Power Distribution Board on 31 August. The list of members was discussed with Lord Midleton and consisted of Chamberlain, Midleton, Sir Charles Allen, William Crooks, and either John Hodge or Stephen Walsh. The Ministry of Munitions identified Lord Midleton's membership as the main source of their concern, for his appointment had destroyed the concept of a Chairman and two independent assessors. Sir Hubert Llewellyn Smith, Secretary of the Ministry of Munitions, informed the Minister, Edwin Montagu, 'I had hoped for a Board of three Members at most, without any fanatical advocates on either side, but I fear that if Lord Midleton is to be a Member this hope will not be realised.'[8] On the following day Montagu informed Hankey, 'I have never liked the suggestion, of Lord Midleton, whose whole experience and therefore whole bias will be in favour of the War Office.'[9] Reluctantly, on 1 September, Montagu was forced to accept Midleton's appointment as a 'settled fact'. Consequently, Llewellyn Smith advised Montagu that the appointment of a 'definite Munitions advocate' should be sought. Colonel Sir Charles Allen was known primarily as a former Territorial officer, and rather less for his chairmanships of Sir Henry Bessemer and Company and the Ebbw Vale Steel, Iron and Coal Co. Ltd. Both he and the suggested alternative Hardy, a glass manufacturer, were described by Llewellyn Smith as 'comparative nonetities' in the munitions industry.[10] Instead of these Midleton nominees, the Ministry of Munitions sought the appointment of Arthur Balfour.

The 'great Sheffielder' had gained much experience of wartime munitions work as a member of the industry advisory committee to the Treasury. His services were secured as the 'munitions advocate'. The Ministry of Munitions also had a close interest in the appointment of a 'good Labour advocate' to the Board. Like all other trade unionists considered for incorporation within the government's conduct of the war effort, William Crooks had taken a firmly patriotic line, but by the autumn of 1916 he was in ill-health and without wide industrial experience.[11] The Labour Adviser to the government and President of the Board of Education Arthur Henderson was asked to advise on the appointment of two representatives of Labour to the Board. The Ministry of Munitions was fully satisfied with the recommendation that George Barnes should join the Man-Power Distribution Board. In 1915 he was sent on missions to Canada and to the British armies in France to seek the recruitment and return of skilled mechanics to British industry.[12] In the context of the Board's formation these missions were regarded as valuable and relevant experience which later drew him into the higher conduct of the war. He was joined by Stephen Walsh who, like Crooks, had campaigned vigorously on recruiting platforms during the period of voluntary recruiting for the army.[13] Lord Derby knew Stephen Walsh personally for they had shared public meetings in Lancashire in 1914, and Derby had publicly commended him for his recruiting work. Walsh also supported conscription, and the appointment of 'patriotic labour' representatives who fully supported the employment of all the nation's resources for the effective prosecution of the war balanced their more direct interest in the 'protection' or exemption of engineers and miners from military service.

On 22 September the War Committee accepted the further appointments of Arthur Balfour, George Barnes and Stephen Walsh as members of the Board.[14] Despite the alterations in the representation of industry and labour, Midleton's intention to reflect a generalised geographical 'mix' of members' political interests and backgrounds was retained. Chamberlain 'represented' the Midlands and Midleton the 'South', though the latter's political base was more narrowly confined to landownership in west Surrey and southern Ireland. Walsh and Balfour represented the interests of Lancashire and Yorkshire respectively. Midleton considered it important that Scotland should be represented as he thought that it had done well in the recruiting campaigns, and Barnes was a Glasgow MP.

The original Derby list which Hankey had circulated, in his usual state of ignorance about industrialists and labour leaders, had been much modified by effective pressure from the Ministry of Munitions. Consequently, industrial and labour 'advocates' had been appointed, though Barnes and Walsh had participated fully in the recruitment of men for the army. Midleton had exerted some influence on the composition of the Board. His presence augured well for the military authorities who looked forward to a close investigation of the available manpower in civil industry with a view to debadging some occupational age groups in order to release fit young men for the army. Midleton's close relationship with the War Office suggested that the feasibility of further legislation to redirect men according to the requirements of the war effort would be seriously considered. Furthermore, 'industrial conscription' might be introduced if no other way could be found to bring the British armies up to strength for the spring campaign planned for the Western Front in 1917. Robertson had remarked to Midleton on the task which lay before the Board, 'There is much to be done, and the sooner a beginning is made the better. The whole manhood of the nation needs to be organised, and every man put in his proper place.'[15] A start was made with the appointment of joint-secretaries to the Board. The Prime Minister's youngest son, Captain Cyril Asquith, who was not medically fit for service abroad, and E. A. Sandford Fawcett, who as a munitions official had been dealing with exemption cases, were appointed. In the provision of joint-secretaries it was clear that the tension between the Ministry of Munitions and the War Office had not been resolved and that their submissions would dominate the initial proceedings of the Man-Power Distribution Board.

In late September 1916 Austen Chamberlain emphasised that he could not foresee what developments might eventually take place and it was 'not considered advisable to lay down any hard-and-fast rules at present'.[16] In the light of these uncertain preliminary statements some doubt was cast on the capacity of the Board to identify quickly the main issues concerned in the distribution and supply of the remaining manpower in civil life. Consequently, the presentation of evidence and subsequent submissions to the Board assumed a significance which would not have been so apparent had either Chamberlain or Midleton any expertise in the work of essential war industries or the impact of military demands for munitions on the recruitment of men for the army. Between 26 September and 29 November 1916 departmental ministers were called and examined by the Man-Power Distribution Board, although the main evidence was collected by 20 October.

On 26 September Sir Nevil Macready and Auckland Geddes met the Board at the India Office to discuss the military situation. Their evidence clearly indicated the embattled position of the War Office *vis-à-vis* other government departments. Furthermore, it was significant that the Adjutant-General's evidence, supplemented by that of the Director of Recruiting, provided the starting point of the Board's investigation into the distribution of manpower. Macready explained that the War Office spent its time 'in internecine warfare with every other Department of the State in order to obtain what is absolutely necessary for the defence of the State'.[17] As a result the British forces in France were short of 80,000 men. He estimated that no more than 35,000 general service men per month would be sent to France in the following three months. He attributed this sorry state of affairs to the lack of co-ordination between departments, the unilateralist acts of the Ministry of Munitions and the difficulties which the War Office had experienced with the tribunals. Macready countered the contention that the War Office wished to be 'masters of everyone', by observing that the War Committee needed to assume a greater role in this aspect of the war effort. The Adjutant-General indicated that

it is for the Cabinet . . . to say which is the most important thing, and where the men are to go to, and all I ask is that I should be able to get the men who are to be made into soldiers and not get old gentlemen with large families instead.[18]

It emerged at this early stage of the Board's existence that the War Office wanted all men of twenty-five years and under to be released from their civil work for service in the army.

Macready's main dispute with the Ministry of Munitions lay in his contention that he had no power to question a certificate of exemption from military service in cases where the local recruiting officer felt that it had been issued without precise knowledge of the man's work. Consequently, the lack of co-ordination between the two departments was most apparent where the munitions industry sought to expand a production programme at the inevitable cost of a reduced level of recruitment of skilled men into the army. In this context Macready referred to the much enlarged heavy artillery output, which was negotiated without reference to the needs of the army for skilled artificers. He claimed that new artillery batteries were being sent to the British armies in France without any skilled engineers at all. This situation was a prime example of the impact of the complete absence of any administrative machinery to distribute manpower. However, the War Office exaggerated its criticism of the Ministry of Munitions when its officials were accused of 'approaching soldiers in the streets who are on furlough and asking them if they would not prefer to work in Munition factories'.[19] The army looked to the Board to guarantee future drafts of skilled men, as it did to curtail the semi-autonomous position of the tribunals. The War Office noted that 'It is hardly an exaggeration to say that the Tribunal system has stood between the nation and complete success in the summer campaign.'[20] Military representatives, attached to local and appeal tribunals, complained that the award of temporary exemption for three months was frequently granted to delay or frustrate the eventual enlistment of older men for the army. Conversely, tribunals complained that they were required to review the exemptions granted to older men, while young unmarried men in essential war industries remained exempt from military service. By September 1916 some tribunals in urban areas were threatening strike action. The tribunals were administered by the Local Government Board and although serious problems existed they broadly reflected, rather than contributed to, the difficulties inherent in a situation where general principles of manpower utilisation were minimal.

The last substantial complaint raised by the Adjutant-General on 26 September concerned the excessive number of men of military age which was retained in government departments. The War Office estimated that 130,000 men might be made available for general service from this source. The impact of this observation was somewhat tempered by the knowledge that there were 900 men of military age at the War Office in London, including at least 200 who were known to be fit for service in France. The Board's members were known to be concerned about the adverse impact on public opinion of the retention of men of military age in administrative posts in Whitehall. One early conclusion which the Board drew was that the process of substitution could be extended, so that men were replaced by women in selected areas of military employment in Britain.[21] The Man-Power Distribution Board was surprised that as a result of the phenomenal growth in the size of the army, its administrative services in Britain numbered 295,000 men. It requested more information on these figures and urged that men should only be employed in hospitals and kitchens in work which women could not do. Some substitution had taken place in hospitals, but Austen Chamberlain urged that women clerical workers ought to be more widely employed by the War Office. Whereas Chamberlain argued that the process of substitution could be managed more effectively by the military authorities, both Macready and Geddes emphasised that the pool of recruitable men for the army was severely restricted by the 'empire-building' activies of the Ministry of Munitions.

However, Addison had urged that the principle of releasing men fit for active service whose places could be filled without a reduction of industrial output could be applied equally to ancillary services in the army and navy. In his submission to the Board on 27 September he pointedly noted,

it should not be in the national interest that men should be taken from the manufacturer of munitions to the detriment of output while men fit for active service are utilised in the Army for clerical and menial services.[22]

Here again, on the second day of evidence to the Board, was talk of the apparently irreconcilable two watertight compartments, one an army problem and the other a munitions problem. Addison had been associated with the provision of labour for the munitions industry since the formation of the separate Ministry in May 1915 and he was distrustful of the influence which the War Office might exert on the Man-Power Distribution Board. He therefore attempted to divert the Board from the consideration of its own powers to redistribute labour, by recommending the principle that each department should be required to create machinery to secure the most economic and useful employment of the manpower at its disposal in relation to its specified duties. The Ministry of Munitions had established an internal Combing-Out Commission, details of which it gave to the Board.[23] In part the Ministry of Munitions highlighted this administrative innovation to demonstrate that its labour supply branch was the most effective machinery for the control of manpower in essential war industries. Addison emphasised that the ministry had a shortage of 35,000 skilled and unskilled operatives and that an additional 100,000 men would be required in the near future to meet the labour requirements of an increased munitions programme. Addison's main message to the Man-Power Distribution Board was absolutely clear. Any future proposal for the 'release of men from vital munition works should be carefully scrutinized in relation to the full programme of munition requirements'.[24] Finally, Addison indicated that 'cartloads' of badges were not being issued by controlled establishments in the munitions industry. The total number of badges issued to men of military age was 880,176, of which approximately one-half were for men directly employed on work for the Admiralty and the War Office.

The First Report of the Man-Power Distribution Board was circulated on 30 September. It accepted the War Office's argument that the debadging of skilled workers in civil industries would substantially alleviate the military manpower problem. It also foresaw the growing importance of identifying priority areas within the war effort. In this context the report recommended that the Allies be informed, and Russia in particular, 'that demands for supplies in excess of those to which we are already committed, may entail a reduction of our military effort'.[25] Although the retention of five divisions for Home Defence in addition to the garrisons of defended ports was criticised by the Board, the two main recommendations of the report substantially reinforced Macready's position. Firstly, it recommended that the construction of new factories should not be sanctioned since they could not expect to begin production before the end of the war. Fortuitously this point was rejected by the War Committee. Secondly, the Board proposed and the Cabinet accepted that in future all large orders for munitions should be referred to the Adjutant-General, 'in order to ascertain how his recruiting figures would be affected, both by the increased demand on the Army and the increased demand of the labour market'.[26]

The effect of this decision was twofold. Firstly, despite the constitution of the Board, this recommendation encouraged the military and munitions authorities to disregard the Board as an irrelevance or, more accurately, an intruder into their domain. In practice, the supply and distribution of manpower had been effected by the two departments in a state of uneasy co-existence since May 1915. Secondly, the Board's recommendation reinforced the War Office's continuing assumption that it had first call on the remaining manpower because the successful outcome of the war was perceived to depend on the reinforcement of the British armies in France. Consequently, the Man-Power Distribution Board was initially supportive of the military requirements for manpower and less certain about the place of manufacturing industry in the overall war effort.

On 13 October 1916 Addison wrote a troubled entry in his diary: 'The Man-Power Board without consulting us is now rumoured to be contemplating the entire cessation of badges of exemption.'[27] The rumour was in fact true. The Second Report of the Man-Power Distribution Board of 12 October requested the War Committee to agree that no further badge certificates should be issued so that the Board could consider fully the question of debadging. It noted that 'experience shows that when once a man has been badged it is extremely difficult to get him unbadged, or if unbadged, to secure him for the Army'.[28] The Board was told by Sir Mortimer Durand, chairman of the defunct Badge Committee, that 1,000 to 1,500 war service badges were being issued by the Ministry of Munitions each day.[29] The Board's growing interest in the establishment of a debadging programme to release young men for service in the army received a considerable boost from the seemingly impartial evidence of the Board of Trade.

Prior to the creation of the Man-Power Distribution Board, the Board of Trade was generally acknowledged to be a 'general manpower authority' for the civilian sphere of the war effort. It retained statutory obligations under the Military Service Acts to provide certificates of exemption from enlistment for essential war work. This function was mainly carried out by the Reserved Occupations Committee. It prepared and revised lists of classes of work considered essential for the maintenance of the commercial and industrial capacity of the nation, excluding the munitions, coal-mining and railway industries. In September 1916 the Reserved Occupations Committee noted:

The present position of the trades of the country is remarkably satisfactory, in view of all the circumstances, and the Committee are of the opinion that still more men can be released without bringing the trade and industry of the country to the verge of collapse.[30]

The Board of Trade concluded that there was no evidence to suppose that the existing level of protection for war work was inadequate. It maintained an outlook which was much more optimistic than the munitions perspective, in spite of the acute disagreements which had marred ministerial relations between Runciman and Kitchener. In January 1916 the Board of Trade had calculated that 1,230,000 men could be taken from industry for the army provided that it supervised the sources and methods by which the men were taken. By the end of August 860,000 men had been obtained by the army. Yet despite the expansion of the munitions programme, the Board of Trade was prepared to contemplate a further withdrawal of 400,000 men from industry during the remaining months of 1916. It even suggested that the outlook for

1917 was so favourable that 100,000 men might be spared for the army in January 1917. In fact the Reserved Occupations Committee had only very loosely supervised the withdrawal of men from industry. Consequently, the impact of the work of the recruiting officer on the output of the munitions industry was under-estimated by the Board of Trade. The department exuded a misplaced confidence in the adaptability of industry.

The Board of Trade's advice and statistical data was double-edged, but the department was in a position to appreciate the theoretical value of the Man-Power Distribution Board. If departments continued to act independently and use *ad hoc* methods to secure labour from commerce and non-essential trades, only to utilise wastefully men recruited for the army and the munitions industry, the manpower situation would indeed worsen quickly by the spring of 1917. The Board of Trade urged that the demands of the War Office and Ministry of Munitions would be best dealt with as a whole, so that they 'may be regarded for the purpose of winning the war on land as one Department, and some agreement should be made as to relative requirements for fighting men and munition workers'.[31] It was hardly feasible to contemplate the unification of the military and munition authorities for manpower purposes. The main implication of the Board of Trade's statements was that the Man-Power Distribution Board would succeed in the efficient distribution of labour where the Reserved Occupations Committee had failed. Runciman argued, like the military authorities, that in order to organise the remaining labour supply, men who were protected by badges in the munitions industry must be released. The Board of Trade's attitude to the problem of debadging was influenced by the results of its piecemeal approach and abortive schemes early in 1916. In this 'game of musical chairs' recruiting officers did not locate men who were debadged by their employers. It concluded that 'After much expenditure of time and money men have been combed out at one place and have readily found work elsewhere',[32] often at neighbouring works.

As a result of the evidence which was obtained from the War Office and the Board of Trade, Chamberlain appreciated that a debadging policy would release further men for military service. Therefore, after four months training, substantial drafts would be available for the spring campaign in France in 1917. His opinion was abundantly clear on 6 October when he cross-questioned

Llewellyn Smith on the withdrawal of exemptions and the concomitant fear of 'industrial conscription'. Chamberlain declared,

Is not this the proper way to look at the problem; men of military age should by law be in the Army, but the law makes exceptions with regard to certain men, because if they work at their own trades they will be more useful out of the Army. The only reason for their exemption for military service is that they are doing work of a particular kind outside the Army.[33]

The Second Report of 12 October recommended that no badge certificates should be issued pending an investigation of the system. Montagu opposed the report and reminded the War Committee that Chamberlain's proposal contravened Asquith's pledge to the trade unions of 28 September that no skilled man would be taken into the army except in his skilled capacity.[34] On 27 October the Ministry of Munitions ceased to issue badges to unskilled men under thirty years of age for two weeks, provided that men removed from munitions work by recruiting officers were replaced by suitable substitutes by the War Office. The arrangement gave Montagu and Addison a short time to attempt to counter the support which Chamberlain and Midleton were able to obtain at the War Committee for the Board's debadging plan. Addison complained that the Board's practice of initiating change in the organisation of industrial manpower, without consulting munitions officials, endangered complex agreements which the ministry had concluded with trade unions since May 1915. By 23 October Addison was providing Montagu with evidence of disrupted production in the hope that the ministry's trenchant objections would be expressed at Cabinet level. Montagu was advised by Addison to remonstrate with the Man-Power Distribution Board and inform Chamberlain

that it is quite impossible for you to be responsible for the production of munitions if your arrangements with labour which have been gradually built up under the greatest difficulties during the last fifteen months are to be upset or interfered with by the Man-Power Board issuing instructions which throw the machinery of the Ministry out of gear and at the same time antagonise labour.[35]

While relations between the Man-Power Distribution Board and the Ministry of Munitions deteriorated severely, the suggestion that the substitution of men by women in spheres of civilian and military work might be more rigorously implemented was pursued. Indeed, though a comprehensive scheme of substitution was not to be adopted, the discussions which the Board initiated marked the beginning of a movement to bring the question of the widespread employment of women within the context of the efficient distribution of the nation's manpower resources. Within two weeks of the Board's establishment Austen Chamberlain received a detailed memorandum from Mrs Katherine Furse on the organisation and employment of women.[36] In 1914 she had organised the first Red Cross Voluntary Aid Detachment (VAD) to be sent to France and by the end of the year she had returned to London to organise the VAD recruiting office. Mrs Furse proposed that to accelerate the combing-out of fit men of military age in government departments, and in military work 'at the back of the army', women should be allowed to enrol in a uniformed 'State Service' administered by a Central Women's Department.[37] The work of small organisations which supplied volunteer women for government work was stifled by the attitude of the military authorities and the restricted range of tasks which women were allowed to undertake. As a result the recruiting procedures of women's voluntary organisations entailed long delays and unnecessary expenditure in the compiling of waiting lists which were swiftly rendered obsolete.

Katherine Furse was critical of the War Office, and the Man-Power Distribution Board was keen to receive evidence of the obstructive attitude of the department in retaining fit men for clerical duties in Whitehall. She complained,

It really is rather a shame that we women should still be civil subordinates. The VAD and the Women's Legion have a semi-official status but at any moment – when it suits the War Office – they are merely civilians and can be dismissed with a week's notice.[38]

Mrs Furse was particularly anxious that the recruitment of women for government work, as cooks, nurses, motor-drivers or whatever their role might be, should not be indiscriminate but regularised. If this reform was achieved, *ad hoc* appeals for labour, which were often vastly over-subscribed, could be avoided. On 6 October the Board of Trade was invited to comment on Mrs Furse's plans but it had no previous direct contact with women's organisations which carried out semi-military work. Within the context of the existing limited process of substitution Miss Durham, Chief Woman Inspector, was reluctant to support organisational change. She wrote, 'It may safely be asserted that the systematic measures already taken and machinery set up by the Employment Department are sufficient to meet the demands for women's labour as they extend both in industry and commerce.'[39] This statement evaded the issue of supplying women for semi-military work.

The Board of Trade acknowledged that its Labour Exchanges, even in co-operation with the War Office and the British Red Cross, would not suffice as a recruiting agency if large numbers of women were encouraged to enlist 'for the period of the war'. The distinction lay between the recruitment of women for ordinary industrial work, for which there was no shortage which could not be handled by the Central Advisory Committee for Women's Employment, and extending the process of substitution in non-combatant branches of the military war effort. In the latter case the need for the increased recruitment of women was pressing, but Mrs Furse's plan for a uniformed women's service was utterly dependent on the goodwill of the military authorities which had not so far been forthcoming.

Austen Chamberlain accepted that the substitution of men by women was likely to be much further extended before the war ended. On 19 October he requested that a scheme which could efficiently recruit 200,000 women should be drawn up, but the War Office was not represented at the meeting.[40] In view of the suggested first step of appointing dilution officers to find out where men were doing work which women ought to be doing, for example in pay offices and canteens, this was rather an oversight. In the short term Katherine Furse's plan for a uniformed women's service, using the VAD as a model, was dismissed by the Adjutant-General. He was not persuaded that the manpower problem was sufficiently serious to warrant such a dramatic change in the provision of ancillary services for the military war effort. However, the serious attention given to the employment of women by the Man-Power Distribution Board ensured that reform would again be suggested as the level of recruitment for the army fell during 1917 and as the War Office's resistance to organisational change weakened.

The Board suffered serious constitutional defects in its relations with major 'labour-employing' departments, such as the Admiralty, Ministry of Munitions and the War Office. However, some departments which suffered from inherently weak political positions benefited from the existence of the Board. For the first time they gained the opportunity of drawing some attention to their own special work and problems. Neither the Reserved Occupations Committee nor the Badge Committee were impartial bodies because they were supervised by large departments with vested

interests in the allocation of manpower. The Air Board, for
example, was able to request assistance to obtain skilled labour for
manufacturers in this new industry. During the debadging controversy the dislocation of aero-engine production was feared.
Austen Chamberlain informed Llewellyn Smith, 'A certain amount
of skilled labour comes into the pool at present and we have the
complaint that it is not fairly divided amongst those who require it
– the Admiralty, the Air Board, Munitions and so on.'[41] In the face
of lack of interest from munitions officials, the Board ensured that
the aeronautical industry was allocated the 6,000 skilled men it
required, thus publicising, effectively, 'the paramount importance
of maintaining and developing the equipment of the Air Services'.[42]

A similar indication that the threefold priority in manpower
allocation of the army, navy and munitions was being undermined
came from the interest which the Board took in agricultural work.
The Board of Agriculture was extremely critical of the uncertain
position of the farmers in relation to the military requirements for
men. Auckland Geddes, Director of Recruiting, claimed that some
rural areas still had a 'fair margin' of men that could be recruited
from agriculture. Lord Crawford, President of the Board of Agriculture, informed the Man-Power Distribution Board that if a
home-grown food supply was considered an essential part of the
war effort sufficient men must be left on the land for this purpose,
especially to maintain the acreage of arable land.[43] Temporarily,
Auckland Geddes agreed to the cessation of recruitment from the
land so that a survey could be made of the level of remaining labour
in the agricultural industry.

The lengthy deliberations of the Board during October and
November 1916 encouraged detailed quantitative assessments to be
made of many aspects of the government's conduct of the war.
Though these were not independent studies of the efficiency of
government departments in their supervision of war work, the
investigations placed the sectional interests within the context of
the overall prosecution of the British war effort and the supply of
vital war material to the Allies. Hitherto, the role of the
aeronautical and agricultural industries had been under-rated, but
the Man-Power Distribution Board asserted their importance as it
pursued its central aim of promoting the effective allocation and
economic utilisation of manpower. The *raison d'être* of the Board,
namely the settlement of disputes between departments, had been

severely curtailed by the inexperience of its members and the continuing impasse between the Ministry of Munitions and the War Office.[44] However, departments which had previously been perceived to be of secondary importance in the allocation of manpower were recognised by the end of 1916 as vital aspects of the war effort which had to be sustained in the long conflict with Germany.

In October 1916 the Board attempted to secure general approval for establishing new local manpower committees under its direct control to deal with exemptions. Chamberlain intended that they would implement the debadging programme, but the problems of control and representation were immediately encountered. The War Office feared that if manpower committees were to be representative of the departments concerned, the wrangles that were confined to Whitehall would swiftly be extended to the localities. The Ministry of Munitions attacked the scheme to allocate manpower by local committees for two reasons. Firstly, it suggested that the plan did not fall within the Board's terms of reference, which was arguable. Secondly, the scheme opposed Montagu's contention that the 'ministry must control its own labour'.[45] Arthur Henderson initially supported the scheme for local machinery, but just before the publication of the plan he observed, 'our existing machinery affords no assurance that the P[rime] M[inister]'s pledge to the skilled men would be observed, and I am afraid that the latest proposals will not help me to remove it'.[46] The Board was reminded about the strength of labour opinion on the importance of the pledge when it received a deputation from the Amalgamated Society of Engineers (ASE). Brownlie, the Chairman of the ASE, complained that his members were being recruited daily for non-mechanical units despite the pledges given by the Prime Minister that a man with a badge and certificate would not be conscripted into the army. The deputation expected the Board to over-ride the judgment of departments and impose a clear procedure based on well understood principles. The absence of a uniform pattern of regulations sorely disappointed the ASE. It was informed by Chamberlain, 'Our terms of reference do not constitute us as a body with autocratic authority to direct the man power of the whole nation spontaneously where we think it ought to go.'[47] To the departments this conclusion was already self-evident.

The last major report of the Board appeared on 9 November. The Third Report enshrined its obsession with debadging and the creation of localised machinery. It recommended that all unskilled and semi-skilled men under twenty-six years of age should permanently lose their badge and certificate of exemption. To provide 80,000 general service men for the army within two months the scheme was to be supervised by local committees, with the addition of an appeals procedure to a District Referee. Montagu was unsurprisingly severe in his general criticism of the report. He told Chamberlain, 'Of course I can't agree to your proposals which will, as I think, destroy Munitions output just as we are all coming to the conclusion that this is a war of material.'[48] Addison observed, 'The Minister is as worried as ever over the man power question . . . I wish he were not so jumpy, however.'[49] The scheme was also opposed by the major 'labour-employing' departments because it ignored a prior agreement on substitution. Consequently, the appointment of superintending factory inspectors as direct local representatives of the Board would serve no useful purpose. By seeking to ignore the Labour Exchanges and create new machinery the Board divorced the related questions of the supply and the demand of labour in industry. The only local repositories of considerable industrial experience were the Labour Exchanges, which were maintained by the Employment Department of the Board of Trade. They had become by 1916 a familiar, if unloved, national institution in the ever-changing circumstances of the government's interventionist role in the economy in wartime.

The Man-Power Distribution Board's propensity to disregard existing machinery maintained by government departments, while being unable to institute alternative administrative structures which commanded general support, illustrated its inherent weakness. Without any greater access to the War Committee than such departments as the Board of Trade, it suffered from an inability to implement its proposals at the local level. No national system of local manpower committees was established by the Board. In part this problem was caused by the Board's terms of reference which did not categorically give it a right to initiate administrative change in the allocation of manpower in industry. The problems encountered suggested that, at this stage of the war, any movement towards the notion of a single central manpower authority faced severe opposition from departments who considered their claim for additional manpower to constitute the most urgent demand on the labour supply. The Man-Power Distribution Board noticeably failed to report on the relative importance of each department's demand for men.[50] Consequently, both the War Office and the Ministry of Munitions continued to assume that their own systems of local representation, via recruiting officers and dilution officers, could best supervise the withdrawal of men from industry for the army.

It was ironic that in attempting to locate men who could be conscripted into the army, predominantly through debadging, the Board received so little support from the War Office. The recruiting officers were completely distrusted by the trade unions. Chamberlain was informed by John Hills of the Boilermaker's Society that,

> we do not agree with what is going on at the present time, namely, that everybody should be put under a military contract and dominated by the Military authorities, and without regard to what is in the best interests of industry.[51]

The Man-Power Distribution Board was caught, and held responsible, between the growing militancy of the engineering trade unions and the arbitrary intervention of recruiting officers in the munitions industry. Undue optimism in the power of the Board to curb the recruitment of skilled men for the army and the labour movement's hostility towards the process of debadging were major contributory factors in the strike in the engineering industry in Sheffield on 16 November 1916. The Ministry of Munitions had been instructed by the War Committee not to issue badges of exemption from recruitment. Addison remarked that in this situation the trade unions 'could get no satisfaction out of the War Office and the Man-Power Board, insisting on pursuing its course of colossal stupidity, did nothing either.'[52]

The Sheffield strike brought into sharp focus, not so much the stupidity of the Board, but its utter powerlessness to deal with the manpower issue on equal terms with other departments. The immediate cause of the strike was the recruitment of Leonard Hargreaves, who was a fitter at the Vickers works, into the Army Service Corps. He was debadged in violation of the pledges given to skilled men.[53] The government's response was co-ordinated by an emergency Cabinet committee which demanded that the army should immediately return Hargreaves to Sheffield. Lord Derby also proposed that the ASE should issue 'trade cards' to its skilled members, which would be a surety against their enlistment. Under this arrangement trade union officials undertook to recruit men for the artificer grades of the army from their members who were not employed in munition works. These points formed the basis of the Trade Card Agreement which was concluded on 18 November 1916 between the government and the ASE. On 22 November Lloyd George extended the agreement to thirty-two trade unions in the Engineering Unions Federation. Significantly, the Trade Card Agreement was associated with Lloyd George and Derby as War Office ministers. The Ministry of Munitions distrusted the political repercussions of the agreement. It did not have a well-defined principle. Trade unions agreed to the arrangement, primarily because their members with cards were guaranteed exemption from military service. They were less interested in providing skilled men for the technical corps of the army.

The Man-Power Distribution Board was not directly involved in the negotiations to end the strike, although Austen Chamberlain was a signatory to the agreement. At the same time Montagu vehemently opposed the Board's third report which was discussed by the War Committee on 17 November. He complained that it impeded direct discussion between the Ministry of Munitions and the War Office on debadging. Accordingly the War Committee agreed that Montagu and Derby should meet to discuss the issue, which resulted in the withdrawal of badges from unskilled and semi-skilled young men with the objective of the gradual release of men under thirty-one years of age who were fit for general service. It was planned that 50,000 men would be released for the army by the end of January 1917, not 100,000 men which the Board of Trade had originally envisaged. In the course of these bi-lateral meetings in late November 1916 the function of the Board was eclipsed by the two departments.

Discredited by its inability to stop the strike at Sheffield and isolated by the withdrawal of support from the War Office, the Board had outlived its usefulness as a subordinate adviser to the War Committee on manpower questions. By this time Austen Chamberlain was deeply concerned with the military operations which lay within the responsibility of the India Office. Chamberlain's chairmanship of the Board was a heavy addition to his ministerial duties and it 'was one of the chief causes of the temporary breakdown which sent him to Broadstairs shortly afterwards.'[54] He confessed his exasperation at the treatment of the Board's work to Walter Runciman,

The Man-Power Board has had an extraordinarily difficult and contentious task before it. We have done our utmost to preserve good relations with all the

Departments concerned. I am sorry if we have failed to obtain the good-will of the Board of Trade.[55]

This letter was written to a minister who had supported fully the formation of the Board. Greater antagonism to the Board existed in the major 'labour-employing' departments which were rarely prepared to accept its decisions. Consequently, it rapidly became of little value to the military authorities for, as Robertson bluntly recorded, 'it had no power to enforce them, it was not of much value.'[56]

The Man-Power Distribution Board's investigations into the provision of men in civil industry was motivated primarily by the necessity of ensuring that sufficient drafts of men would be trained and available to reinforce the British armies in France in the spring of 1917. Under the prevailing strategic plans the maintenance of the military war effort became the Board's prime consideration. However, the long-running controversy on the issuing of badges to regulate the retention of men in industry on both skilled and unskilled work by no means satisfied the army's demand for recruits. Macready noted that to keep the armies up to strength to 30 June 1917 and provide for the continuing expansion of the Royal Artillery and the Royal Flying Corps, 385,000 general service men were required between September 1916 and March 1917.[57] With the passing of several months this problem grew more acute. Derby pronounced,

I see every Department struggling for men, Munitions, Agriculture, Ship-building, and last but not least the Army and knowing that there are sufficient men in this country to supply the wants of all I look to see the controlling hand which will give to each its proper quota.[58]

The Board was a valuable experiment but at no time offered the prospect of a 'controlling hand' because it was not empowered to allocate rigid quotas of men for the military and industrial components of the war effort. It was heavily criticised from the perspective of sectional interest by departments which were not forced by the War Committee to submit to the machinery of arbitration provided by the establishment of the Board. The War Office and the Ministry of Munitions were notable examples of departments which assumed that their interests would be furthered by the Board and realising their mistake, grew impatient with its proceedings. For many ministers the rapid demise of the Man-Power Distribution Board became an illustration of the problem of policy-making which the 'Wait and See' government did not solve. Although the Chairman was of ministerial rank the Board was not granted parity of esteem with the departments, and apart from its two leading members consisted of men who had little experience of administrative practices in Whitehall. They found support for their recommendations difficult to secure once the content of the First Report was effectively resisted. It suffered the isolation which similarly afflicted the new Food and Air administrations. Unlike the provision of the food supply and the development of an aircraft industry, the organisation of manpower cut across all aspects of the war effort. The Board was a bold experiment which needed the closer attention of the Prime Minister. In not being accorded the status of separate Cabinet rank, the Board's functions narrowed and it became a limited administrative innovation characteristic of Asquith's reluctance to modify the existing, sectionalised departmental responsibilities on manpower. Initially, it represented the ability of the government to respond coherently to identified problems in the war effort, but its decline was interpreted by critics of Asquith's premiership as one further example of his inability to vigorously prosecute the war effort.[59] In fact the opposition which led to the collapse of the Man-Power Distribution Board reflected the continuing scale of the compartmentalisation of decision-making within the war effort which persisted in proving insurmountable. Asquith failed to break down the boundaries of departmental self-interest, but it was a problem which Lloyd George would find no easier to overcome.

Notes

1 Harcourt mss. dep. 514, Minute to Harcourt, 2 August 1916, unsigned; Addison mss. Box 46, Minutes of Cabinet Committee, 2 August [1916].
2 Addison mss. Box 46, Minute, Tallents, 1 August 1916.
3 Austen Chamberlain mss. AC 16/1/2, Asquith to A. Chamberlain, n.d.
4 C. Petrie, *The Life and Letters of Sir Austen Chamberlain*, London, 1940, II, pp. 47–8.
5 Midleton mss. PRO 30/67/25, Asquith to A. Chamberlain, 23 August 1916.
6 Midleton mss. PRO 30/67/25, Curzon to Midleton, 21 August 1916.
7 Robertson mss. I/35/84, Robertson to Midleton, 7 September 1916, signed copy.
8 Addison mss. Box 46, Minute, Llewellyn Smith to Montagu, 31 August 1916.
9 Addison mss. Box 46, Montagu to Hankey, 1 September 1916.
10 Addison mss. Box 46, Minute, Llewellyn Smith to Montagu, 31 August 1916.

11 *Dictionary of Labour Biography*, London, 1971–82, II, pp. 110–1. See also W. Crooks, *The British Workman Defends His Home*, London, 1917.
12 G. N. Barnes, *From Workshop to War Cabinet*, London, 1924, pp. 114–34.
13 *Dictionary of Labour Biography*, IV, p. 189.
14 PRO MUN 5/66/322/146, Memorandum on the Formation of the Man-Power Distribution Board, Minutes of the War Committee, 2 September 1916.
15 Robertson mss. I/35/84, Robertson to Midleton, 7 September 1916, signed copy.
16 PRO MUN 5/66/322/146, *op. cit.*
17 IWM MPDB 77/66/1, Man-Power Distribution Board, evidence of C. F. N. Macready, 26 September 1916.
18 *Loc. cit.*
19 IWM MPDB 77/66/1, Man-Power Distribution Board, First Day, evidence of A. Geddes, 26 September 1916.
20 IWM MPDB 77/66/1, Army Needs and Available Man Power, [War Office], 16 September 1916.
21 Beveridge mss. IV.10 (Part ii), Enlistment and the Industrial Situation, Professor Chapman, 4 October 1916.
22 Addison mss. Box 46, Statement addressed to the Man-Power Board, Addison, n.d. From the minutes of the Board in IWM MPDB 77/66/1 this statement was made on 27 September 1916.
23 Addison mss. Box 46, Minute, H. H. Piggott, 28 September 1916; PRO MUN 5/66/322/145, Man-Power Distribution Board, Memorandum prepared for Addison, 21 September 1916, unsigned.
24 Addison mss. Box 46, Statement addressed to the Man-Power Board by Addison, n.d.
25 Austen Chamberlain mss, First Report of the Man-Power Distribution Board to the War Committee, 30 September 1916.
26 *Loc. cit.*
27 C. Addison, *Four and a Half Years*, London, 1934, I, p. 256.
28 Austen Chamberlain mss. Second Report of the Man-Power Distribution Board to the War Committee, 12 October 1916.
29 Addison mss. Box 46, H. M. Durand to Long, Report of the Badge Committee, 15 September 1916.
30 Beveridge mss. IV. 9, Reserved Occupations Committee, Constitution and functions of the Committee, etc., 20 September 1916, unsigned.
31 Beveridge mss. IV. 10 (Part i), Board of Trade Note bringing up to date the Note of April 1916, Beveridge, 3 October 1916.
32 *Loc. cit.*
33 Beveridge mss. IV. 10 (Part ii), Man-Power Distribution Board, Fourth Day, 6 October 1916.
34 *History of the Ministry of Munitions*, VI, part 1, pp. 14–17.
35 Addison mss. Box 22, Addison to Montagu, 23 October 1916, signed copy.

36 See K. Furse, *Hearts and Pomegranates, The Story of Forty-five Years*, London, 1940, pp. 310–25.
37 IWM MPDB 77/66/1, Memorandum, Katherine Furse, 25 September 1916.
38 IWM MPDB 77/66/1, Katherine Furse to Mrs F. S. Oliver, 21 September 1916.
39 Beveridge mss. IV. 9, Note on Substituting women and its future extension in connection with the utilisation of Manpower, Miss F. H. Durham, 10 October 1916.
40 IWM MPDB 77/66/1, Man-Power Distribution Board, Ninth Day, 19 October 1916.
41 IWM MPDB 77/66/1, Man-Power Distribution Board, Fourth Day, 6 October 1916.
42 IWM MPDB 77/66/1, H. P. Harvey to E. A. Sandford Fawcett, 28 September 1916.
43 IWM MPDB 77/66/1, S. Oliver to Sandford Fawcett, 25 September 1916.
44 Beveridge mss. IV. 9, F. Macleod to Beveridge, 29 September 1916.
45 Austen Chamberlain mss. AC 16/1/3, Montagu to A. Chamberlain, 30 September 1916.
46 IWM MPDB 77/66/2, Henderson to A. Chamberlain, 10 November 1916. See also IWM MPDB 77/66/1, G. M. Young to Sandford Fawcett, 31 October 1916.
47 IWM MPDB 77/66/1, Man-Power Distribution Board, Eleventh Day, 3 November 1916.
48 Austen Chamberlain mss. AC 16/1/7, Montagu to A. Chamberlain, 9 November 1916.
49 Addison mss. Box 99, Diary, 10 November 1916.
50 IWM MPDB 77/66/2, Memorandum, Man-Power, Montagu, 20 November 1916.
51 IWM MPDB 77/66/1, Man-Power Distribution Board, Fifteenth Day, evidence of J. Hills, 15 November 1916.
52 Addison, *Four and a Half Years*, I, p. 262.
53 See C. J. Wrigley, *David Lloyd George and the British Labour Movement*, Hassocks, 1976, pp. 171–4; *History of the Ministry of Munitions*, VI, Part 1, pp. 35–41; J. Hinton, *The First Shop Stewards' Movement*, London, 1973, pp. 162–77.
54 Petrie, *The Life and Letters of Sir Austen Chamberlain*, II, p. 55.
55 Austen Chamberlain mss. AC 16/1/10, A. Chamberlain to Runciman, 1 December 1916, signed copy.
56 Robertson, *Soldiers and Statesmen 1914–1918*, I, p. 301. See also Bonham-Carter, *Soldier True*, p. 161.
57 IWM MPDB 77/66/1, Army Needs and Available Man-Power, [War Office], 16 September 1916.
58 Derby mss. 920 DER(17) 26/19, Memorandum, Derby, n.d., [November 1916].
59 Addison, *Four and a Half Years*, I, p. 267.

4

Manpower and the political crisis
December 1916

In November 1916 France was exhausted, the political outlook in Italy was poor and Russia was on the verge of revolution. These conclusions were reached by Lord Lansdowne, whose reassessment of the state of the British war effort led to a frenzied debate on the future course of the war. He honestly expressed his apprehensiveness about Britain's prospects in 1917 and demanded a thorough 'stock-taking' in order to estimate how much better the Allied position would be at the end of a further year of fighting. Lansdowne plainly asked, 'Let our naval, military and economic advisers tell us frankly whether they are satisfied that the knock-out blow can and will be delivered'.[1] He was sceptical of the value of 'paying the same sort of price for the same sort of gains' as during the 'advances' on the Western Front in 1915.[2] In effect his memorandum was a thinly-veiled piece of speculation on the possibility of a peace settlement. It was circulated to the War Committee, and Robertson was outraged that this question could be raised at Cabinet level at all.

Robertson rejected the notion that an outright military victory, or 'break-through', could not be achieved on the Western Front. He attacked the discussion of the terms on which peace might be concluded and later informed Lansdowne,

I considered it my duty to point out, what is common knowledge, that the nation is not really at war as yet and that until it is we cannot expect to win ... Many of our business people and railway authorities tell us that there is more business of a non-war nature now being carried on than before the war commenced. I am glad to think that steps may shortly be taken to remedy this and to put forth the full strength of the Nation.[3]

This was highly improbable by any known measure of non-war output. Robertson completely overstated his case as a result of his private sources grossly misinforming him on the maintenance of non-essential manufacturing capacity. However, his intention was clear. Robertson was both startled and angered by Lansdowne's memorandum and he sought to obtain the government's commitment to a comprehensive control of economic activity in wartime Britain. He therefore worked to reinforce the position of the War Office in relation to the civil departments. During 1917, 940,000 men were required for the army. Robertson felt that the measures taken by the War Committee to recruit men had proved inadequate and that the nation should be organised in the interests of the military effort so that the idea of 'business as usual' could, finally, be overturned. As with previous plans for operations on the Western Front, the summer campaigns of 1917 were designated of crucial importance by the General Staff in France so that a period of additional strain on the nation's manpower would be required. This type of statement was usually accompanied by the notion that the scale of sacrifice earlier in the war was insufficient. These discussions were no exception, for Robertson reminded the Secretary of State for War that 'Up to the present time the people of this country have not been called upon for such sacrifices as I believe them to be capable of bearing and willing to make.'[4]

In the aftermath of Lansdowne's memorandum Lloyd George encouraged the military members of the Army Council to go beyond a statement of the recruiting problem, and advance recommendations on the means of obtaining the necessary number of men. This instruction was a departure from previous practice whereby the military authorities had stated the total requirement of recruits and reminded the War Committee of its duty to provide the drafts. The military members went much further on 28 November on this crucial issue in their conclusion

that unless steps are taken *at once* by His Majesty's Government to introduce some better system of utilizing the manhood of the nation, untrammelled by conditions that in practice now nullify to a great extent the object of the Military Service Acts, it will be impossible after April next to keep the armies up to strength.[5]

As 2,500,000 men of military age were still in civilian life the military members of the Army Council considered that there was no reason why 940,000 men could not be obtained for military service. They suggested that the upper military age should be raised to fifty-five years, and men up to that age should perform 'National

Service' essential to the effective prosecution of the war. This call for compulsory National Service was directly related to the principle that the army should have 'first call' on the services of every man between the ages of eighteen and forty-one years. The employment of other men on 'National Service' would be designed to release every man who could be spared from naval duties or other indispensable employment. Taking advantage of the disintegration of the Man-Power Distribution Board, which had been established to allocate the labour requirements of each department, the War Office proposed the drastic solution of National Service to the problem of recruiting.

Despite the failure of the Somme offensive 'to produce visible results in any way proportionate to its cost',[6] the invasion of Roumania by German forces and the realisation that French reserves were substantially depleted during the Verdun campaign gave considerable weight to the opinion of the military authorities that it was imperative that the British armies on the Western Front should be maintained at full strength. Although the issue of compulsory National Service was discussed at the War Committee on 21 November, this dramatic initiative was moulded in the War Office and reflected Lloyd George's political opposition to the structural conduct of the war. In the autumn months of 1916 the War Office was the main source within the government of the criticisms of Asquith's premiership.[7] Lord Derby was Lloyd George's most important supporter of the reorganisation of the higher direction of the war. Throughout November 1916 the possibility of the resignation of the Secretary of State and the Under Secretary of State for War, however slight, was a potent threat to the survival of Asquith's Coalition government. Consequently, the demand of National Service was partially a device which would help to secure Lloyd George's wider objectives. To his surprise agreement was reached rapidly on this issue.

Asquith understood the importance of the military demand for men, despite some well-founded reluctance to believe in the promise which Robertson made of a 'break-through' on the Western Front in 1917. Two days after the memorandum of the military members was circulated, the War Committee agreed in principle to the introduction of compulsory National Service for all men up to sixty years of age. Hankey recorded in his diary, 'Epoch making War C[ommit]tee which decided on the Restriction of R[ailwa]y

Traffic & Compulsory National Service for Industry & Agriculture. This is splendid & we may yet win the war hands down.'[8] Even writing in retrospect, Robertson declared, 'No better day's work was done in London at any time during the war.'[9]

In view of the criticism levelled at the government that it was unable to respond rapidly to the changing condition of the war, it was significant that this decision occurred as a response to the impending defeat of Roumania, the German *levée en masse*, and the deteriorating food and shipping situation. The 'Wait and See' government had adopted compulsory national service not only to stifle criticism from the War Office, but to prosecute more effectively the nation's war effort. The government had taken a step towards civil industrial enrolment as a bid to maintain munitions output during the forthcoming period of increased recruitment for the army.

The vigorous response of the military authorities was not the only one which was made to Lansdowne's interest in a peace settlement. The second reaction tended to reinforce the military critique of the war effort. Lord Robert Cecil's importance as a government minister far outweighed the intrinsic value of his duties since July 1915 as Under-Secretary at the Foreign Office. On domestic isues he provided highly regarded independent assessments and his 'Note' of 27 November received close attention. Cecil shared Lansdowne's pessimism on the course of the war, but argued that it could be pursued more successfully if drastic changes were made in the organisation of civil society. With the debate on compulsory National Service in mind, he noted, 'Very possibly we shall have to adopt what is called industrial conscription. Quite certainly we shall have to make great innovations in our industrial organisation.'[10] Increasingly, considerable pressure had mounted on the government to extend its direct control of industries, some of which had already been, in effect, nationalised. The purpose of this pressure from the ranks of Unionist backbench MPs was to ensure the most economical use of manpower. Cecil echoed this viewpoint, and he indicated the feasibility of such industrial control through the establishment of a Cabinet committee on civilian organisation. Composed of three members, Cecil proposed that it would work in close collaboration with the War Committee.

Asquith accepted the idea of a Cabinet committee which would 'deal with domestic questions of national organisation.'[11] Hankey accepted the implications of this scheme, as a two-committee structure, by commenting that it was 'to do for the internal situation what the War C[ommit]tee is supposed to do for the War.'[12] Furthermore, its composition suggested that Asquith was prepared to allow Lloyd George, as Chairman, a degree of initiative in the development of a coherent form of industrial control. Its members were to be Lord Robert Cecil, Austen Chamberlain, Walter Runciman and Herbert Samuel. The proposed Civil Committee included all the main antagonists on the issue of the future utilisation of labour and the feasibility of central manpower planning. Although Herbert Samuel, the Home Secretary, did not dissent from the decision to introduce compulsory National Service, he had immediately circulated a paper which suggested an alternative course. Rather than compel labour to work in essential war industries, he proposed that the government should prohibit employers from recruiting labour for non-essential industries. Samuel argued that this method of manpower control in the economy would render unnecessary 'long lists of work-people, held under State control, ... who could be used – and many Trade Unionists are convinced would be used – for objects hostile to fundamental labour interests.'[13]

The proposed membership of the Civil Committee promised an explosive interaction. It reflected the range of opinion which existed on Lloyd George's interest in the mobilisation of labour. Samuel was not the only Cabinet minister and Liberal politician who supported fully Asquith's premiership, but resented the enormous War Office demand for men for 1917. On the mobilisation of the nation's industrial potential there had arisen special differences of opinion which aggravated already worsening relationships in the War Committee. The intention to introduce National Service was a component which featured prominently in the disunity of the government in Asquith's final week as Prime Minister. Walter Runciman refused to concur in the adoption of the principle. His opposition resuscitated Lloyd George's belief that since the out-break of war the Board of Trade was nothing more than a sanctuary for Liberal 'backwoodsmen'. In his letter to Hankey on 30 November, Runciman was particularly critical of the War Committee's failure to consult the Board of Trade, the Industrial Commissioner and the representatives of organised labour.[14] Hankey later added a note to Runciman's letter which stated,

It was alleged by some people in a good position to judge, though denied by Mr Asquith, that this letter precipitated [sic] the crisis, which ended in the fall of the Asquith Government. This is my view, as the letter exasperated Mr Lloyd George into taking action.[15]

Potentially the two decisions, to accept National Service and form a Civil Committee of five members at the end of November, provided the opportunity for the transformation of the direction and organisation of the war effort. However, the foremost critic of National Service was a prospective member of the Cabinet committee which was expected to implement it. The problems of establishing the Civil Committee and its relationship to compulsory National Service were rapidly apparent to Asquith's critics. The functions of the Civil Committee were yet to be defined. In certain situations it might have an adverse impact. If a scheme of substitution on a large scale was introduced to release men from industry, the process would hardly benefit from the separation of executive powers of decision-making for domestic and overseas questions, or between the industrial and military aspects of Britain's contribution to the Allied conduct of the war. Furthermore, the practical difficulties of implementing National Service included the wholesale cancellation of government pledges to the trade unions. Edwin Montagu was appointed Chairman of the sub-committee of representatives of eight government departments to work out the legislative framework of the scheme. The War Office appreciated that the opposition of Runciman and Samuel might delay the implementation of National Service. Consequently, Hankey was pressurised to push forward the committee work and ensure that the legislation could be enacted before Christmas.[16]

For ministers critical of Asquith's chairmanship of a large Cabinet which devolved initiative to 'labour-employing' departments and avoided adjudicating on differences between them, the failure and legacy of the Man-Power Distribution Board was a constant reminder of the need for change. Lloyd George noted, 'The departments all compete with each other and there is no one to settle their difference. Things look very bad.'[17] By the beginning of December 1916 important decisions on the control and allocation of manpower had been taken, but the entire conduct of the war remained unchanged and, indeed, uncertain. The main impression which the government gave was that it consistently failed to organise the available supply of labour in civilian work. Lloyd George was not the only minister who accused Asquith of procrastination and indecision. After a prolonged debate the Ministry of

Munitions assumed responsibility for the supply of aeroplanes in early December. Addison wrote, 'As this diary has shown for about two months now, the reports and recommendations of the Man-Power Board have been before the War Committee with nothing decided.'[18] On the same day Addison canvassed Liberal MPs to establish how many would actively support a Coalition government formed by Lloyd George. Fear that the policy decisions on National Service and the Cabinet structure would not lead to dramatic change in the short term infuriated Lloyd George into, in Hankey's words, 'taking action'.

The crisis in relations between Asquith and Lloyd George started in earnest on 1 December when the Secretary of State for War gave the Prime Minister an outline of his 'triumvirate scheme' for a supreme War Council. Instead of forming a Civil Committee to supplement the War Committee, Lloyd George proposed that the overall direction of the war should be conducted by a Council of three or, at most, four ministers, none of whom would have departmental duties. Asquith countered Lloyd George's plan with the reminder that the War Committee was being reconstructed through the creation of a committee to deal with domestic issues. This was not entirely the case, and on 3 December Lloyd George had a further interview with Asquith. The War Council plan was discussed again and disagreement on the exclusion of the Prime Minister from the proposed War Council persisted. No agreement was reached on the membership of the War Council, although Lloyd George believed that his plan was being seriously considered.

At this point in the crisis some politicians, implacably committed to Asquith's removal, feared that any compromise agreement reached by the two protagonists would result in the maintenance of the *status quo*. During 1916 Lord Milner had formed and led a 'revived opposition' in the House of Lords which was publicly critical of Asquith's premiership. On 29 November he was offered the post of Food Controller, but after meeting Lloyd George to discuss the appointment he rejected Asquith's offer.[19] Milner dreaded a 'Patch-Up' and on 3 December he wrote, 'Of course the loss of time is *AWFUL* – with the Germans already in Bucharest. But I had rather have six weeks of chaos followed by six months of Energy than any further prolongation of pure Squashiness.'[20]

Asquith's grasp of the political situation was slipping and the fear of a compromise being reached was illusory. On Sunday 3

December and the following day Lord Crewe, a close political confidant of Asquith and Lord President of the Council, was belatedly drawing up a plan to implement the two committee scheme. He was led to assume that the Prime Minister would be chairman of both. Lloyd George's position was significantly reinforced by the ambivalent attitude of Bonar Law, Leader of the Unionist Party, towards Asquith, second, Addison's canvas – which indicated a solid basis of support for him in the Liberal Party – and third sympathetic support from such senior Unionists as Arthur Balfour, Walter Long and Lord Derby.[21]

On 5 December Asquith resigned. He refused to serve under either Bonar Law or Lloyd George. Bonar Law was unable to form a government and on 6 December Lloyd George accepted the King's invitation to form a government. During the crisis in relations between Asquith and Lloyd George in the first week of December, the predominant dispute concerned the search for the most effective means of managing the war effort. Disagreement occurred on the scale of restructuring which was envisaged by the Secretary of State for War. In turn the dispute on the structural framework of Cabinet decision-making affected the movement towards National Service and the co-ordination of the manpower supply. Runciman sought to reverse the decision on the greater control of industrial output, and few ministers expected Asquith to implement it in an undiluted form. Indeed, his critics suspected that the creation of Montagu's committee was prevarication of the highest order. There was a schism in the government on the need for National Service and Lloyd George received support from Milnerite critics of the government who looked forward to 'War business' being conducted on 'business lines'. Consequently, among the complex interplay of factors, in the first week of December the manpower problem played a significant part which has hitherto been under-rated and neglected. Hankey considered Runciman's attitude on a scheme of civil industrial enrolment to be important, while the eclipsing of anti-conscriptionists and liberal economic non-interventionism was also observed by Beatrice Webb. She noted on 7 December, 'Asquith and his lieutenants are mildly against any interference with anyone or anything: the Lloyd George–Curzon group want to mobilise labour whilst retaining for the ruling class property intact and the control of trade and industry.'[22] William Pringle, a maverick Liberal MP and one of the most active backbench critics of the operation of the Military Service Acts throughout the war, located two immediate reasons for the fall of Asquith. They were the government's treatment of the manpower issue and the direction of the war. He laid great emphasis on the existence of a 'ginger' group, comprising Unionists, as a factor which 'insisted on a system of universal National Service as the only method to "counter Hindenburg"'.[23] The same group suggested that Montagu's committee was evidence of the government's 'slowness'. Pringle had a political record of staunchly independent action which did not endear him to his constituency party in North-West Lanarkshire and he did not support Lloyd George's bid for the premiership.[24] Consequently, his evidence was not overtly partisan in a controversy which deeply concerned the political principles of the Liberal Party.

It was confidently assumed that the new government would immediately introduce National Service. Lloyd George drew a considerable amount of support from politicians and observers who put the manpower requirements of the army first and thought that Lloyd George would do so too. On 1 December Lord Burnham, proprietor of the *Daily Telegraph*, told Lloyd George that the only chance of a 'break-through' on the Western Front was to attack all along the line. This totally uninformed opinion from a sympathetic observer of the military interest was based on the assumption that 1,500,000 men could be recruited for this grand campaign. Lloyd George was informed that the 'Army looks to you to get the men'.[25] The dilemma created by Lloyd George's rhetoric in justification of introducing National Service was that it concealed his private criticism of the use of manpower in the British armies abroad and especially on the Western Front. Beyond the acute and very real differences of opinion between Lloyd George and Asquith on the control of manpower at the highest level, Lloyd George was reluctant to reflect on the full implications of compulsory National Service. For example, it would inevitably be denounced by engineering trade unions as 'industrial conscription'. Lloyd George's real perspective was recorded by C. P. Scott, the editor of the *Manchester Guardian*, following a conversation sometime between the momentous events of 3 December. It again indicated the centrality of the issue of manpower as Asquith's political significance waned,

In regard to Conscription a mere tightening of the screw w[oul]d be useless. If he h[a]d power he w[oul]d seek to make it more discriminating – There were limits to what the country c[oul]d do in regard to supplying men – Three tasks were sought to be imposed on us (a) to keep the seas (b) to finance the Allies & provide them with munitions (c) to provide an army on the full continental scale. We c[oul]d discharge any two of them, but not all three.[26]

In the two weeks before he became Prime Minister, Lloyd George's call for the effective conduct of the war placed him in the invidious and false position of his support being claimed for the maintenance of the British military presence in France at the established level of 1,500,000 men. However, during his period at the War Office Lloyd George had resented the considerable prestige which Robertson and Macready enjoyed at meetings of the War Committee. He was less anxious to maintain the army on a full continental scale than observers of the military scene such as Lord Burnham and Lord Esher appreciated.[27] Indeed, Lloyd George was determined that the allocation of manpower released through the National Service scheme would not be primarily determined by the constant demand of Haig and Kiggell for more men. Although Lloyd George was extremely critical of the persistent failure of the War Committee to implement the plans of the Man-Power Distribution Board, he was also wary of any scheme which would guarantee the Army Council an unrestricted supply of men for service in France.[28]

Compulsory National Service, as Lloyd George understood it, would be a civilian directed scheme which would enable the government to respond swiftly to the changing circumstances of the war by reallocating its mobile supply of labour. In this context the manpower issue played an important part in Lloyd George's appointment as Prime Minister. The failure of the Man-Power Distribution Board, from which Lloyd George successfully distanced himself, damaged the ability of the War Committee to take any further initiative in this crucial sphere of the war effort. Instead, the demand for National Service drew opposition from ministers who enjoyed the political support of the Prime Minister. Asquith's Coalition government was reluctant to carry out the necessary Cabinet and departmental reconstruction which was essential if the notion of National Service, as yet undefined, was to stand any chance of success. In contrast, with the supporters of the more 'total' organisation of the nation's manpower and material resources on his side, Lloyd George epitomised the movement to conduct the war effort on a more efficient level if the Allied operations were to have any chance of military success in 1917. It was therefore assumed that Lloyd George as Prime Minister would introduce a comprehensive scheme of National Service.

Lloyd George's request for the support of the Labour Party on 7 December marked a crucial stage in the consolidation of the new Coalition government. His approach was made more difficult by the critical attitude which the TUC had adopted in relation to Lloyd George during the political crisis.[29] Lloyd George sought the support of the Labour Party with tangible offers of ministerial places and less certain assurances about his future policy intentions. Sidney Webb believed that he was both non-committal and evasive in his statement to senior Labour figures at the meeting.[30] Beatrice Webb sketchily noted, 'All he definitely promised was a Ministry of Labour and a Food Controller – whilst he clearly intimated compulsory mobilisation of labour.'[31] The new War Cabinet was to consist of five members. Arthur Henderson was appointed to it and Lloyd George offered the newly created Ministry of Labour and one other ministerial office to Labour politicians. Of almost greater importance, in view of the resolutions passed against 'industrial conscription' at successive Labour and Trades Union congresses, was the question of National Service. Lloyd George treated the subject with considerable circumspection. He certainly intimated his intention to introduce National Service which, he reminded his cautious audience, was agreed in principle by Asquith's War Committee. However, the late government's resolution was nothing more than a general intention.

The Labour MPs and trade unionists which assembled at the War Office on 7 December did not refuse their assent to the Prime Minister's manpower plans. More significantly, to give some assurance on this issue, Lloyd George agreed to the suggestion 'that just as the enforcement of military compulsion had been preceded by a period under the Derby scheme of voluntary enrolment with a time limit, so a similar procedure might be adopted in the present case.'[32] It was not to be the last time that the Derby scheme, as the final stage of voluntary recruiting for military service, was regarded as a suitable method of transition from the notion of voluntarism to the principle of compulsion. Lloyd George's assurance that a period of voluntary civil enrolment would precede the compulsory transfer of labour marked a departure from his statements on National

Service over the previous two weeks. It was expedient for some
reassurance to be given, at a crucial point in the formation of the
new government, that the Prime Minister was not committed to a
policy which would be confronted by labour with extreme hostility
in the engineering works and the munitions factories. Lloyd George
continued to employ the rhetoric which forecast dramatic changes
in the organisation of manpower for civil war work, but one week
after his appointment the statement of intent on National Service
was still without any practical substance.

It was soon apparent that Lloyd George needed to be reminded
that the deteriorating military manpower situation in France
required an immediate response. Lord Rhondda, President of the
Local Government Board and one of Lloyd George's 'businessmen',
informed the Prime Minister with almost indecent haste, 'The
question of Man-Power, National Service and especially the supply
of men for the Army seem to me to be among the most pressing
problems at the present moment.'[33] Rhondda urged that the
experience of his department should be used to enable the government to start to meet the demand of 940,000 new recruits in 1917.
Haig sought reassurance from Lord Derby, now Secretary of State
for War, that the government appreciated his concern regarding the
reinforcement of the British armies in France. Derby assured the
anxious Commander in Chief that the War Cabinet would find a
satisfactory solution. Also, in placatory Derby style, he agreed with
Haig, 'that the question of man-power is the most difficult problem
to solve, & one which must be solved if we are to give you an
effective force during the whole of next year'.[34]

The most immediate and direct challenge to Lloyd George to
reassure the military authorities was issued two days after he
became Prime Minister. In an impressionistic way Robertson told
Lloyd George that the supply of manpower should be organised in
Britain to eradicate the still prevalant 'business-as-usual' approach.
He complained, 'We can only expect *just* to win through and no
more, and yet things in England are going on much the same to-day
as two years ago.'[35] The latter part of this statement was manifest
nonsense, and it reflected the failure of the Army Council to
appreciate the importance of the basic manufacturing industries to
the overall war effort. The note was an exhortation in the classic
Robertson style that, despite the difficult next few months, an
earnest government with audacity, courage, a definite plan and a

commitment to the Western Front would create the 'right conditions' for the defeat of Germany in 1917.

A more concrete review of the manpower position was circulated on 12 December by the Director of Recruiting, Auckland Geddes. The review noted that of the 11,050,000 men employed in Britain 3,352,000 worked in trades and industries of 'relatively small National Importance'.[36] This category of men employed in non-essential industries, as defined by the War Office, included 1,226,000 men in the amorphous area of Hotels, Entertainments, Stockbroking and Professional occupations. Auckland Geddes concluded that to provide recruits for the army, men in less vital trades must be transferred, by voluntary or compulsory means, to essential industries to release men fit for military service on a large scale. This was the most authoritative statement available in support of the urgent implementation of a comprehensive scheme of National Service. Geddes forcefully noted, 'The problem of recruitment for 1917 when reduced to its essentials therefore is to effect the transference of approximately 1,000,000 persons from the non-essential to the essential industries. Nothing less will enable the Armies to be maintained.'[37] At the earliest stage of Lloyd George's premiership the War Office worked hard to re-establish the pre-eminent importance of its own manpower requirements in relation to the labour demands of the civil departments. Similarly, its demand for 940,000 men was seen as the prime and wholly legitimate reason for the introduction of National Service. Even if it was to be a voluntary campaign in the first instance the War Office assumed that the logical result of National Service would be the compulsory transfer, or mobilisation, of labour from trades and occupations of small national importance to essential industries.

Montagu's committee was empowered by Asquith to work out the details of the National Service scheme including the establishment of upper and lower age limits, the advisability of extending it to female labour and the drafting of a bill.[38] Proposals were discussed at its main meeting on 1 December and the committee, which included Austen Chamberlain and Walter Long, expressed a preference for a form of National Service which was strictly limited to the enrolment of male workers in non-essential trades. This plan arose out of the experience of the Reserved Occupations Committee and suggested that the potential value of compulsory enrolment had been seriously over-estimated by the War Office. As far as can be ascertained Montagu's committee did not meet on 4 December and at the height of the political crisis no alternative meeting could be arranged. Of all the senior Liberal ministers who enjoyed close political relations with Asquith, Montagu was the least anxious to follow the former Prime Minister to the opposition front benches.[39] As he did so he wrote a valedictory memorandum and draft Bill on National Service which formed the basis of the War Cabinet's initial discussions on the control of manpower. Montagu acknowledged that disagreement had occurred on whether the Directorate of National Service as a central manpower authority should be a recruiting agency for both civil and military forms of war work.[40] Geddes had urged that this should be the case, but in general terms the draft Bill was designed 'to regulate the supply of workers and men for all industries, occupations, and services (including the naval and military services) . . . having regard to the needs of the country at the moment'.[41] A voluntary campaign would initially take place with provision for the compulsory movement of labour if it proved necessary. Many of the complicating factors which Montagu raised were overlooked by Lloyd George, who felt that National Service gave the government an opportunity to be seen to be both dynamic and innovative in tackling a major problem.

In the minutes of the War Cabinet meeting on 14 December no mention of National Service was made without the prefix 'compulsory'.[42] The three members present, Lord Curzon, Lord Milner and Arthur Henderson, accepted the principle that there should be both military and civil sides to National Service. The creation of the Ministry of Labour had led to a temporary dislocation of the civil sphere in the administration of the manpower supply. Consequently, the War Office occupied a position of considerable strength at a crucial stage in the development of the new government's manpower plans. Lord Curzon also told Lloyd George, 'we were all agreed in pressing upon you the extreme desirability of persuading Montagu to be the new Director of National Service . . . The scheme is Montagu's. He is a firm believer in it.'[43] Certainly no one knew better than the former Minister of Munitions the practical difficulties which represented the reality of the situation far more closely than the false expectations which were invested in the scheme.

However, Montagu was aware that the scheme would draw criticism from departments as it sought to balance the military and civil demands on National Service. Without Montagu's appointment the introduction of this vital component of the government's aim to win public approval at an early stage would be far more difficult to achieve. Henderson thought that his appointment would be welcomed by the labour movement. Hankey wrote a eulogy on Montagu's qualities including his 'tremendous grip & power of work & knowledge of Government & power of handling men'.[44] With so much at stake for the government, Montagu came under considerable pressure to accept the post of Director of National Service.[45] No other appointment caused quite as much difficulty and no other Asquithian Liberal received as much attention from the government as Montagu did after 14 December. Two places were available in the government for former Liberal colleagues of Lloyd George, one of which was intended for Montagu. Despite his reluctance to withdraw from ministerial life, Montagu's personal bond with Asquith was strong, and the government's appeals were to no avail.[46] The scheme of National Service had suffered a severe setback.

During the same period that Montagu withstood pressure to rejoin the government, Austen Chamberlain was engaged in an efficient lobbying process. He initiated a process which led inexorably to the appointment of his half-brother, Neville, as Director-General of National Service. On 17 December Austen Chamberlain first put forward his half-brother's name to Lord Curzon. On the following day he wrote in the same vein to a second member of the War Cabinet, Lord Milner, who was informed:

You know something of Neville and his ability. He made a remarkable address last summer to the Trade Unions Congress when welcoming it to Birmingham, and I have learned from labour Members – Henderson and Barnes included – that they were very much struck by the courage, sympathy and novelty of his welcome.[47]

Both Curzon and Milner 'independently' suggested his name to the War Cabinet. On 19 December it resolved that Neville Chamberlain should be offered the post. At 2.30 p.m. that day Austen Chamberlain contacted him at Paddington shortly before his departure for Birmingham, [48] and at 4 p.m. his appointment was announced in the House of Commons, as part of Lloyd George's parliamentary statement on government policy.[49]

Immense pressure was placed on Neville Chamberlain in the course of a short interview with the Prime Minister. He was told that the organisation of National Service was 'Imperial work' and therefore more important than his municipal duties in Birmingham. He was not given more than ten minutes to consider the offer because Lloyd George needed to announce the appointment as part of his package of plans on future policy. Furthermore, he was told nothing about the details of his future government work. That night Neville Chamberlain noted, 'I don't suppose there is a more miserable man in Birmingham tonight than I.'[50] Although he was fortified by the thought that he had not sought the post, he contemplated his removal to 'that odious London' with trepidation. Neville Chamberlain was elected to Birmingham City Council in 1911. One month before his appointment as Director-General of National Service he was returned for a second term of office as Lord Mayor. His pre-war city 'town-planning' schemes had won national interest and his innovative attitude to local government continued into 1916 with the establishment of the Municipal Savings Bank in Birmingham. In this latter scheme Milner piloted the Bill through the House of Lords and told Chamberlain, 'I have so much sympathy [for] your public work & the spirit in which you set about it.'[51] The Lord Mayor of Birmingham also enjoyed close political relations with Leo Amery, one of Milner's coterie and a Birmingham MP. During 1915 they corresponded on the wartime organisation of industry and the need after the war for the more harmonious relationship of 'Capital and Labour'. This theme formed part of Chamberlain's address of welcome to the TUC in September 1916, which was widely reported.[52] In it he urged that positive steps should be taken to improve relations between employers and employed; for example, through the retention of administrative controls which had originally been established for the duration of the war. Inevitably, as Lord Mayor Chamberlain was Chairman of the Local Tribunal.[53] His position as a provincial political figure of some importance was recognised in that he was a member of the Central Control Board (Liquor Traffic).[54]

It would certainly be an exaggeration to perceive Neville Chamberlain as a national figure in the first two years of the war. The House of Commons was astonished that he should be appointed to introduce National Service. However, through his wartime work which had reasserted the Chamberlainite Liberal Unionist tradition in Birmingham, he had won considerable esteem in the Milnerite circle.[55] He was also known, through his brother, to senior

Unionists, who distrusted Bonar Law's ability to oppose Lloyd George when conservative principles on such questions as land reform and Ireland were endangered. In common with many backbench Unionists, Neville Chamberlain's opposition to Asquith's premiership was emphatic and without qualification. On his resignation Chamberlain noted 'Thank heaven. At last we shall have a chance of success.'[56]

Neville Chamberlain looked forward to the formation of the new government, not realising the part he would play in it. On 17 December 1916 he wrote,

I feel for the first time that the Cabinet will really attend to the business of waging war & will think out decisions & enforce them on the Departments. On the other side the Departments (or some of them) have men at their head who understand their business and are free from the shibboleths.[57]

Two days later he was the Director of a new government department. From the first year of the war he had been interested in the issue of 'National Organisation'. Untainted by direct contact with the national political scene and largely 'free from the shibboleths', he joined the 'War-business' government as an expert on the reorganisation of industry and labour. Alongside the creation of the Ministry of Labour, Neville Chamberlain's appointment reflected the War Cabinet's realisation that National Service would only succeed if it received the unqualified support of the labour movement.

The government's concern about the attitude of labour was reflected in the War Cabinet's discussion on 19 December, but not in the Prime Minister's speech later the same day. The War Cabinet decided that the Prime Minister should make no mention of a time limit for the voluntary campaign to achieve the required results, which if unsatisfactory would be replaced by a scheme of compulsory enrolment. Henderson reported that his party was opposed to any scheme which resembled 'industrial conscription'. The War Cabinet was reluctant to jeopardise the political position of the Labour ministers so soon after the formation of the broad-based Coalition government and, consequently, the scheme's success was wholly dependent on voluntary enrolment.[58] For military service in January 1917 100,000 fit men were required.

The diluted scheme of National Service was not conveyed by the Prime Minister in his long statement on the constitution and war policy of the new government on 19 December. Bonar Law told the King, 'The most important subject . . . was the declaration that the Government intended to take steps to secure universal national service.'[59] For the purpose of maximum impact Lloyd George justified the 'more drastic steps' to correct the 'imperfect organisation of our industrial manpower' by comparing the experiences of life on the Western and domestic fronts.[60] By highlighting the scale of 'sacrifice' on the Western Front in pursuit of the nation's just cause, the Somme battles were used as the embodiment of the ultimate expression of devotion to the interests of the state. The Prime Minister appealed to the 'unfit man and the exempted man' to reflect on the life of the soldiers in France, who

are enduring much, they are hazarding all, whilst we are living in comfort and security at home. You cannot have absolute equality of sacrifice. In a war that is impossible, but you can have equal readiness to sacrifice from all.[61]

He sought to implant the notion of sacrifice in domestic war work so that opposition to the call for men to render service to the state would be defused. In effect, labour was informed that conditions at home could never be worse than the situation in the front line. This speech therefore attempted to inform the domestic workforce that the more 'total' organisation of resources would be needed to secure victory and therefore the further loss of individual rights at the workplace would be necessary.

Lloyd George's rhetorical embellishments not only heightened the dramatic impact of Chamberlain's appointment, but completely overstated the potential value of the voluntary campaign to the conduct of the war. His flourishes included the incredible statement,

I hope before Parliament resumes its duties in another few weeks we shall be able to report that we have secured a sufficiently large industrial army in order to mobilise the whole of the labour strength of this country for war purposes.[62]

This pronouncement was duly emphasised in the newspaper reports of the speech on the following day. The reports failed to note the paradox by which the voluntary enrolment of labour would establish an 'industrial army'. Some newspapers commended this 'Derby-type' scheme because 'it is necessary to have some drastic method of maintaining discipline and steady work in the industrial ranks'.[63] The inevitability of compulsory powers being introduced in the near future was widely emphasised. This was reflected in the different titles of Chamberlain's post which were in circulation. Among them the description 'Civil Controller of Mobilisation' was most at variance with the duties of the Director of National Service.[64] The 'Derby scheme' which led to the imposition of compulsory military service without serious unrest was cited as a precedent which should be followed in the case of National Service. Similarly, the use of the phrase 'industrial army', implying the mobilisation of labour and a disciplined workforce, encouraged the universal expectation of an immediate reorganisation of manpower utilisation in Britain.

An important reason for the heightened expectations of National Service in Parliament and the press lay in its presentation as a specific British response to the introduction of the National Civilian Service Law in Germany. On 30 November the War Committee referred to the '*levée en masse* in Germany' as a major factor which influenced its acceptance of the principle of National Service.[65] However, the Auxiliary Service Law did not come into operation in Germany until 5 December. Every German male between the ages of seventeen and sixty who was not in the army or navy became liable for National Service.[66] The German law embodied the intention of enabling the state to decide where every worker should be placed to be of maximum value to the conduct of the war effort. At the same time the law was not intended to interfere with the right of labour to organise, nor were workers to become subject to military discipline in industry. Furthermore, *The Labour Gazette* noted,

Enrolment for National Service is to be effected [in Germany] in the first instance by voluntary enlistment in response to appeals issued by the government. If these appeals should fail to meet with a satisfactory response compulsion will be applied.[67]

The law was administered by the newly formed War Department of the Prussian Ministry of War and was described in Britain as the foremost example of Prussian militarism at work in civil society. It was widely interpreted as being draconian in its impact on the civil population in Germany and the occupied territories. In his policy statement Lloyd George encouraged this viewpoint by stating that it was 'necessary to make a swift and effective answer to Germany's latest move'.[68] Newspapers concluded that Chamberlain's appointment was 'the answer to Hindenburg's mass levy'.[69] In fact the law far from threatened a *levée en masse* and its contribution to the recruitment of men for the German army remained secondary to the impact of the military conscription laws. Writers such as Beatrice Webb overestimated the Ministry of War's ability to impose industrial conscription on the civil population without reference to the wartime aspirations of

the German labour movement.[70] Evidence on its limited impact
was collected through such official channels as the Foreign Trade
Intelligence Department of the Foreign Office.[71] In fact, in their
references to voluntarism there were sharp similarities between the
German Auxiliary Service law and the British National Service
scheme. The British scheme was a reaction to the complexity and
indecision of manpower co-ordination under Asquith's premiership
rather than a direct response to the German law. However, the
scale of publicity it received in official speeches was deliberately
designed to convey the existence of an integrated military and
industrial war effort in Germany which would also have to be
secured in Britain.[72] This propagandist manoeuvre indicated the
government's determination to ensure that the scheme of voluntary
National Service quickly enjoyed the complete confidence of
recruiting officers, munitions officials, employers and trade
unionists.

On a troubled Christmas eve in Birmingham Neville Chamberlain
reflected on his new post and concluded,

I have never had even a scrap of paper appointing me or giving me any idea
of where my duties begin and end. I don't know whether I have Ireland or
Scotland as well as England. I don't know whether I have Munitions
volunteers. I believe I am to have a salary but I don't know what. I suppose
I can be dismissed by someone but I don't know who.[73]

Chamberlain later observed that 'the difficulties literally bristle. At
every turn one is held up by somebody's pledge & the pledges have
always been in the direction of bribes to the proletariat.'[74] He
received details from the War Cabinet Secretariat of the work of
the Man-Power Distribution Board, whose archives were eventually transferred to the National Service Department. Unlike his
brother at the Board, however, Neville Chamberlain' powers and
responsibilities were not carefully defined. Nor did his work enjoy
any greater prestige because his office was not of ministerial rank
and his department was not directly answerable to Parliament.
Furthermore, with the exception of Milner, Neville Chamberlain
did not have the political support necessary, to establish the
autonomy of his department or resist the 'hustle' of the Prime
Minister. Chamberlain complained that he was 'faced with a
demand for a scheme to be produced instantaneously'.[75]

Neville Chamberlain was less disturbed than Montagu had been by the indication that the department should obtain and regulate the supply of men for military and naval service in addition to ensuring the more equitable provision of manpower for all civilian industries, occupations and services. At this stage it was fully intended that the National Service Department would be obliged to assume control of the military Recruiting Department. On 22 December Chamberlain met Nevil Macready and Auckland Geddes. He was most impressed with Geddes, who as Director of Recruiting was the prime candidate for the post of Military Director at the department.[76] Regular contact with the military authorities inclined Chamberlain to disregard Montagu's cautious advice of starting the scheme by gradually classifying industries and registering volunteers. Instead of Montagu's plan of exploiting the voluntary association of civilians with the more effective management of the war effort, Neville Chamberlain developed an unhealthy interest in the notion of an 'industrial army'. He wrote on 2 January 1917, 'I am evolving vast and revolutionary notions of turning the whole war industry of the country into a State owned concern in which every one should be only an officer or a private – and all the surplus should go to the State!!!'[77]

He outlined his scheme for an 'industrial army' with three grades of pay to his shocked and disturbed deputy James Stevenson. In Chamberlain's search for a systematic approach to the allocation and control of manpower, he wanted to abolish the various wage rates in order that men 'drafted' from non-essential industries into agricultural and munition work would receive the same payment. Following his discussion with Stevenson, Chamberlain noted,

He says the Unions wouldn't stand it for a minute & moreover it wouldn't supply the demand because you couldn't put the Industrial Army men at army pay alongside munition workers who are earning their £3 to £8 a week. I agreed but suggested that the Army might work in National factories. But he says the Unions wouldn't allow that either.[78]

Chamberlain promoted the idea of equality of sacrifice and sought to impose a form of mobility in manpower control which would effectively inter-relate the separate military and civilian war institutions. He foresaw the development of parity of treatment between men in the army and in munition factories. Despite his expressions of goodwill to the labour movement he failed to sufficiently realise that he threatened the autonomy of the civil worker and raised the fear of 'industrial conscription'. By the first week of January 1917 Chamberlain had considered a number of 'revolutionary' schemes which had the appearance of securing the control of labour rather than controlling the general relationship of 'Capital and Labour'.

There were two reasons for Chamberlain's interest in grandiose schemes and the development of an 'industrial army'. Firstly, civil government departments continued to fail to establish any common ground of agreement on the value and relevance of National Service to their war work. Secondly, Chamberlain was sceptical that a voluntary campaign would significantly add to the available supply of manpower. He reflected, 'I don't believe we shall get much out of volunteering but Ll[oyd] G[eorge] says we can't have compulsion without legislation & as the House is up we can't get that before the end of February.'[79] The inherent drawback of Chamberlain's political position was that his office symbolised the government's reluctance to clarify the relationship of its adoption of compulsory National Service with the development of voluntary methods of intervention in essential war industries. In particular, the creation of the National Service Department – without a specific act of legislation – at sub-ministerial level and represented by the Home Office in the House of Commons, indicated the continuing degree of uncertainty which existed on this issue. It was quickly understood in Whitehall by ministers and civil servants alike that Chamberlain was unlikely to obtain compulsory powers while the extent of the transfer of labour from non-essential industries to work of national importance remained in doubt.

Some light was shed on the animosity shown towards the concept of National Service by some departments in Whitehall in the difficulties which were encountered by Chamberlain in recruiting staff for senior posts. The Ministry of Labour was formed around the Employment Department of the Board of Trade and the new ministries for Shipping and the Coal Mines drew on the experience of departments which had formerly held responsibilities for these aspects of the overall war effort. In contrast, the National Service Department did not inherit the personnel of the Man-Power Distribution Board. Furthermore, other ministers were reluctant to make their staff available for organising the voluntary campaign of National Service. Montagu had suggested that James Stevenson, a munitions official and previously the manager of whisky distillers John Walker & Sons, should be appointed Civil Director. In the course of 22–30 December 1916 manoeuvre and counter-manoeuvre took place as Chamberlain demanded and Addison, now Minister of Munitions, resisted the claim for Stevenson.[80] The whole issue was even discussed at one of Lloyd George's notorious breakfast meetings without result. Despite the Prime Minister's intervention it was not until the end of December that Addison 'finally agreed however, that he [Stevenson] should assist him as adviser for a *short* time until he got his schemes started'.[81] Under considerable pressure Stevenson agreed to act as Deputy Director but he only remained at the department until 1 February 1917. Throughout January his position was uneasy because he was critical of the voluntary campaign and the probability that it would entice skilled labour from munitions factories for alternative war work. The problem of providing the department with permanent staff at the highest level was indicative of the distrust which greeted the arrival of this innovative scheme in Whitehall. This wrangle delayed the appointment of other staff and led to a deterioration in relations with the Minister of Munitions who at an early stage privately accused Chamberlain of being 'utterly incompetent'.[82]

At the end of 1916 the future of the government's manpower plans was uncertain. The basic problem of the failure to co-ordinate the labour demands of the departments was still clearly apparent. The promise of change through the much-heralded National Service scheme remained theoretical and was far from becoming an actuality. The first three weeks of the department's existence had suggested a want of prime ministerial direction and support, apart from the assertion that the separate spheres of military and industrial war work would be completely integrated through the creation of a 'total' organisation for the pursuit of the war effort. In a bid to establish a policy direction Chamberlain subordinated the method of voluntarism to a grand scheme which aimed at the total state ownership of essential war industries and the control of labour through the provision of an 'industrial army'. This departure from Montagu's recommendations disregarded the practical obstacles which prevented the wholesale movement of labour. By the end of December 1916 Labour advisers had not been appointed to the National Service Department, and the Labour Party and the TUC remained unaware of Chamberlain's assessment of the industrial situation.

Furthermore, schemes created by the central administration to classify the importance of industries and move labour to vital war work could not be implemented without the development of local machinery. At the forefront of its tasks, the National Service Department faced the daunting challenge of facilitating the recruitment of 100,000 men for military service during January 1917. The actual test of the new department was the extent to which reinforcements would be provided for the British armies in France in sufficient time for the opening of the Allied military offensive on the Western Front. At the end of December 1916 the National Service Department was poorly equipped and badly prepared for assuming these tasks through the effective distribution of labour in accordance with occupational priority areas. The department lacked the powers to act independently as well as the standing, *vis à vis* established departments, to hold its own in the event of disputes with them. In effect, National Service remained an idea without a practical plan, a theoretical commitment without a clearly defined industrial need and an innovatory ministry without the general support of departments concerned with the allocation and control of manpower.

Notes
1 PRO CAB 37/159/32, Terms on which a peace might be considered etc., Lansdowne, 13 November 1916.
2 *Loc. cit.*
3 Robertson mss. I/21/47, Robertson to Lansdowne, 1 December 1916, signed copy. See also Robertson, *Soldiers and Statesmen*, I, p. 304.
4 Robertson mss. I/6/7a, Robertson to Lloyd George, 24 November 1916, signed copy.
5 PRO WO 162/28, Supply of Men for the Army, Memorandum by the Military Members of the Army Council to the Secretary of State for War, 28 November 1916.
6 Liddell Hart, *History of the First World War*, p. 295.
7 Riddell, *War Diary*, entry for 26 November 1916, pp. 222–4; J. M. McEwen, 'The struggle for mastery in Britain : Lloyd George versus Asquith, December 1916', *Journal of British Studies*, XVIII, 1978, pp. 137–41.
8 Hankey mss. HNKY 1/1, Diary, 30 November 1916.
9 Robertson, *Soldiers and Statesmen*, I, p. 304.
10 PRO CAB 37/160/21, Note on War situation, need for industrial conscription and Cabinet Committee on civilian organisation, R. Cecil, 27 November 1916.
11 PRO CAB 37/160/30, Asquith to King George V, 30 November 1916.
12 Hankey mss. HNKY 1/1, Diary, 29 November 1916.
13 IWM MPDB 77/66/2, National Organisation, H. S[amuel], 30 November 1916.

14 Hankey mss. HNKY 4/8, Runciman to Hankey, 30 November 1916.
15 Hankey mss. HNKY 4/8, Note by Hankey, 1 June 1917. This signed note was written on Runciman's letter to Hankey of 30 November 1916.
16 Hankey mss. HNKY 1/1, Diary, 30 November 1916.
17 Quoted in Riddell, *War Diary*, p. 222.
18 Addison mss. Box 99, Diary, entry for 4 December 1916.
19 P. A. Lockwood, 'Milner's entry into the War Cabinet, December 1916', *Historical Journal*, VII, 1964, pp. 121–8.
20 Milner mss. dep. 353, Milner to Lady Edward Cecil, 3 December 1916.
21 K & J. Morgan, *Portrait of a Progressive*, Oxford, 1980, p. 54.
22 Beatrice Webb mss. Harvester microfilm Mf685, Diary, 7 December 1916.
23 Pringle mss. VI, Reasons why the Asquith ministry fell in December 1916, Pringle, n.d., microfilm.
24 Pringle mss. II 24, Pringle to J. Rabine, Secretary of the Coatbridge Liberal Club, 11 December 1916, signed copy, microfilm.
25 Riddell, *War Diary*, entry for 1 December 1916, p. 225.
26 C. P. Scott mss. Box 133, Political diaries, 3 December 1916.
27 Oliver, Viscount Esher (ed.), *Journals and Letters of Reginald, Viscount Esher*, London, 1934–8, IV, Esher to Lord Murray of Elibank, 28 November 1916, p. 69.
28 Lloyd George, *War Memoirs*, II, p. 1035.
29 See Minutes of the Parliamentary Committee of the TUC, Harvester microfilm M769, 6 December 1916.
30 See Report of 16th Annual Conference of the Labour Party, 1917, in P. Stansky (ed.), *The Left and War : The British Labour Party and World War I*, London, 1969, pp. 171–99.
31 Beatrice Webb mss. Harvester microfilm Mf685, Diary, 8 December 1916.
32 Bonar Law mss. 81/1/36, Curzon to Bonar Law, 10 December 1916. Curzon enclosed a 'Memorandum of Conversation between Mr Lloyd George and certain Unionist ex-Ministers', 7 December 1916. See also H. A. Taylor, *Robert Donald*, London, 1934, p. 134.
33 Lloyd George mss. F/43/5/3, Rhondda to Lloyd George, 15 December 1916.
34 Derby mss. 920DER(17) 27/2, Derby to Haig, 13 December 1916, unsigned copy.
35 Robertson mss. Robertson to Lloyd George, 'My views on the situation', Final draft, 8 December 1916.
36 A. Chamberlain mss. AC 16/1/24, General Review, Man-Power Position, D[irector of] R[ecruiting], [A. Geddes], 12 December 1916.
37 *Loc. cit.* See Appendix 2.
38 See K. R. Grieves, 'The British Government's political and administrative response to the man-power problem in the First World War', (Ph.D. thesis, University of Manchester, 1984) pp. 108–16.
39 S. D. Waley, *Edwin Montagu*, London, 1964, pp. 106–7; Addison, *Politics from Within*, I, Diary, entry for 9 December 1916, p. 272.

40 IWM MPDB 77/66/2, National Service, Montagu, 5 December 1916.
41 Lloyd George mss. F/79/19/2, National Service, Draft of a Bill, 5 December 1916.
42 PRO CAB 23/1 W.C.7, 14 December 1916.
43 Lloyd George mss. F/11/8/2, Curzon to Lloyd George, 14 December 1916.
44 Hankey mss. HNKY 4/8, Hankey to Lloyd George, 14 December 1916, signed copy.
45 Hankey mss. HNKY 4/1, Diary, 17 December 1916.
46 'An account of the crisis', Montagu, 9 December 1916, in Waley, *Edwin Montagu*, p. 114.
47 Milner mss. dep. 144, A. Chamberlain to Milner, 18 December 1916.
48 For Austen Chamberlain's account of the events of the afternoon of 19 December 1916, see Petrie, *The Life and Letters of . . . Sir Austen Chamberlain*, II, pp. 64–6.
49 Neville Chamberlain mss. NC 1/18/2/10, N. Chamberlain to Norman Chamberlain, 7 January 1917.
50 N. Chamberlain mss. NC 1/20/1/107, N. Chamberlain to Mrs Mary Carnegie, 19 December 1916.
51 N. Chamberlain mss. NC 7/11/9/11, Milner to N. Chamberlain, n.d.
52 N. Chamberlain mss. NC 2/20, Political journal, 17 September 1916.
53 N. Chamberlain mss. NC 1/26/80, N. Chamberlain to Anne Chamberlain, 3 March 1916.
54 J. Turner, 'State purchase of the liquor trade in the First World War', *Historical Journal*, XXIII, 1980, p. 606.
55 N. Chamberlain mss. NC 8/5/1/41, N. Chamberlain to Milner, 18 December 1916, unsigned copy.
56 N. Chamberlain mss. NC 2/20, Political journal, 13 December 1916.
57 N. Chamberlain mss. NC 18/1/93, N. Chamberlain to Hilda Chamberlain, 17 December 1916.
58 PRO CAB 23/1 W.C. 11, 19 December 1916.
59 Bonar Law mss. 77/2, Bonar Law to George V, 19 December 1916, unsigned copy.
60 88 H.C. Deb. 5s, Col. 1350, 19 December 1916.
61 *Ibid*. Col. 1348.
62 *Ibid*. Col. 1353.
63 N. Chamberlain mss. NC 15/1(b), Press cuttings, *Yorkshire Herald*, 20 December 1916.
64 *Daily Telegraph*, 20 December 1916.
65 PRO CAB 23/1 W.C. 3, 12 December 1916, Appendix II, Extract from War Committee proceedings of 30 November 1916.
66 G. D. Feldman, 'The political and social foundations of Germany's economic mobilization, 1914–1916', *Armed Forces and Society*, III, 1976, pp. 137–9.
67 Board of Trade, *The Labour Gazette*, XXV, February 1917, p. 47.
68 88 H.C. Deb. 5s, Col. 1351, 19 December 1916.
69 N. Chamberlain mss. NC 15/1(b), Press cuttings, *Eastern Daily Press*, 20 December 1916.

70 Beatrice Webb mss. Harvester microfilm Mf685, Diary, 7 December 1916.
71 PRO NATS 1/1071, German Patriotic Auxiliary Service Law, Summary from Daily Notes, Miss Logan, 21 February 1917.
72 Labour Party Cuttings Collection 24/2/30, National Service Pamphlet, 'Notes to Speakers on National Service', n.d. [January 1917].
73 N. Chamberlain mss. NC 18/1/95, N. Chamberlain to Ida Chamberlain, 24 December 1916.
74 N. Chamberlain mss. NC 1/18/2/10, N. Chamberlain to Norman Chamberlain, 7 January 1917.
75 N. Chamberlain mss. NC 1/20/1/109, N. Chamberlain to Mrs Mary Carnegie, 25 December 1916.
76 N. Chamberlain mss. NC 1/26/92, N. Chamberlain to Anne Chamberlain, 22 December 1916.
77 N. Chamberlain mss. NC 1/26/96, N. Chamberlain to Anne Chamberlain, 2 January 1917.
78 N. Chamberlain mss. NC 1/26/95, N. Chamberlain to Anne Chamberlain, 1 January 1916. This letter should be dated 1 January 1917.
79 N. Chamberlain mss. NC 1/26/94, N. Chamberlain to Anne Chamberlain, 28 December 1916.
80 Lloyd George mss. F/1/3/4, Addison to Lloyd George, 23 December 1916 & F/7/1/1, N. Chamberlain to Lloyd George, 25 December 1916; Addison mss. Box 99, Diary, entries for 23 and 27 December 1916.
81 Addison mss. Box 99, Diary, entry for 30 December 1916.
82 Addison mss. Box 99, Diary, entry for 28 December 1916.

5

The introduction of Chamberlain's National Service appeal
January – February 1917

Launched amid a flourish of publicity, the National Service Department embodied the intention of the 'Do it Now' government to mobilise the civilian working population and relate its efforts more closely to the conduct of the war on the Western Front. However, the means of facilitating 'labour fluidity' were not yet available. For example, while he indulged in the consideration of fanciful schemes the implementation of the scheme of voluntary enrolment for vital war work was far from the forefront of Chamberlain's work. The difference between the expectation of an advanced form of industrial organisation and the problems of policy-making which he encountered in early January 1917 was observed with concern from the vantage point of the War Office.

General Sir William Robertson informed General Sir Archibald Murray, Commander in Chief in Egypt, 'We have had many changes here lately owing to the change of Government but so far things go on much the same as ever. The desire was to get a business government and the result is I think that we have got one which mistakes bustle for business.'[1] This state of affairs was partially relieved by the peace which reigned at the War Office now that Lloyd George had been succeeded by Lord Derby as Secretary of State for War. While plans for future military operations were being discussed Robertson was entirely dissatisfied with the refusal of the War Cabinet to attend to the worsening military manpower position. He told General Sir Charles Monro, 'The one thing I cannot get them to touch is the question of men and that happens to be the most important of all. Before Lloyd George became Prime Minister he was very keen about the Man Question. He now declines to touch it.'[2] Monro was commended for raising some additional units in India which Robertson hoped would be followed by a considerable expansion in the size of the Indian Army, assisted through the provision of British officers and rifles by the War Office. However, with the evacuation of Indian infantry from France in 1915, the availability of Indian manpower no longer had such a direct bearing on the provision of men for military service on the Western Front, despite the substitution for British battalions in Egypt and Mesopotamia of units of the Indian Army.

The Army Council informed the War Cabinet that if the forces in France were to be maintained in the months of April, May and June it was necessary to recruit 450,000 men in the first three months of 1917. Of this total figure 350,000 category 'A' recruits were required. In the absence of a coherent government policy on manpower the War Office placed great reliance on the work of the National Service Department. According to Chamberlain, Lord Derby 'expressed himself as most anxious to help. Especially if there should be any friction with the W[ar] O[ffice] he begged me to let him know as he was determined that there should be no sand in my wheels.'[3] Derby's response was not merely genial. It reflected the profound sense of anticipation with which news of the appointment of Chamberlain was received by the military authorities in London and on the Western Front. By assisting the National Service schemes Macready sought to deflect criticism of the military enlistment procedures. Military plans and, in particular, the immediate task of obtaining a sufficient number of substitutes to enable the agricultural, munition and shipbuilding industries to release the men required for the army, demanded the rapid introduction of the national campaign for volunteers.

On 12 January 1917 Lloyd George arranged a conference which enabled Chamberlain to consult other ministers concerned with the supply and distribution of manpower. It decided that the Director of National Service should prepare his proposals on the organisation required for obtaining National Service volunteers, the method of allocating labour to vital war work and the measures to be taken to provide recruits for the army.[4] This instruction constituted the best, and certainly the most reliable, definition of Chamberlain's task since his appointment. It emphasised the importance of utilising the remaining voluntary capacity of the adult male population, through effective central and local bureaucratic assistance, to increase substantially the process of substitution in essential war industries.

Beneath the formality of the conference, Lloyd George was
dissatisfied with the apparent lack of progress at this crucial
juncture. Hankey wrote on 12 January, 'The Director of National
Service (Neville Chamberlain) made a very bad impression on all
concerned at the morning meeting. Ll[oyd] George told me he was
very much depressed. He did not seem to have made any progress at
all in working out his scheme.'[5] In the *History* of the National
Service Department, which in most respects was merely a
chronological outline, the author barely concealed his disgust that
'although he [Chamberlain] had been told beforehand by the
Secretariat of the War Cabinet that he would not be required to
produce a scheme for that meeting, he was asked by the P[rime]
M[inister] at the meeting for the outlines of his Scheme'.[6]

Notwithstanding Chamberlain's failure to appreciate the urgency
of the volunteer scheme, Lloyd George was principally at fault in
his conduct of the debate on implementing National Service, for
two reasons. Firstly, the deliberations of the War Cabinet were in a
chaotic state for most of January 1917, which Hankey attributed to
Lloyd George's 'unbusinesslike habits'.[7] Hankey admired the
amount of work which Lloyd George had undertaken in the first six
weeks of his premiership.[8] His criticism, however, was specifically
directed at the constant dislocation of the Cabinet's business by the
coverage, without notice, of unimportant issues on the insistence of
the Prime Minister. At an early stage the War Cabinet manifested
inherent weaknesses which eventually led to the arbitration of
inter-departmental disputes by individual members of the Cabinet,
most notably Milner, outside the framework of the reformed
wartime executive. Secondly, the Prime Minister failed from the
outset to invest the work of the Director of National Service with
the authority and prestige of a parliamentary office. Other departments concerned with manpower supply remained uncertain
whether the new 'Controller of Man-Power' differed to any great
extent from the administrative and subordinate position formerly
held by the chairman of the Man-Power Distribution Board. At
least six separate authorities were still vying with each other for
manpower, and the willingness of departments to further the
National Service appeal was tempered by the realisation that the
most effective way of protecting their 'sectional' interest, whether it
was coal-mining or merchant shipbuilding, was to retain their
autonomous control of the appropriate labour force free from

interference.[9] Neville Chamberlain sought advice from his brother Austen on his political situation. He was mistakenly reassured that it was unnecessary for him to become a Member of Parliament and that definite powers would be available when his scheme was submitted to the War Cabinet.

This was a somewhat circular proposition. In the meantime, most departments feared the effect of the national appeal for volunteers on their workforce, except the War Office which had everything to gain from National Service. The Ministry of Munitions and the Board of Agriculture were particularly worried by the implications of the new manpower authority. The Ministry of Munitions was determined to ensure that its existing agreements with trade unions in the industry continued without hindrance. Its Labour Supply branch was responsible for the allocation, dilution and transfer of manpower engaged in the manufacture of munitions. This arrangement was consolidated in an agreement with the National Service Department on 1 January 1917.[10] The departments disagreed on whether a scheme could be introduced which had not obtained the approval of the Minister of Munitions.[11] Disagreement also arose on the vital issue of the control of manpower after it had been allocated to war work by the Director of National Service. Addison continued to be upset by the temporary loss of James Stevenson and described Chamberlain as a man who was 'aghast at the magnitude of the job in front of him and who is leaning against any available support with his hands hanging limply at his side'.[12]

Addison remained singularly unimpressed with the news he received on the preparation of an organisation to administer National Service. His main informant was James Stevenson who was in any case deeply antipathetic to his new work. By 9 January Addison believed that Chamberlain would 'try to set up an organisation which would see that farmers, ourselves, the Navy and everybody else would make the proper use of the labour which he supplied. The whole suggestion is too grotesque to be worth discussing.'[13] Addison's sense of foreboding was partly based on a realistic assessment of the inherent difficulties of creating a mobile supply of labour entirely through voluntary civil enrolment. Addison saw Lloyd George on 10 January and expressed such a degree of concern that the Prime Minister asked Chamberlain for his programme. Consequently, at the conference which followed,

Addison had manoeuvred Chamberlain into a position in which he appeared more unprepared and less in control than was actually the case.

In addition to the vociferous criticism which Chamberlain encountered from Addison, the Board of Agriculture was also concerned that the National Service scheme would inevitably impinge on the food production programme for 1917. To reduce the impact of the removal of skilled labour from the land for military service Rowland Prothero, President of the Board of Agriculture, pursued two courses of action. Firstly, an agreement with Field Marshal Lord French on the employment of men from the Home Army on farm work. Secondly, the recruiting of 100,000 local women and 40,000 town women for agricultural work. The latter plan was suspended while Chamberlain developed his schemes with the result that the supplementary supply of labour was too late to increase the amount of land under the plough in time for the harvest in 1917.[14]

Consequently, plans to reduce the dependence on imported supplies of food while continuing to release fit men of military age, which was always an uneasy question of manpower priorities, was further complicated by the intervention of a third department. Planning for the centralisation of enrolment procedures at the National Service Department effectively disrupted departmental manpower plans, in several key areas, in the first quarter of 1917. In the case of agriculture, Prothero was advised by the Prime Minister to disregard the contribution which enrolled volunteers might eventually make to food production. He was also advised to request the Home Army to provide working parties of men unfit for general service for work on the land, and to take steps to enrol volunteers for agriculture work.

On 19 January the War Cabinet met for the single-issue agenda of National Service. In fact over twenty ministers and senior civil servants discussed Chamberlain's First Report which had been circulated three days earlier. It was generally agreed that the 'Main feature consisted in a proposal that all exemptions for men under 22 should be withdrawn'.[15] Chamberlain recommended that all exemptions issued by, or under the authority of, government departments to men born in the years 1895–98 should be cancelled immediately. He included in this proposal all men in the age group who held Tribunal certificates of exemption. Speed was of the essence and Chamberlain therefore indicated that the 'clean cut' should be operated to release 280,000 men in civil life between the ages of nineteen and twenty-two years who were fit for general service.[16] This scheme arose from the necessity of responding to the intense pressure of the War Office which sought a guaranteed flow of recruits for the British armies in France. The 'clean cut', with a few excepted categories, was the central area of conflict which arose in the discussion of the report. Addison wrote,

I pointed out that we already had an arrangement about exempting skilled men and that his [Chamberlain's] proposal would involve sweeping at least 70,000 skilled men who had been through apprenticeships into the rank and file of the army. This, I am glad to say, killed the proposal so far as the skilled are concerned.[17]

Addison's firm ground from which he argued against the 'clean cut' included its 'desolating' effect upon output and the broken pledges which would be incurred.[18] Though the War Cabinet agreed that Chamberlain's plan would make men available for the army it accepted Addison's contention that some areas of vital war work would collapse.

Consequently, the significance of the meeting lay in its wish to retain skilled men in industry. More surprisingly, the War Cabinet reached agreement on the major occupational priority areas which comprised the well-worn phrase 'work of national importance'. The War Cabinet decided that the essential war industries were 'men employed in the production of steel, in the occupations covered by the trade card scheme, and in agriculture, mines and quarries, railway shops, transport work and shipyards'.[19] Addison was relieved that munition and shipbuilding trades won renewed recognition of their vital importance to the Allied war effort. In that these industries were substantially covered by the trade card scheme, the War Cabinet's decision was by no means a departure from the agreements of late November 1916 between the War Office and the Ministry of Munitions. In identifying industries where skilled labour of all ages was required, the prospect of introducing the 'clean cut' had disappeared. The rejection of this major part of Chamberlain's plan for the recruitment of men for the army diminished his contribution to the development of new policy.

Instead, the War Cabinet decided that the requirement of 100,000 men for the army in January should be met by the release of men from civil work in quotas. Addison was informed that 50,000 semi-skilled and unskilled men in munition factories should be made available. The Board of Agriculture's quota was 30,000 men and to the chagrin of Sir Richard Redmayne at the Home Office, 20,000 men were required from the coal-mining industry.[20] This quota arrangement was confirmed rather than initiated by the War Cabinet. Most of the consultations had taken place on an inter-departmental basis prior to the agreement and the rate of release of men from munition work, coal-mining and agriculture depended on *ad hoc* arrangements with the War Office. The absence of Neville Chamberlain in a mediating role was most marked in the quota plans.

The War Office remained the principal department concerned with the distribution of manpower, favouring the military war effort at the expense of industrial purposes. Its pre-eminence was confirmed with the decision that its Recruiting branch was not to become part of the organisation of National Service. The removal of this function from the orbit of Chamberlain's interests reinforced the implicit and growing disregard of the department's initial value as an 'arbiter' on manpower. His position certainly contrasted strongly with the Prime Minister's ideal definition of the National Service Department as 'an instrument in charge of all the nation's man-power'.[21] Chamberlain's intentions on the 'clean cut' and as an arbiter of manpower distribution were barely recognisable at all. Although the function of the department to organise a 'great patriotic appeal' to recruit a volunteer 'Industrial Army' for the process of substitution remained intact, its potential contribution to the economic use of manpower remained nebulous. The department was devoid of commonly accepted principles on which to act and, *vis à vis* other ministries, Chamberlain's position was worsened by the morass of precedence, procedural disputes and departmental 'empire-building' which characterised the issue of manpower policy development and implementation in the third year of the war.

The development of the scheme of National Service was severely hampered by the basic distrust of Chamberlain's role in long-established departments. Nowhere was this more apparent than in the Ministry of Munitions. Addison feared that the enrolment of National Service volunteers, who would act as substitutes for the 50,000 men released from munition work, involved 'his going into all sorts of works, farms, shipyards, munition works, etc. to see that the men whom he had supplied were being properly employed. This

I pointed out was an impossible proposal in that it could not possibly be done.'[22] The problem of the eventual control of enrolled labour after its allocation to work of national importance was the main area of discord between the National Service Department and the Ministry of Munitions. Much work was done by senior officials of both departments on the contentious statements in the Director's first report.[23] As Addison regarded the proposed National Service scheme purely as an additional source of manpower he was opposed to any 'interference' in the internal direction of labour on munition work. Two paragraphs of the report were re-drafted to reflect this situation.

Addison and his senior officials assumed that the National Service appeal would have only limited value in providing skilled substitutes. With the problem of obtaining replacements in mind, the Minister of Munitions was angered by the activities of the Recruiting Department which he regarded as 'thoroughly truculent and inclined to pass off on anybody available the deficiencies of their own organization, which are pretty manifest'.[24] He fully defended his district officials from the charge that they were less than whole-hearted in facilitating the release of 50,000 men from essential war work.[25] Macready sent evidence to the Ministry of Munitions of remarks which were alleged to have been made to recruiting officers by local munitions officials. For example,

I cannot understand how you people ever entered into the agreement about the release of the 50,000 men by the end of January. I was personally concerned in erecting the barbed wire fence which we have put around them and I can tell you that you will never get them.[26]

The Ministry of Munitions was dismayed that the War Office did not understand that once this quota was released no guaranteed source of skilled replacements would be immediately available to maintain output. Arrangements on substitution whereby men fit for general service were released from factories and exchanged for unfit men who were supplied to employers by recruiting officers had developed from local schemes between the two departments. This procedure collapsed during the creation of the quota release scheme, but the charge of passive resistance was hardly appropriate to the complexity of manpower distribution between the military and industrial war effort.

Macready was reminded that the system of medical examinations administered by the Recruiting Department was 'hopelessly behindhand'.[27] The names of 102,063 men had been forwarded to the military authorities by 6 January 1917 in line with the recommendation of the Man-Power Distribution Board. The Labour Supply branch provided evidence that during that time only 12,883 men were medically examined of which 5,351 were found to be suitable for general service.[28] These details corresponded closely to the complaints which trade unions raised on the effectiveness of military trade-testing centres. They endeavoured to comb out skilled men in line regiments for service in technical corps, with the aid of lists of skilled union members supplied by trade societies. Derby admitted that only 9,600 men were reallocated to skilled work in the army in November and December 1916.[29]

Chamberlain did not participate in the detailed discussions which took place on a bi-lateral basis between the War Office and the Ministry of Munitions. Stevenson was restored to the Ministry of Munitions at the end of January, and as the department no longer incorporated a 'military side', the removal of Auckland Geddes to fill the post of 'Chief of the Staff' at the National Service Department was vigorously opposed by Derby and Macready.[30] Lloyd George was irritated by the long-running absence of a permanent Deputy Director, which was unwittingly revealed by Chamberlain when he reported an interview at which 'the P[rime] M[inister] said "I thought Mr Chamberlain would have known someone in the Midlands"'.[31] A reluctant Ernest Hiley, Chairman of Glover and Main, Ltd., engineers and appliance manufacturers, and Town Clerk of Birmingham from 1908 to 1916, was pressurised into accepting the post. With the business community of Birmingham providing both the Director and Deputy Director of National Service, Whitehall decided that it had still more reason to remain cautious and distance itself in its relations with this new ministry.[32]

The weakness of the National Service Department during the preparatory stage of the appeal for volunteers was further illustrated in the controversial enlistment of agricultural workers for military service. Prothero told the Council of National Unionist associations that he was not responsible for the quota of 30,000 men.[33] His protest at the War Cabinet's decision won support from Unionist landowners who were concerned with the diminishing supply of skilled labour in relation to their commitment to increase the acreage of cultivated land in 1917. Lloyd George warned Derby, 'I am receiving representations from every quarter about the calling up of the 30,000 men from Agriculture. The country is frightened, and rightly so, as to food supplies and the submarine menace is becoming more and more formidable.'[34] Lloyd George told the War Office that the 30,000 men should be called up slowly over two or three months, which halted the prospect of the quota arrangement securing sufficient men for the army in the first month of 1917. On 22 January the importance of increased food production was embodied in the War Cabinet's decision that the Home Army should provide 15,000 substitutes to offset the eventual withdrawal of 30,000 labourers from agriculture.

The contribution of the National Service Department towards the settlement of the dispute was extremely limited and its assistance was neither immediate nor tangible. On 25 January the War Cabinet decided that in the forthcoming general appeal for volunteers special emphasis should be laid on the needs of agriculture.[35] As the appeal to rural labourers to enrol for National Service was likely to be attractive in view of their low wages, the potential benefit to farm work of the envisaged campaign was arguable and far from apparent to the Board of Agriculture.

As the reluctance of the Ministry of Munitions and the Board of Agriculture to release men became clear, the use of manpower already in uniform was reviewed. Lloyd George expected Chamberlain to undertake periodic examinations of the degree to which manpower was economically allocated in separate spheres of the war effort. At the point that manpower in civilian work was being re-examined, the National Service Department was ill-prepared for participating in the much needed reassessment of the role and size of the Home Army. Civil departments were critical of the employment of fit and unfit men on home defence duties in preference to vital war work and had achieved limited success in the return of skilled men to the civil components of the war effort. Hitherto, the War Office had been secure in the knowledge that the Home Army lay fully within the sphere of military jurisdiction, beyond the scrutiny of other government departments. Its sanctity as an integral element of the war effort was confirmed on 23 August 1916 when the War Committee decided that no reduction should be demanded in the number of trained men allocated to Home Defence. It was argued by the General Staff that Germany had sufficient transport to convey a seaborne force of 160,000 men across the North Sea. British experience of landings at Antwerp and Gallipoli did not lead the military authorities to realise the improbability of such a German move – still more of its success.

Yet on 22 January 1917 the Admiralty and the General Staff reported that the premise of the manpower calculations for home defence was unchanged. The Grand Fleet would not guarantee that German landing operations would be interrupted within one day of the invasion force being sighted. Neither the Admiralty nor the War Office would state that an invasion was out of the question. Consequently, Lord French, as Commander in Chief, Home Forces, maintained that a force of 500,000 men was still required in Britain for the threefold purpose of repelling an invasion, the garrison of defended ports and the provision of air defence.[36] However, on 19 January the War Office decided to consider whether better use could be made of the number and classification of men retained for Home Defence.

The investigation implied that the home forces should be reduced in size and this theme concerned the ever-vigilant Walter Long. He entered the debate to provide Lloyd George with a helpful memorandum on the difference between an 'invasion' and a 'raid'. Long was familiar with the opinions of 'great military commanders', who all agreed that an invasion of 300,000 to 500,000 men was 'practically impossible'. However, he argued that a raid of 100,000 to 120,000 men was quite feasible. He concluded 'I for one hope that whatever steps are taken in regard to the forces in the country, nothing will be done which is likely to unduly weaken our powers of defence.'[37] Two days later Robertson was directed, against his own advice, to send two divisions from the Home Army to France, which reduced the number of mobile divisions in Britain to seven. Long and Robertson believed strongly that the solution to the problem of providing fit men for the army in France was not to be found in the reassignment of roles for military formations at the behest of the War Cabinet. Nevertheless, the use of military manpower, as determined in accordance with the offensive preparations made each spring on the Western Front, was belatedly becoming of interest to the Cabinet.

In private Lloyd George condemned the notion prevalent at GHQ in France that manpower recruited for the army and subsequently allocated to a specific unit in a theatre of war could never be subject to civil scrutiny. Robertson attempted to counter the increasing tendency towards the flexible reallocation of military labour, most frequently for agricultural purposes, on the broad and ill-defined argument of 'military efficiency'. In so doing he reflected the strongly held view at GHQ that the issue of military manpower was unrelated to the labour demands of the civil departments. At an early stage in his premiership Lloyd George noted the 'exclusivity' of army control over newly recruited and trained military manpower. In France there was the additional factor of bureaucratic remoteness. The supervision of manpower in the British armies in France was completely autonomous, with the exception of the provision of reinforcements.

Lloyd George's frustration with the restrictions placed on the War Cabinet's supervision of manpower could be gauged from a record of his conversation with Frances Stevenson on the subject of the level of British casualties in operations on the Western Front. He privately accused Haig of not being unduly concerned about the 'wastage' incurred in the offensives during 1916. Lloyd George declared,

He [Haig] seems to think they are his property. But if they are his property, I am their trustee. I will never let him rest. I will raise the subject again & again until I *nag* him out of it – until he knows that as soon as the casualty lists get large he will get nothing but black looks and scowls and awkward questions.[38]

This report of Lloyd George's view reflected the minimum influence which he exerted over the formulation of offensive activity and its manpower implications on the Western Front. Certainly, the Prime Minister's rhetoric was more pronounced than his ability to reduce the casualty lists at this stage of the war.

Due to the delays encountered in withdrawing men from factories and agriculture the War Cabinet had no option but to order the embarkation of the 66th and 67th Divisions for France to meet the immediate demand for trained reinforcements. At Horse Guards Lord French did not protest about the substantial reduction of trained manpower available in Britain for home defence. He noted, 'I have agreed to this on the understanding that it is certainly a risk and that the Defence of the country is not adequately provided against an invading force of 150,000 men. In sending these divisions we have however incurred a minimum of risk.'[39] The departure of two divisions from Southampton had ramifications far beyond the arrival of a further 25,000 British troops in France. At the end of January Robertson foresaw no improvement in the recruiting position and he informed Murray, in Egypt, that 'we are very short of men'.[40] Derby had arranged with Macready that eighteen year old recruits should be used to reinforce the depleted Home Army after a shortened period of training. The reduction in its size reflected the Home

Army's less vital role in the war effort. As the manpower shortage grew more acute the 'indivisibility' of providing men for military service was more frequently questioned, as the War Cabinet endeavoured to reassert political control over the formulation of strategic plans and, in particular, the supervision of joint military plans with the French Army. Lloyd George's rise to the premiership and the creation of the National Service Department far from consolidated the military priority for men which, initially, the War Office had assumed to be the rationale behind the adoption of National Service. Consequently, inside the War Office the issue of manpower preoccupied the Army Council to the exclusion of a comprehensive re-examination of the Allied chance of a 'break-through' on the Western Front in 1917.

The greatest disappointment which the War Office expressed on the issue of National Service was the insufficiency of Chamberlain's powers to execute an appeal for volunteers, let alone to come to terms with the complexity of compulsion. In particular, Chamberlain remained ill-prepared to determine which industries and services were of national importance and which could be deemed non-essential. The fear that National Service would inevitably give rise to a series of mistakes arising from a weak local administration ignorant of complex industrial processes was articulated most clearly by Professor Adams. As the process of preparing the scheme to enrol National Service volunteers reached its final stages, the intention of the National Service Department was closely monitored by the Prime Minister's Secretariat. It kept Lloyd George informed of the work of departments and provided an independent source of advice on chief policy issues.

W. S. G. Adams was eminently well-qualified to monitor Chamberlain's work and warn the Prime Minister of the dangers which lay ahead. He was previously Chief Statistician at the Board of Agriculture in Ireland, first Gladstone Professor of Political Theory and Institutions at Oxford University and a labour adviser at the Ministry of Munitions.[41] He joined Lloyd George's Secretariat, or 'Garden Suburb', as principal additional private secretary with responsibility for Ireland, labour affairs and agriculture.[42] In the first two months of 1917 Adams provided Lloyd George with a series of memoranda on the general principles and practical implications of National Service. He also wrote notes on the subject for Lloyd George's speeches.

On 16 January Adams warned that the introduction of industrial compulsion, after voluntary enrolment was presumed to have failed, would provoke the deep hostility of the labour movement. He argued that such latent strength of feeling should not be aroused on the misguided assumption that National Service would be no more difficult to impose than compulsory military service. Adams noted that the conscript soldier had 'a definite round of duties, prescribed by a perfectly definite end; he has rights established by long tradition; and he lives a common life, which secures his rights & mitigates his hardships. The industrial conscript has none of these consolations.'[43] The experience Adams gained at the Ministry of Munitions was reflected in the four main points he raised against the manipulation of National Service to establish a disciplined mobile supply of labour. Firstly, the labour movement would oppose the transfer of men to private firms which were unregulated by the government. Secondly, the separation of the male wage-earner from his family would cause financial hardship and exacerbate existing housing shortages in urban manufacturing areas. Thirdly, the work allotted to the transferred man could be completely inappropriate to his skill and previous experience. This was related to the fourth point which suggested that mobile labour was manifestly an inefficient or wasteful form of work management, suitable only in emergency conditions.

Although these points concerned compulsory National Service he raised them to draw attention to the problems which would be encountered during the campaign of voluntary enrolment. Whether compulsory or voluntary, a serious threat to the increased mobility of labour lay in the extent to which a detailed definition of 'work of national importance' could be provided by the department. The classification of industries according to their contribution to the war effort could only proceed effectively in association with the higher direction of the Allied military plans. Adams foresaw the problems which would arise from the inability of the government to successfully relate the importance of civil work to the overall war effort. Consequently, the notion of National Service appeared destined to alienate industries from the continued exploration of the best means to secure an adequate supply of men for military service in France.

On 20 January 1917 Neville Chamberlain spoke for the first time in public since his appointment. He chose the inaugural meeting of the National Alliance of Employers and Employed at Central Hall,

Birmingham as the first forum to speak on his task of forming an
'Industrial Army'. Chamberlain thoroughly enjoyed the enthusiastic reception he received in his home city and pronounced the
'Capital & Labour' meeting 'a great success'.[44] F. S. Oliver, the
Tory intellectual and political confidant of Milner, told Chamberlain that his speech, 'struck absolutely the right note. I could say
much of it but will content myself with saying ditto to the
gentleman in the audience who said that you were "your father's
son". He was quite right.'[45] Chamberlain described his task as 'a
dentist to the nation' and he was much enamoured with this
analogy. He expanded the idea at great length, culminating in the
vivid expression that he was 'extracting teeth with as little incon-
venience to the victim as possible and providing a reasonably
satisfactory set of artificial ones'.[46] In *The Observer* he was
commended for tackling the problem of arousing enthusiasm 'for
measures which must be unpleasant to be sound'.[47] He did not
describe in any detail the organisation of his scheme for National
Service but emphasised the importance of a nation organised for
war providing, in abundance, men for the army, munitions and
money through the maintenance of the export trade. He warned his
audience that the government would take steps to introduce
compulsory National Service if there was an inadequate response
to the voluntary appeal. This warning was repeated at many
meetings in the course of the campaign. The speech falsely suggested that Neville Chamberlain already possessed wide terms of
reference which entrusted him with the direction of manpower in
civil industries. It also led his audience to presume that a
comprehensive and virtually all-embracing system of National
Service would shortly be implemented.

The complexity of Chamberlain's work contrasted strongly with
the straightforward viewpoint of adherents to the 'westerner' cause.
They argued that the war could be won in 1917 by the rapid
enlargement of the British army in France and its unrestricted
reinforcement throughout the duration of military operations. The
Birmingham Post drew attention to the antagonism which Chamberlain's broad view had incurred from 'agitators more militarist
than the military authorities'. They were identifiable as members of
the Unionist War Committee. It was a backbench group which was
determined to focus parliamentary attention on the interests of
GHQ in France.[48] They had numbered 150 members in March

1916 and following the 'nation's dentist' speech, the Committee was derided as 'Agitators of the "hang the halfpence"' school, who shout in the same breath for every man to be thrust into the fighting line and for more money to be raised, [and] are not at all pleased with the breadth of Mr Neville Chamberlain's declaration'.[49] Through his reference to the department's intention to contribute to military operations, munitions production and the export trade, Chamberlain attempted to indicate that his work would transcend and override sectional interests. Newspaper speculation reinforced Chamberlain's initial attempt to convey the potential significance of relating the economic condition of the nation to the overall war effort through the introduction of National Service. He also sought to indicate that success in the priority areas of the war effort would hinge on the substantial reduction of manpower levels in non-essential industries. With such little information from the department and high expectation of radical change the momentum of supposition that the conduct of the war was about to undergo an extraordinary transformation was maintained by journalists who wrote articles on 'Mobilising Labour'. The *Daily Telegraph*, which was sympathetic to the 'Hang the Halfpence' school, pronounced on 30 January

It is clear, then, that we have not to do, as many people seem vaguely to believe, with some experiment in man-power, some administrative 'side show', but with a sweeping policy affecting every person in this country who is not now engaged in 'work of national importance'.[50]

Such was the scale of newspaper interest in 'a sweeping policy', which remained vaguely-formed despite countless articles, that Lloyd George took the initiative and used the issue of National Service as the centre-piece of his first speech to his constituents since the formation of his government. Privately he was perturbed and impatient about this central innovation. Lloyd George told C. P. Scott that 'he was pleased with the results of most of his outside appointments to business men, but was rather disappointed with Neville Chamberlain'.[51] However at Caernarvon on 2 February he said, 'Let all roads lead to the Industrial Army, and let the Industrial Army pave the road to peace.'[52] Lloyd George projected a vision of a disciplined and mobile workforce, despite the more cautious view of his Secretariat, which would reflect the civilian population's acknowledgement of the right of the government to demand specific work 'for the good of the State'. He exerted moral pressure on men too old for military service in the audience who should be ready to enlist in the 'great industrial army'. His constituents were told, 'We have suffered in our past efforts by the non-mobility of labour, and if the industrial army is to successfully carry out its campaigns its members must be ready and willing to go where they are told.'[53]

In his speech Lloyd George introduced a contentious point in impressing upon his audience that although they may be currently employed in essential war work they must not be deterred from enrolling because their skill or labour might be more urgently required elsewhere. This statement renewed Addison's opposition to the establishment of a general purpose 'Industrial Army'. If volunteers were to be invited to enrol without regard to their occupation, logically, Chamberlain would be empowered to decide whether the volunteer's existing work was important enough for him to be retained at his current workplace. The threat of 'outside' interference in munition factories was again raised and Addison was not placated by the fact that the invitation to comment on the National Service enrolment form was not issued until after the draft was sent to the printers. He noted, 'I must say that it is impossible for one to carry the enormous responsibilities of the Ministry of Munitions if, without any consultation with us, large masses of labour are to be liable for disturbances of this kind.'[54] The organisation of munitions production was particularly vulnerable to intervention because it comprised an easily identifiable and comprehensively registered concentration of adult male labour, some of whom were young and exempted from military service.

As Lloyd George had put pressure on Chamberlain to complete his plans for the appeal for volunteers, so did the Army Council. The military authorities were more pessimistic in early February 1917 than at any stage since the formation of Lloyd George's government. Robertson believed that memoranda from the Army Council had played a significant part in the reviews of military manpower provision which took place in 1916. Its note of 6 April 1916 had brought full military conscription and its paper of 28 November 1916 had brought compulsory National Service in principle and the change of government. He was less hopeful about the impact of its 'third effort' on 2 February 1917 which noted that only 50,000 men were recruited for general service in the preceding month.[55] The War Cabinet was therefore informed that the required number of recruits for February would be raised from

120,000 to 170,000 men. The Army Council predicted that as soon as heavy fighting commenced in April on the Western Front the British armies in France would fall below strength. Robertson privately concluded that Lloyd George's government was remarkably similar to Asquith's period of office in that the supply of recruits was not being guaranteed. The Army Council urged that all existing exemptions should be cancelled by successive age groups, whether they were issued by departments or tribunals, and that compulsion should be introduced to require men to undertake essential war work if the appeal failed.

Following these cumulative pressures from the Prime Minister, Ministry of Munitions, Army Council and the press and in the absence of any agreed principles which governed the distribution of manpower for military and civil purposes, Chamberlain recommended that there should be a gradual cancellation of exemptions from military service. His Second Report envisaged the progressive release of age groups to twenty-six years by June 1917 to provide 590,000 men for the army.[56] This estimated figure would only be 10,000 men below the level required for military service by June and Chamberlain planned to fill their places through the 'great patriotic appeal'. Initially, the War Cabinet responded to this proposal by urging the War Office to consider the possibility of reducing the number of battalions in each division, instructing the Home Secretary to review all tribunal exemptions held by men under thirty-one years and applying voluntary National Service to Ireland.[57] However, the War Cabinet also decided to cancel the exemptions of all men up to and including twenty-two years of age, with the exception of the categories of occupations already defined as essential war work.[58] Chamberlain had secured the major recommendation from his First Report, although it did not amount to the 'clean cut' due to the categories of skilled labour which were exempt from military recruitment.

The exemption cancellation programme was the crucial prerequisite of the appeal for volunteers because the places of men fit for general service who were removed from industry would need to be filled. However the Labour Supply branch of the Ministry of Munitions feared the extreme disruption of output. Its Director, Stephenson Kent, drew Addison's attention to industries basic to Britain's role as the arsenal of the Allied war effort, where semi-skilled and unskilled men who were not 'protected' were engaged in essential output by their very familiarity with the work process. The Trade Card scheme protected skilled men in the foundries, but with the removal of 1,005 semi-skilled men under twenty-three years of age the disruption of the industry was severe. Similarly, in gas works most stokers were fit for general service, but substitutes were not efficient. Consequently, munitions output was affected where neighbouring gas works were inefficient. In the engineering trades the problem was more acute as the cancellation of exemptions was carried out on a far larger scale. Recruiting officers were no longer bound by the substitution agreement. They arbitrarily called up skilled men in brass castings, aluminium and other metal trades which disrupted aeroplane-engine production and gun repair work.

Sir William Weir, Controller of Aeronautical Supplies, noted that men employed on vital war work were not as a matter of course in exempted occupational categories.[59] The withdrawal of sixteen men from Rolls-Royce in one day had completely stopped all deliveries of magnetos. The reduction of aeroplane construction was not envisaged as a direct outcome of the enlistment of munition workers.[60] The reappearance of 'eternal wrangles' between the Ministry of Munitions and the War Office led to a modification of the scheme whereby men alleged to have been improperly called up had their cases investigated before enlistment took place.[61] Unresolved disputes in aeroplane production wre referred to Lord Cowdray, President of the Air Board, and to Neville Chamberlain for problems in all other manufacturing areas. Shortly afterwards, this review procedure was dismantled.

Chamberlain's attempts to secure a supply of men for the army in advance of his appeal for industrial workers suffered from the failure of the War Cabinet to define the relationship between recruiting and the production of munitions. He wrote on 10 February,

attempts have been made to render me powerless which have failed. In short as things are at present I get backing as between Dept and Dept; it is only when I recommend things that would really bring the country face to face with realities that other considerations (as to the importance of which I have not sufficient information) prevail.[62]

The lack of information was pertinent for without it the National Service Department was powerless to determine the distribution of manpower. Furthermore, without a satisfactory plan to reinforce the British armies in France from civil industries, the prospects for effectively allocating and employing labour recruited for voluntary service was significantly reduced. Within the higher conduct of the war, manpower

planning still did not have a place. Without the full commitment of
the War Cabinet, ardent compulsionists such as Austen Chamberlain[63] and Walter Long[64] doubted the efficacy of launching so
great a scheme as National Service on a voluntary basis. This
concern was voiced in *The Times* as 'The fear in the minds of many
people is that we may waste a year, as we did in 1915 in the case of
recruits for the Army, in appeals for volunteers which will not give
the numbers needed.'[65] In a context where decision-making on
manpower remained so confused, the inability to resolve inter-
departmental disputes did not auger well for the patriotic appeal
for labour.

The National Service scheme was launched on 6 February 1917 at
the Central Hall, Westminster. The main speeches to promote the
national campaign were made by Lloyd George, Arthur Henderson,
Neville Chamberlain and John Hodge, Minister of Labour. The
Archbishop of Canterbury and the Lord Mayor of London were
also present, for no major national campaign during the war was
complete without their presence on the platform. 'God and mam-
mon' were employed in equal share at the inaugural meeting and
during the promotion of the appeal at the local level.
    By this stage the object of securing a mobile reserve of civilian
labour for the substitution and reinforcement of labour in essential
national industries was well known. This scheme provided the
means for the government to appeal to the whole male population
between the ages of eighteen and sixty-one to enrol, even if they
were already on work of national importance. A decision on the
enrolment of women was postponed until the scheme was successfully implemented. Local authorities were called on to help the
appeal by establishing National Service Committees, which would
supervise the campaign in each town and district. Men who
enrolled agreed to take work for any department or employer
named by the National Service Department. The wage level was
calculated at the existing district rate for the trade and a minimum
wage of twenty-five shillings would be paid to all volunteers
regardless of the work performed. Travelling and subsistence
allowances were available.[66]
    The local National Service Committees were solely concerned
with the organisation of public meetings, canvassing and publicity.
Consequently, the key element of the local administration was the

Employment Exchanges. The Ministry of Labour agreed that the manager's task was to allocate individual volunteers to local vital war industries and administer the system of allowances. The right of appeal existed for both the employer and the volunteer but Chamberlain told Lloyd George, somewhat optimistically, that men would be given work for which they had expressed a preference and close to their homes, but neither could be guaranteed. At the same time, Chamberlain undertook to grade industries on the simple criterion that 'What is less important must give way to what is more important.'[67] Schedules were prepared to differentiate between essential and non-essential trades so that a definitive list was available for the Employment Exchange managers.

A much encouraged Prime Minister commended Chamberlain's explanation of the scheme on 6 February for its 'hereditary lucidity'. Lloyd George directed his attention to the more general aspects of the appeal,[68] and argued that the country was 'Entitled to [the] utmost help of every member which partakes of its life'.[69] The obligation of each man to enrol was portrayed as a universal remedy which would restore the nation's fortunes in war, and, more specifically, counter the German submarine campaign by increasing the acreage of land under cultivation and shipyard output. For men over military age the civil enrolment scheme was held to embody the notion of 'sacrifice', even if in Britain it merely entailed discomfort. Speakers at National Service meetings were advised to tell their audience, 'Having enrolled their conscience is clear that they have offered themselves and their work to the country, and whether they are called up . . . or perhaps not required at all – let them at least have the comforting reflection, "Anyway, I was willing".'[70]

Although the scheme was not universally beloved, Chamberlain was pleased that he had obtained favourable expressions of support from some ministers instead of the studied contempt which hitherto greeted his plans. He recorded

Ll[oyd] G[eorge] smiles upon me most benevolently and not only expressed his own approval & congratulations in Cabinet but stated that many others had spoken to him about the speech very warmly & he was satisfied that it had created an excellent impression.[71]

However, his contention that no serious criticism of the scheme could be found was not supported by the attitude of the partisan press at either the national or regional level. Certainly some newspapers exhorted its readership to enlist. For example the *Hull Daily News* noted, 'We hope to be able soon to report that Hull's army of volunteers for National

Service is a formidable one.'[72] Nevertheless, newspapers which held opposing viewpoints on the role of compulsion in civil society were quick to criticise the appeal. The *Morning Post* argued that 'nothing but compulsory national service will meet the need' in order to 'break the German lines in the West'.[73]

In the immediate term, however, the possibility of a consensus of support for National Service was threatened more by the opponents of 'industrial conscription' than by the proponents of compulsion. *The Star* regarded it as 'indefinite, unspecified work' which corresponded closely to Adams's prophecy that the appeal would be too indeterminate.[74] The *New Statesman* compared it to the 'sacrifice' of a five per cent return for those who could afford to assist the war effort by subscribing to the war loan.[75] Several newspapers revealed that the scheme was not so much a national campaign, in that all social classes were likely to participate, as one designed to secure the most economic use of the working population. The satisfactory transfer of men to essential war production required local bureaucracies which understood the division of work skills in industry. The *Sheffield Independent* vigilantly opposed the slightest manifestation of 'industrial conscription'. It noted on 7 February,

If Mr Chamberlain or any other magician of organisation could sweep away the limitations of specialised labour then it might be possible easily and quickly to divert energy from one channel to another. This cannot be done. Labour is not a fluid. It cannot be poured like water from a vase to a bucket.[76]

For this reason radical and unionist journals alike argued that the scheme to transfer labour was less desirable than the reduction of manpower levels in non-essential industries by the prohibition of selected manufactured goods.

In the full glare of press scrutiny, not least from antipathetic newspapers, Chamberlain set out to promote the enrolment campaign for National Service. The Parliamentary National Service Meetings Committee was created by the Whips of all parties to supply speakers for the major meetings and organise smaller gatherings through the local parliamentary agents.[77] This approach closely resembled the activities of the Parliamentary Recruiting Committee and three of the four secretaries of the Meetings Committee had assisted the Derby scheme. The Meetings Committee criticised the dependence of the scheme on the system of local government and urged that success could only be secured if the National Service appeal was conducted in a similar way to the

Derby scheme. The initial number of public meetings was low, due in large part to the disintegration of the national network of Unionist and Liberal agents by 1917. On 20 February Lloyd George expressed his disappointment that hundreds of meetings had not taken place and told Chamberlain, 'I sincerely trust therefore that whoever is in charge of organising the effort to stir up public interest in the enrolment of this volunteer army will put a good deal more life into it.'[78] Between 17 February and 1 March Chamberlain addressed large public meetings at Bristol, London, Glasgow, Sheffield and Cardiff. However, the number of meetings held by local National Service Committees totalled only twenty-four by 27 February, with another forty-nine arranged. Furthermore, no locally arranged meetings had been held in Wales and in eleven English counties there was still no prospect of a major public meeting.[79]

Lloyd George was kept closely informed on the progress of the scheme by Adams, but neither of them appreciated the difficulty of organising a door-to-door canvass by voluntary workers in the third year of the war. Eighteen months after the local implementation of the National Registration Act, a canvass without reference to any statutory obligations was an unrealistic objective in some districts. Lloyd George unfavourably compared the National Service appeal to the victory War Loan scheme which he launched on 11 January.[80] However, the War Loan plan did not require a canvass and offered rather more attractive terms than National Service, where much depended on the ability of public speakers to highlight its 'dramatic qualities'. The Prime Minister's anger was fuelled by early indications that the response to the general appeal was limited and fell far short of the rate of enrolment required for the target of 500,000 volunteers by 31 March 1917. Adams told Lloyd George on 1 March,

up to date 91,400 volunteers have been enrolled. Of this number only a very small percentage – Mr. Hiley will not put it at present at more than 5% – can be considered as effectives. A very large number will, it is expected, be found to be engaged on work from which they cannot be removed.[81]

By 8 March 114,800 volunteers had enrolled for National Service and the department had stopped its reference to 31 March as the final enrolment day. In the press there were persistent reports of silent, and occasionally more vociferous, opposition in specific districts to the locally organised appeal. On 10 March *The Times* reported,

Out of more than 8,000 circulars issued to persons between 18 and 61 in Chiswick, asking for information as to the time they could devote to National

Service, only 2,000 have been returned filled up, and of these only 50 state they can give their whole time to it.[82]

The *Manchester Guardian* noted the remarks of R. J. Davies, chairman of the Manchester and Salford Labour Party, on the appeal. Davies stated, 'He knew that in some workshops and factories there was a sullen hostility to the whole thing, and that but for regulations there would be trouble in those places about it.'[83] During the period 7 February to 31 March, 206,000 men were enrolled as National Service volunteers, including 39,109 who volunteered in the first week. The number of men enrolled whose applications were considered by Employment Exchanges during the same period totalled 92,489 volunteers. One-half of these applicants were already employed in the 'protected' trades and of the total applicants considered, just 388 men were placed in employment as National Service volunteers.[84]

At an early stage in the enrolment campaign Addison confirmed Lloyd George's view that blunders could not be afforded in the 'muddled' areas of National Service and Food Control. In early March 1917 they both hoped that Liberal MPs who had remained loyal to Asquith could be persuaded to leave the opposition benches. Consequently, they feared the damage which might be caused to the government's unsecured, but self-proclaimed, reputation of prosecuting the war more effectively than its predecessor, should the cornerstone of National Service collapse within three months of its celebrated adoption. Addison reported that Lloyd George 'was as disgusted with Neville Chamberlain's performance as I was and had evidently been stafing [sic] his Department pretty vigorously for sometime'.[85] Unsupported by other departments and distrusted by the Prime Minister, National Service became the epitome of a misdirected national initiative which bore poor comparison with the Derby scheme. The expectation of a swiftly enrolled 'industrial army' was not aided by the information that three dukes, two admirals and a director of the Bank of England had enrolled for National Service.[86] Did these eminent public figures have any intention of being interviewed at their local Employment Exchange and placed on essential war work at the district rate? The advertisements asked, 'Are you Fiddling while Rome is Burning? Or have you put your name down for National Service?'[87] In the face of the unimpressive enrolment returns the publicity produced by the department took on a farcical complexion which Chamberlain was unable to eradicate in his remaining months as Director of National Service.

The 'drama' of National Service was an essential contribution to the image of the government as an executive reorganised along 'business lines' for the more effective prosecution of the war. The scheme was an exercise in the preparation of the civil population for the escalation of the British military war effort in France. The introduction of National Service was also intended to convey the necessity for a more direct, albeit voluntary, association of increased munitions output with the forthcoming offensives on the Western Front. Before it was launched Chamberlain was satisfied that the scheme was workable. More than that, he assumed that the provision of men for the army was dependent on the successful outcome of his campaign. The government portrayed National Service as an opportunity for every class to 'contribute men and women ready to place their labour at the disposal of the State'.[88] Instead of moribund notions of planning manpower provision, Chamberlain looked forward to a form of organisation which would make Britain the definitive 'nation-in-arms'. On 6 February 1917 the 'Do it now' government had focused the nation's attention on an innovative mechanism which would deliver the knock-out blow to Germany 'between the eyes'.[89] In so doing the government completely misjudged the ability of the voluntary campaign to manipulate the remaining patriotic good-will in the nation in the third year of the war.

The implementation of National Service encountered problems as a result of both the organisation and the objectives of the scheme, which led to the failure of the appeal for a mobile reserve of civilian labour. The public spectacle of the demise of voluntary National Service tarnished the assumption that Lloyd George's appointment as Prime Minister guaranteed that the conduct of the war effort would be pursued on an immeasurably superior level. For, it had been asked, what could be worse than the continuation of Asquith's government? As far as the development of manpower plans was concerned, the creation of 'new ministries' had not led to a dramatic improvement in the management of labour. The absence of Cabinet supervision ensured that, initially at least, the distribution of men for military and industrial purposes was no more effectively accomplished than under Asquith's premiership.

Notes

1 Murray–Robertson mss. Add. Ms. 52462, Robertson to Murray, 10 January 1917.
2 Robertson mss. I/32/52, Robertson to Monro, 12 January 1917, signed copy.

3   N. Chamberlain mss. NC 1/26/95, N. Chamberlain to Anne Chamberlain, 1 January 1916. This letter should be dated 1 January 1917.
4   PRO CAB 23/1 W.C.33, Appendix IV, Proceedings at a Conference, 12 January 1917.
5   Hankey mss. HNKY 1/1, Diary, 12 January 1917. See also his diary entry for 14 January 1917.
6   N. Chamberlain mss. NC 8/5/4/1, History of National Service, n.d. This outline was written by Arthur Collins, Secretary of the National Service Department, soon after Chamberlain's resignation and privately circulated to former senior officials.
7   Hankey mss. HNKY 1/1, Diary, 12 January 1917.
8   Frances Stevenson mss. Diary, typescript, 1 February 1917.
9   Riddell, *War Diary*, entry for 14 January 1917, p. 238.
10 Addison mss. Box 46, Summary of a Conference of 1 January 1917, 2 January 1917, unsigned.
11 Addison mss. Box 46, Minute, F. Kellaway to Addison, 3 January 1917.
12 Addison mss. Box 98, Diary entry, 6 January 1917.
13 Addison mss. Box 98, Diary entry, 9 January 1917.
14 Lloyd George mss. F/15/8/3, Prothero to Lloyd George, 11 January 1917.
15 Milner mss. dep. 23/1, Typescript copy of the diary kept by Sir Hugh Thornton, 17 January 1917. Thornton was Private Secretary to Milner.
16 N. Chamberlain mss. NC 8/5/4/2, National Service, Report of the Director-General on his Proposed Organisation, N.S.R.1, N. Chamberlain, 13 January 1917.
17 Addison mss. Box 98, Diary entry, 19 January 1917.
18 Addison, *Politics from Within*, II, p. 121.
19 PRO CAB 23/1 W.C.39, 19 January 1917.
20 Milner mss. dep. 23/1, Thornton's diary, 18 January 1917. See also R. A. S. Redmayne, *The British Coal-Mining Industry during the War*, London, 1924, p. 146.
21 Lloyd George, *War Memoirs*, III, p. 1360.
22 Addison mss. Box 98, Diary entry, 19 January 1917.
23 Grieves, 'The British Government's political and administrative response to the man-power problem in the First World War', p. 164.
24 Addison mss. Box 98, Diary entry, 24 January 1917. This entry was not written until 1 February 1917.
25 Macready, *Annals of an Active LIfe*, I, pp. 263–4.
26 Addison mss. Box 25, Substitution in Munition Works, Part 2, n.d. unsigned. This memorandum was written by Macready shortly before 17 January 1917.
27 Addison mss. Box 98, Diary entry, 24 January 1917.
28 Addison mss. Box 54, Memorandum on Adjutant-General's comments, unsigned [Addison], n.d.
29 Addison mss. Box 70, Minutes of Proceedings at a Conference with the Engineering Trade Unions on Obtaining Skilled Men for the Army, 17 January 1917.
30 Lloyd George mss. F/27/3/8, Henderson to Lloyd George, 20 January 1917.

31 N. Chamberlain mss. NC 18/1/98, N. Chamberlain to Hilda Chamberlain, 27 January 1917.
32 See L. S. Amery, *My Political Life*, London, 1953, II, pp. 100–1.
33 Bonar Law mss. 81/2/18, Pike Pease to Bonar Law, 19 January 1917.
34 Lloyd George mss. F/14/4/16, Lloyd George to Derby, 22 January 1917, unsigned copy.
35 PRO CAB 23/1 W.C.45, 25 January 1917.
36 PRO CAB 23/1 W.C.40, 22 January 1917.
37 Lloyd George mss. F/14/4/24, Memorandum [On the man-power problem and risk of invasion], Long, 20 January 1917. See also Robertson, *Soldiers and Statesmen*, II, pp. 1–18.
38 Frances Stevenson mss. Notes of a conversation with Lloyd George, typescript diary, 15 January 1917.
39 French mss. Box 75/46/2. Diary, O, 22 January 1917.
40 Murray–Robertson mss. Add. Ms. 52462, Robertson to Murray, 31 January 1917.
41 Bonar Law mss. 81/2/15, A. Steel-Maitland to Bonar Law, 13 January 1917; J. A. Turner, 'The formation of Lloyd George's "Garden Suburb": "Fabian-Like Milnerite Penetration"?', *Historical Journal*, XX, 1977, pp. 177–8.
42 J. Davies, *The Prime Minister's Secretariat 1916–1920*, Newport, 1951, p. 63; J. Turner, *Lloyd George's Secretariat*, Cambridge, 1980, pp. 19–20.
43 Lloyd George mss. F/79/20/11, Difficulties of Compulsory National Service, Adams, 16 January 1917.
44 N. Chamberlain mss. NC 2/20, Political journal, 21 January 1917. Among those on the platform were F. Dudley Docker (President of the Federation of British Industries and a director of BSA Co), H. W. Sambridge (President of the Birmingham Chamber of Commerce) and Ernest Hiley.
45 N. Chamberlain mss. NC 7/11/10/1, F. S. Oliver to N. Chamberlain, 21 January 1917.
46 Labour Party Cuttings Collection (LPCC) 24/2/30, *Birmingham Post*, 22 January 1917.
47 *The Observer*, 21 January 1917. Quoted in C. E. Playne, *Britain Holds On 1917, 1918*, London, 1933, pp. 27–8.
48 *The Times*, 7 January 1917.
49 LPCC 24/2/30, *Birmingham Post*, 22 January 1917.
50 *Daily Telegraph*, 30 January 1917.
51 Wilson (ed.), *The Political Diaries of C. P. Scott*, Diary entry, 28 January 1917, p. 259.
52 Lloyd George mss. F/79/20/1, Suggested notes re. National Service, For Caernarvon Speech, unsigned [Adams], n.d.
53 *Loc. cit.*
54 Addison mss. Box 25, Addison to N. Chamberlain, 2 February 1917, signed copy.
55 PRO CAB 23/1 W.C. 55, Appendix One, Memorandum by the Army Council regarding the Supply of Men for the Army, Brade, 2 February 1917. See Appendix 5.

56 N. Chamberlain mss. NC 8/5/4/2, Second Report of the Director-General of National Service, N. Chamberlain, 3 February 1917.

57 PRO CAB 23/1 W.C. 55, 5 February 1917. See also Milner mss. dep 23/1, Thornton's diary, 7 February 1917.

58 *The Times*, 6 February 1917.

59 W. J. Reader, *Architect of Air Power. The Life of the first Viscount Weir of Eastwood*, London, 1968, pp. 55–68.

60 Addison mss. Box 65, Minutes of Proceedings at the Ministers' Fortnightly Meeting with Heads of Departments, 13 February 1917.

61 Addison mss. Box 98, Diary entry, 12 February 1917.

62 N. Chamberlain mss. NC 18/1/101, N. Chamberlain to Hilda Chamberlain, 10 February 1917.

63 A. Chamberlain mss. AC 16/1/26, Note on Man-Power, A. Chamberlain, 6 February 1917.

64 A. Chamberlain mss. AC 16/1/28, Memorandum by the Secretary of State for the Colonies, Long, 10 February 1917.

65 *The Times*, 29 January 1917.

66 N. Chamberlain mss. NC 8/5/4/11, Memorandum [Review of the policy and operations of the Department], unsigned [Ernest Hiley], 5 April 1917.

67 Lloyd George mss. F/17/16/2, Minute, Adams to Lloyd George, 5 February 1917.

68 LPCC 24/2/30, Minutes of Proceedings of National Service Meeting held at Central Hall, Westminster, on Tuesday, February 6 1917. See also *Manchester Guardian*, 7 February 1917.

69 Lloyd George mss. F/232, Speech notes, Central Hall, Westminster, National Service, Lloyd George, 6 February 1917.

70 LPCC 24/2/30, Notes to Speakers on National Service, n.d.

71 N. Chamberlain mss. NC 18/1/101, N. Chamberlain to Hilda Chamberlain, 10 February 1917.

72 N. Chamberlain mss. NC 15/1(b), Press cuttings, *Hull Daily News*, 7 February 1917.

73 N. Chamberlain mss. NC 15/1(b), Press cuttings, *Morning Post*, 9 February 1917.

74 N. Chamberlain mss. NC 15/1(b), Press cuttings, *The Star*, 12 February 1917.

75 *New Statesman*, 13 January 1917.

76 N. Chamberlain mss. NC 15/1(b), Press cuttings, *Sheffield Independent*, 7 February 1917.

77 PRO NATS 1/577, Signed circular letter to MPs, Lloyd George, 27 February 1917.

78 N. Chamberlain mss. NC 8/5/2/19, Lloyd George to N. Chamberlain, 20 February 1917.

79 Lloyd George mss. F/79/21/4, National Service Meetings, Summary up to 27 Feb. [1917], 1 March 1917.

80 D. Lloyd George, *The Great Crusade. Extracts from Speeches delivered during the War*, London, 1918, p. 59.

81 Lloyd George mss. F/79/29/4, National Service, Adams, 1 March 1917.

See also Lloyd George mss. F/79/20/6, Report on First 3,000 Enrolments, A. Collins, n.d.

82 *The Times*, 10 March 1917.

83 *Manchester Guardian*, 9 March 1917.

84 N. Chamberlain mss. NC 8/5/4/11, Memorandum, 5 April 1917, unsigned.

85 Addison mss. Box 98, Diary entry, 1 March 1917.

86 *Manchester Guardian*, 28 March 1917.

87 *The Times*, 24 March 1917.

88 Lloyd George mss. F/232, Speech notes, Central Hall, Westminster, National Service, Lloyd George, 6 February 1917.

89 N. Chamberlain mss. NC 15/1(b), Press cuttings, *Hull Daily News*, 7 February 1917.

6
The collapse of National Service: a setback for Lloyd George
March – August 1917

As a result of the monumental failure of the appeal for National Service volunteers the department hurried into a prolonged decline which ended in Neville Chamberlain's resignation in August 1917. Before examining the attempts of the department to regain its pivotal importance in the war effort the two levels on which the enrolment scheme failed must be highlighted. Firstly, the conduct of the campaign was plagued by uncertainty and inter-departmental strife. Secondly, the general appeal as a bureaucratic response to the worsening manpower shortage depended on promoting patriotic 'voluntarism' within the framework of 'class unity'. It was a combination which was too intangible to meet the demands of competing compartmentalised elements of the overall war effort. These features of the National Service campaign represented the practical dilemmas of waging a 'total' war effort which the department and its successor strove to overcome to render the conduct of the war more efficient. The failure of National Service suggested that there was much to do before Lloyd George's government could truly claim that it had secured an improvement for Allied prospects on the 'Wait and See' government.

The first level of failure concerned the conduct of the enrolment scheme. It never overcame the high degree of uncertainty and inter-departmental strife which characterised the appeal. The failure to resolve this inherent weakness encouraged scepticism towards the presumption that National Service was central to the preservation, let alone the expansion, of the nation's war effort in 1917. The failure to secure co-operation from the government departments in Whitehall was reflected in their reluctance to encourage their civil servants to enrol in the scheme. Lloyd George informed ministers that an example should be set, but Bonar Law, Chancellor of the Exchequer, was most disturbed at the prospect of Treasury officials being transferred to farm work.[1] Chamberlain was required to give an undertaking that although the government should encourage its employees to volunteer, no Treasury official would be called up without the Chancellor's assent.[2] Addison's description of the volunteer scheme as a 'Stage Army' was widely accepted in Whitehall, for ministers believed that Chamberlain's plans were grounded in fantasy.[3] The Minister of Munitions refused to allow any of his staff to enrol and noted

Their latest performance is that they wish to enrol everybody and anybody, including all those at present in the service of Government Departments, in munition works, etc. etc. It is altogether too silly a performance for words. It means that they will stack their catalogues with thousands of names of people who cannot be moved and hide out of sight those whom they could make some use of.[4]

Addison was the most venomous critic of the full and unrestricted implementation of National Service, for the wholly valid reason that he feared the division of authority in the munition industry. The Ministry of Munitions had been empowered since 1915 to move men from munition work in one district to similar work elsewhere, but Chamberlain expected to reallocate workers who had volunteered for National Service in accordance with his own plans. The problem of the dual control of munition workers remained a constant source of irritation and the removal of skilled men from essential war work did disrupt output. Twenty-two volunteers employed by Mowlem, the building contractors, on the construction of Hereford Filling Factory received notices to transfer to work which was 'deemed to be of greater national importance'.[5] On 10 April the Department of Explosives Supply at the Ministry of Munitions reported that a soap firm had been informed that its National Service volunteers would be transferred elsewhere, which would badly affect the production of glycerine. For over two months the multiplication of categories of transferable labour in the munition industry estranged Addison and his senior officials from the enrolment campaign. By 24 April he was unable to accept the position any longer. Addison threatened to resign if Chamberlain continued to remove workers from the controlled establishments of the Ministry of Munitions. He told Milner, 'One would have a little more patience if one felt that the National Service Department were organised and equipped to be able to do this work in an efficient manner, but I tell you frankly, in my opinion, it is grotesquely incompetent.'[6]

During the first quarter of 1917 Milner adopted a crucial role in the settlement of inter-departmental disputes, particularly on his return to Britain from the Allied mission to Russia.[7] He was keen to avoid the creation of further bureaucratic co-ordinating devices and in the first week of April he struggled to untangle the disputed area of manpower planning. At the end of the week he noted, '"National Service" still very perplexing'.[8] Following Addison's bitter letter on the incompetence of the National Service Department, Milner and Henderson held a conference to resolve the existing strife. It concluded that Chamberlain should not withdraw men from munitions work without consulting Addison. More importantly, the conference decided that any further disagreements should be referred to Milner and Henderson.[9] This decision not only reflected how far short of being an 'arbiter' of manpower Chamberlain actually was, but consolidated Milner's broad supervisory role over the development of initiatives on the shortage of manpower for essential war industries.

Persistent criticism which arose from uncertainty in Whitehall over Chamberlain's role increased his vulnerability to political attack. Chamberlain became distracted from the awkward task of establishing public confidence in the capacity of the appeal to secure men for vital war industries by identifying intrigues against him. At an early stage he expected in the long run to get 'pulled down'. On 4 March he remarked, 'The fact is there are intrigues going on all the time & one has no real chance. If I stop here [in London] it is said I ought to be in the country and when I go to the country the backstairs gentlemen have a fair field.'[10] Five days later he appealed for 'fair play towards his department' in a public speech in Bradford.[11] Increasingly, the 'backstairs gentlemen', not least Lord Northcliffe, found some substance for their criticism of National Service whose implementation was so clearly at odds with the expectation of a swiftly enrolled 'industrial army'. Figures released in the House of Commons on 16 July 1917 indicated that of the department's total expenditure of £163,118, at least £84,491 was spent on advertising work for the enrolment campaign.[12] With some justification, Northcliffe believed that the government's expenditure on advertising National Service amounted to a scandal, but his opposition concentrated on the avoidance of industrial conscription.[13] It was not within Chamberlain's power to introduce compulsion, but he was warned about the urgency of being seen to facilitate the recruitment of men for the army. Leo Amery wrote a friendly warning on 8 March which was based on the observation,

I see the 'Daily Mail' has launched an onslaught on the National Service 'chaps' this morning all the more significant from the fact that it has put this in front of Home Rule and everything else. Northcliffe is evidently going to be out on the rampage for some complete recasting of your scheme or more probably immediate compulsory National Service.[14]

Lord Northcliffe was the self-appointed guardian of the nation's will to prosecute the war effort by 'total' organisation.[15] He was critical of National Service because it had not introduced compulsion into the civilian workplace. More widely, he denounced any maladministered part of the government which might damage the credibility of Lloyd George's premiership. Consequently, National Service was brought to Northcliffe's attention because its defects could be described as a liability to the government. He warned J. T. Davies, principal private secretary to Lloyd George, of 'the grumbling about the Man-Power Department, which the Asquithians hope will bring down the Government. I know nothing of Mr Chamberlain. The only things of his that have come to my notice have been blunders.'[16] In part Northcliffe's fear was substantiated by Chamberlain's belief that a 'radical cabal' existed in the House of Commons which was exploiting his vulnerability 'to pay off old scores against Ll[oyd] G[eorge]'.[17] In fact although some Liberal MPs opposed this latest manifestation of uncontrolled state bureaucracy, the 'cabal' was no more dangerous or, indeed, mysterious than that which criticised the introduction of compulsory military service.

A particularly unfortunate feature of the National Service scheme which gained publicity in the press was the administrative delays which followed enrolment. Letters to newspapers reflected the irritation of being subject to advertisements which stated 'The fate of Britain is trembling in the balance' in the knowledge that 39,000 men who had enrolled three weeks before were still 'idle'.[18] Another advertisement warned 'Hindenburg is watching us', but a correspondent to *The Times* complained, 'It is useless to adjure people by the name of a German Field-Marshal to do their duty while those who have already done it are left in the position of waiting and not seeing.'[19] Such letters indicated the fundamental disincentive of the enrolment campaign.

The difficulty of overcoming the unimpressive image of delay and prevarication was complicated by the question of remuneration. The application of a guaranteed level of pay and the Unemployment Benefit scheme was a remarkable instance of intervention in economic and labour policy by a temporary wartime government department. However, Adams's assessment of the remuneration aspect of National Service related the economic circumstances of the married volunteer to the reluctance of some categories of skilled labour to enrol. He noted, 'It is not enough to indicate a low minimum wage 25/- and leave the rest to the uncertainty of the district rate. More exact information will help a man to make the change and to measure the sacrifice which he can fairly undertake.'[20] Adams's sense of realism was an antidote to the profound sense of uncertainty which surrounded the scheme. When combined with the inter-departmental strife, the department's ability to fulfil its mandate of relieving the worsening manpower position was severely damaged. The enrolment of only 91,400 volunteers by 1 March was the most significant statistical return of the campaign. The problem of uncertainty bedevilled the allocation of work, the question of remuneration and the relevance of the scheme to specific demands for skilled labour. Most of all, the campaign was particularly troubled by the absence of support from the Ministry of Munitions. The disastrous relations between Addison and Chamberlain ranked amongst the most embittered of the clashes of personalities between ministers in the wartime Coalition government.

The second level of the failure of the scheme leaves the specific organisation of National Service to consider the unsatisfactory concept of a 'great Industrial Army'. Undue dependence was placed on propagating the same patriotic principles which had encouraged the recruitment of fit men for military service during the first winter of the war. However, conditions were very different in 1917 and the manipulation of 'patriotic endeavour' and 'national unity' was not a sustainable approach to eradicating the deficiencies of manpower control and allocation. At the core of the scheme for voluntary National Service was the necessity to inculcate

a wholesome sense of patriotism and bring every man and woman in the country to regard any act of excess of any kind, or of indolence or neglect to be a crime against the State, and as such, incurring the strong displeasure of public opinion, if even more drastic measures are not forthcoming. *Per contra*, the propaganda must teach the paramount necessity for every man and woman to work for and live in the National interest.[21]

Although the latent threat of compulsion existed, an essential feature of the appeal was the government's determination to resist the appearance of the scheme as a centrally-managed initiative which impinged on the remaining liberties of the civilian public in wartime.

The National Service Department perceived that a co-ordinated system of localised enrolment campaigns would 'arouse the moral sense of the country also to utilise the immense forces of local patriotism and emulation'.[22] Much importance was attached to the local National Service committees. Theoretically, it was intended that the committees would include representatives of the Local Authority, employers of local industries, trade unionists, women 'of various social grades' and clergymen. This was a far more systematic approach to local organisation than the guidelines which the Local Government Board circulated in 1915 in preparation for the local and appeal tribunals. In practice, the National Service committees developed as an *ad hoc* local response to assist the national appeal. Their level of activity was acutely dependent on the composition of District Councils from which the nucleus of committees were drawn and they were established largely without reference to the importance of a balanced social composition. Nevertheless, the importance of these local 'arms' of the department was that they focused the attention of the town or rural area on the importance of its own contribution to the mobile reserve of civilian workers.

The committees existed to highlight the single most dramatic development in the government's conduct of the war since the creation of the New Armies. Public meetings, the like of which had not been seen since the Derby scheme, were held to promote a 'willing co-operation' in the creation of a spectacular 'industrial army'. Frequently the meetings were most unrepresentative of the locality, but pledged nonetheless, as at Edinburgh 'to give whole hearted and sustained support to all steps and measures necessary in the national interests for the successful prosecution of the war'.[23] The main event which attempted to reaffirm the validity of the call for volunteers was the National Service meeting at the Royal Albert Hall on 17 March, which was graced by the presence of Queen Mary. The role of women in the enrolment campaign remained passive and the meeting was held as a demonstration that 'behind the manhood of England stands the unalterable determination of the women'.[24]

Public meetings attempted to project National Service as a means of transcending the complex area of civil-military relations by exploiting parallels between military service and civilian work. The similarities between Lord Derby's scheme and the enrolment campaign were so striking that Chamberlain represented National Service as a military mode of organisation to the increasing discomfort of his senior officials, Ernest Hiley and Arthur Collins. Chamberlain used the vocabulary of military organisation and his pronouncements were at odds with his department's dependence on the preservation of the voluntary character of National Service. On 4 March he told his audience at Whitefield's Tabernacle in London, 'I have got 100,000 volunteers, five divisions of the new industrial army. I want five times as many as that, and I am going to get them. I am going to get them if I am supported by the general goodwill and patriotism of this country.'[25] This distorted description of voluntary National Service was extremely unsatisfactory. The appeal *en masse* was the only feasible response which could have been made in the time available. However, the mistake in placing reliance on the intangible appeal of patriotism in the enrolment campaign was that the notions of 'self sacrifice' and 'general goodwill' failed to generate a framework of organisational strength. Neither did their encouragement and application to National Service actually survive the disillusionment of administrative delays or the hardship of separation when volunteers were transferred to essential war work. It was no part of even the limited implementation of National Service in Britain to assume that a civilian left at home was a soldier temporarily exempted.

The concept of National Service as it was implemented in Britain enshrined voluntarism. It remained the premier method of government intervention in the restriction of non-war industries, yet Chamberlain employed the rhetoric of military forms of organisation to promote a scheme devoid of statutory obligations. When a speaker told the public meeting for National Service at Mitcham that 'the signatories would be under no legal obligation to answer the call when it was made, many of his hearers interrupted with cries of "What is the good of it, then?"'[26] The restricted impact of the appeal was related directly to its conceptual limitations. The scheme's origins as a political innovation, which was designed to meet the needs of the new government rather than the actual requirements of the distribution of manpower, explain the deficiencies of the concept of National Service. With a degree of philosophical detachment Arthur Collins, General Secretary of the department, concluded, 'this experience as regards raising men for National Service has had to be bought by the Country in much the same way as the nation has paid to discover the best means of raising materials for the purposes of War'.[27] As the collapse of National Service on both levels became plain, the question arose as to whether the department had a viability which would enable it to survive the breakdown of the enrolment campaign.

The search for a revival in the fortunes of the National Service Department led it from the general appeal to special appeals for substitution volunteers. On 1 March it became the controlling authority for the organisation of substitution and Chamberlain started to develop the idea of separate local machinery which would obtain substitutes through the co-operation of employers and trade unionists in the 'restricted trades'.[28] Like the volunteer scheme, the substitutes would take the place of men withdrawn from essential war industries for military service but, crucially, would only be taken from the non-war industries.[29]

During his period in office Chamberlain developed a keen regard for the opportunities for innovation which arose in the execution and administration of wartime policy. To remove recourse to strike action he believed that the government should conciliate between the organised interests of employers and trade unionists, within the broad consensus of support for, and participation in, the government's conduct of the war. In encouraging a heightened sense of co-operation between the representatives of Capital and Labour, Chamberlain actually looked forward to their 'amalgamation'.[30] When in September 1917 Austen Chamberlain sought his advice on plans for post-war reconstruction, Neville Chamberlain told him that industrial conditions must be regulated by supervisory boards, 'representative of employers & employed and their recommendations as to wages and trade conditions could be made compulsory on all registered [factories] in that area'.

Neville Chamberlain's interest in the application of Milnerite, or interventionist, conservatism to the problem of post-war industrial relations was derived, in part, from the creation of National Service Trade Committees. Although this local machinery remained substantially incomplete, it was intended to bring together employers and operatives to locate surplus labour in individual industries. The central feature of the substitution scheme was the extent of 'incorporation' of official trade union leaders in its procedure. For example, once a special appeal was made by a Trade Committee the enrolment and transfer of substitution volunteers was supposed to be managed entirely through the appropriate trade unions.[31]

The severe weakness of the substitution scheme arose where trade unions and, consequently, Trade Committees were poorly organised at a time when the local National Service committees were being dissolved after the compilation of their final report.[32] The impression created by the local machinery available to the department was that it was far less competent than the Employment Exchanges to deal with the transfer of labour to essential war industries. The main problems which Chamberlain encountered while planning the substitution scheme during April 1917 was the non-co-operation of the Employment Department of the Ministry of Labour and the small scale of enrolment. Addison argued that the reform of the National Service Department was insufficient to enable the munition industry to release the men required for military service.[33] In fact, the reason for the reduced level of military recruitment, which had created a deficit of 148,000 men in the first three months of 1917, was the result of the successful 'protection' of skilled workers under the Trade Card scheme. Furthermore, the War Cabinet exacerbated the recruiting problem by its refusal to discuss the related issues of short-term military objectives and manpower provision, beyond the delegation of responsibility in this area to Milner and Henderson.[34]

During his promotion of the Trade Committees as a network of 'balanced' agencies, Chamberlain bitterly resented the scepticism of the Employment Department and the active opposition of its Director, Charles Rey, to his substitution scheme. The Employment Exchanges continued to allocate labour on an individual basis at an approximate rate of 5,000 applications per week which represented at best twelve per cent of vacancies notified to the Exchanges.[35] Despite the distrust of skilled labour, the pre-war foundation and close working relations with private employers in manufacturing industry ensured that the Exchanges were the most efficient means of adjusting the government's labour policy to wartime conditions. The scheme commenced on 1 May, yet once again the vacancies which Substitution officers were expected to locate were not found.

The fate of the Substitution scheme depended entirely on the outcome of extended negotiations, but during June 1917 relations between the National Service Department and the Employment Department dropped to a nadir from which they never recovered. On 13 July Chamberlain reacted angrily to the statement circulated by John Hodge, Minister of Labour, at the War Cabinet that of 2,766 vacancies which the Exchanges had passed to the National Service Department because substitutes were required, only 34 had been filled. These figures did not correspond with the National Service returns which included information on the continuing placement of volunteers and military labour for agricultural work. Chamberlain commented on Hodge's information in a letter to Lloyd George,

I think you may be interested to have the latest figures supplied to me by my officials. These show that since the 1st May there have been 8,106 applications to my officers for labour; 8,694 candidates have been submitted in respect of these vacancies and 4,022 volunteers have been actually placed. Of the latter, 965 are returned as 'substitutes'.[36]

Even this figure revealed that less than twenty-five per cent of all vacancies filled by the National Service Department could be described as the specially recruited substitution volunteers. Whatever the relationship between the notified vacancies and the utilisation of volunteers recruited for all forms of National Service, the overall scale of labour transfer was insignificant in relation to the size of the recruiting problem.

By mid-June Chamberlain's contribution to the withdrawal of labour from less essential trades was dependent on the goodwill of the Employment Department. He believed that the officials in the regional divisions of the Exchanges had secret instructions to disregard the substitution officers as an alternative means of labour placement. More accurately, the increasing disuse of the substitution scheme was the outcome of arrangements secured by the Employment Department and there was very little which Chamberlain could do. On 23 June he decided to 'put in to the Cabinet a memo on the whole position of the N[ational] S[ervice] D[epartment]',[37] having observed on the day before that his ministerial duties had 'been limited to a partial control over such volunteers as I could obtain from trades and occupations not of national importance and to certain military forces temporarily diverted to civilian work'.[38]

Towards the end of June 1917 several statements were circulated in support of the continued existence of the National Service Department despite its parlous state. The most authoritative submission was provided by Milner, who was particularly well-placed to observe the absence of 'any clear conception of its place in the general scheme of things'.[39] Milner acknowledged that at least six departments dealt with different aspects of labour supply. Nevertheless, he argued that the department should be preserved because it would have a valuable role should the political will be found to give one authority comprehensive powers to 'manage' the government's manpower plans. Cecil Harmsworth, brother of Lord Northcliffe and Liberal MP, joined Lloyd George's secretariat in 1917 and assumed responsibility for labour-related aspects of the war effort. He had time enough to observe Chamberlain's work and Harmsworth's support for the department rested on the fear that dissolving the department might injure the government's prestige.[40]

Milner and Harmsworth justified the retention of the National Service Department principally on the grounds that it provided the War Cabinet with a policy-making option. They stated that the department should remain available in case a deterioration in the Allied military position demanded the closure of the semi-autonomous labour supply branches and the direct supervision of labour by a *de facto* 'Controller of Man-Power' office. This view of the department's capacity to eventually assume wide-ranging responsibilities was resisted by Chamberlain. He also opposed the prospect of having to 'mark time' for an indefinite period. Instead, he challenged the War Cabinet to cancel all exemption certificates and 'call up' men for military service in clearly defined stages. In his Tenth Report of 22 June Chamberlain returned to a familiar theme

I wish to repeat my conviction that the policy which I have twice submitted to the Cabinet is the only one which will quickly and certainly provide the men required for the army, and that further, it is one which would commend itself to the majority of the people as, on the whole, the fairest all round.[41]

Without the adoption of his proposal for the recruitment of men in age groups regardless of occupation, which would ensure the rapid deployment of substitutes, Chamberlain saw no reason for the continued existence of his department.

With some justification Chamberlain noted that the declining importance of his work resulted from the War Cabinet's apparent preference for circuitous rather than direct methods of attaining an equitable balance in the provision of manpower for the war effort. The Tenth Report clarified the conditions Chamberlain demanded if he was to remain Director of National Service but it also revealed that his situation was already quite hopeless. He required a decision from the War Cabinet, which had still not considered the report when he wrote an ultimatum to the Prime Minister on 19 July. Chamberlain sought to confront Lloyd George with his 'intolerable' position, and 'unless the Cabinet are able to consider my Report tomorrow and to adopt the policy recommended therein I must ask you to accept my resignation as from the 20th instant and to allow me to state publicly my reasons for relinquishing my office'.[42] Towards the end of July 1917 the work of the National Service Department ground to a near standstill, as momentous reforms were considered by Milner and Derby to determine future recruiting plans and long awaited changes in the supply and allocation of manpower. The National Service Department was vitally concerned in these issues, but until clear recommendations were forthcoming it was not surprising that Chamberlain's attempts to preserve his position on his own terms were ignored.

The main question posed in late July was, for how long could the War Office retain sole responsibility for the system of recruiting for the army in view of the persistent criticism of the decentralised enlistment machinery? On 6 July Derby warned Lloyd George that the existing state of recruiting was far more damaging to the War Office's reputation than its involvement in the conduct of the Mesopotamian campaign. He told the Prime Minister,

we are really in a tight place, not only with regard to the number of men but with regard to the methods we are obliged to adopt to get even those that we are getting. The House of Commons Committee on the Medical Re-examination was as I told you at the time, likely to prove very hostile. It is proving very hostile, . . . and I hope by the evidence we can produce to mitigate some of the charges that are being brought against us. There is no doubt, however, we shall have a great deal of trouble when the report is issued.[43]

Derby referred to the Parliamentary Select Committee which was chaired by the Lloyd George Liberal MP Edward Shortt. It was appointed to investigate the recruiting arrangements at the War Office and, in particular, the working of the Military Service (Review of Exceptions) Act. In the absence of a satisfactory outcome of the National Service volunteer and substitution schemes, Derby, assisted by the Adjutant-General, had campaigned for the legislative extension of compulsory military service. This pressure culminated in May 1917 in statutory provision for the re-examination of men of military age previously discharged as unfit from the army or who possessed exemption certificates on medical grounds.[44]

In the first six weeks of the operation of this Act 70,000 'A' men and 60,000 'B' and 'C' men were obtained for military service through a deeply contentious procedure. They were not secured by removing fit men from categories of 'protected' occupations, but by the re-examination of men who had been discharged on medical grounds from the services during the war. Derby justified medical re-examination by drawing attention to the fraudulent use of 'rejected' papers which could be obtained in some towns at fifteen pounds per set. He observed, 'There is no doubt the Act is very unpopular and it is very easy to get up a cry against it but as a matter of fact it has shown how many men escaped under various circumstances, chiefly fraud, when examined in the first instance.'[45] Although some entries in the register of men who held medical rejection certificates were suspect, the treatment of the one million men listed was of far greater concern for the Parliamentary Select Committee. It uncovered the stringent supervision of the recruiting medical boards by Brigadier-General Auckland Geddes and Surgeon-General Sir Alfred Keogh, Director of Army Medical Services. Geddes told Shortt's committee on 2 July that his guiding principle was 'that there is no man who is able to make his living in civil life who cannot find some employment in the Army'.[46]

Subsequent evidence led the Select Committee to conclude that this 'guiding rule' was actually implemented by recruiting officers with 'blind obedience'.[47] Furthermore, the pressure to re-examine men and place them in medical categories above their discharged grade, to ensure their availability for general service, was reinforced by continuing adherence to Keogh's circular letter of 16 September 1916. It ordered medical boards not to reject any man who could perform military work without danger to himself or others. The chairmen of local medical boards were serving military doctors and they inevitably regarded instructions from senior officers, within the framework of the Royal Army Medical Corps, as orders which they were bound to obey. [48] The chairmen were able to overrule their civilian colleagues on the Medical Boards; consequently, the boards were preoccupied with the fulfilment of the military demand for men and not with rectifying the inequitable treatment of ex-servicemen and young protected skilled men in the essential war industries. The Select Committee observed with disquiet the lack of public confidence in the medical boards, which the most 'visible' part of the localised enlistment machinery.

The Select Committee's mandate to restore public confidence in the conduct of medical examinations was facilitated, quite remarkably, by the War Office's own assessment of its recruiting functions. On becoming Adjutant-General, Macready had recommended that the 'discriminating' work should be placed under civil control, and Geddes's review of the expansion of the work of the recruiting branch since the outbreak of war implied that he wished to stop its direct association with the enlistment machinery.[49] Increasingly in 1917 this function was the cause of severe and effective attacks on the military authorities in the House of Commons.[50] On 19 July the Select Committee sent a resolution to the Prime Minister which urged that the responsibility for military recruiting should be transferred to a civilian authority. Shortly afterwards Derby saw Lloyd George and, in the course of a short taxicab ride, they agreed that the War Office should transfer the whole system of recruiting to a civilian government department.[51]

The Committee had expected some opposition from the War Office, but on 24 July Derby surprised it by agreeing that the recruiting machine 'from A to Z' should be entrusted to civil control. As far as the practical effect of this reform was concerned Derby noted,

it is only after going through all the various processes of seeing whether they can be spared from their employment and whether they are fit for the various categories of service the Army require – when you have done that and passed them through these various stages, then alone should the Army come in.[52]

Unusually Derby took the initiative on this issue. His view on the value of separating the function of recruiting from the vastly expanded administrative work of the military authorities was based on his experience of recruiting in Lancashire. In equating the success of his recruiting work, which was based on his family's historic connection with the north-west, with the renewed promotion of locally-led recruiting campaigns, he overlooked, as Chamberlain had done, the fact that the 'volunteer spirit' was not as prevalent in 1917 as it was in 1914.

Derby embodied the usefulness of the notion of 'civilian control' during his period of office as Secretary of State for War, especially in the uncritical support he provided Sir Douglas Haig and Sir William Robertson at Cabinet level. The War Office was interested in the 'civilian' control of recruiting because it would deflect criticism from the military authorities. The effectiveness of this plan depended on the ability of Derby to influence negotiations so that a close affinity with the ostensibly independent civil authority could be established immediately to protect the military manpower supply. Derby resisted Shortt's suggestion that the Local Government Board should become responsible for the recruiting machinery. Derby's main reason for agreeing to such a dramatic reform in July 1917 was that a special opportunity had arisen. A department with some administrative experience but in terminal decline was available. Derby told Lloyd George on 25 July that the National Service Department should be used, although the army would have little confidence in Chamberlain's supervision of the work. He went on, 'It might, however, enable you to put a new head to the department and really make some use of what is at the present moment a rather useless body.'[53] Harmsworth agreed with Derby though not because the department had a perfect administrative record. Indeed, like Derby, he also ignored Chamberlain's position, knowing that the Director was opposed to any alteration in the work of his department.

By 27 July Neville Chamberlain was not only isolated but thoroughly beleaguered. His Tenth Report had been lodged with Hankey's office for five weeks without being discussed in the War Cabinet although informal responses were drafted by 'labour-employing' departments. Lloyd George asked Chamberlain to delay any final step towards resignation, because he was awaiting Auckland Geddes's report on the future basis for recruiting which emphasised the criterion of occupation, rather than age.[54] The essence of Chamberlain's position was 'After having threatened resignation & being kept waiting for a month I should be dismissed in an atmosphere already prepared for my decease.'[55] Chamberlain had not enjoyed the most cordial of relations with Auckland Geddes. The latter's growing reputation for administrative expertise was based on the solid accumulation of experience under Macready's tutelage.[56] He had contributed to the creation of the Man-Power Distribution Board, the development of the Trade Card scheme and the transfer of Substitution officers to the National Service Department. He had been present at many of the trade union delegations to the War Office and he was a principal figure in the frequent bi-lateral talks with the Ministry of Munitions.

Uninhibited by the constraints on the professional soldier of the deep sense of hierarchical decision-making in military administration and concern over personal prospects for promotion, Auckland Geddes, as a temporary but enthusiastic soldier, grew in confidence and developed an 'interventionist' role in Whitehall. Lloyd George welcomed Geddes's interest in broad manpower issues because the Director of Recruiting was able to comprehend the context within which plans for the allocation of labour evolved. Geddes's report was unremarkable but that was also its virtue. The actual difference between their reports amounted to degrees of emphasis along the spectrum between the poles of 'occupation' and 'age'. Geddes's report was more attuned to the political limitations on the movement of labour, in comparison with Chamberlain's preoccupation with the unrestricted implementation of the 'clean cut'.

Geddes presented his report to the War Cabinet on 3 August and attention centred on his support for the transfer of military recruiting to a civilian organisation. The War Cabinet agreed with this step and the question arose as to which department would assume responsibility for recruiting. In accordance with the series of *ad hoc* arrangements made since Lloyd George became Prime Minister, it was resolved that Milner, General Smuts and George Barnes should decide 'all questions of recruiting and Man-Power'.[57] As chairman, Milner was presented once again with an opportunity of tackling the repercussions of 'the Prime Minister's lack of method and his harum-scarum ways'.[58] Milner would have been even more anxious to leave the government than he actually was, had he not been allowed to resolve problems which arose on the issue of manpower unfettered by the intervention of the War Cabinet. In the absence of a central manpower department headed by a senior ministerial figure, the supervision of initiatives by Milner was probably the most effective response the War Cabinet could make.

Auckland Geddes visited Milner on 4 August and later the same day Milner resisted pressure from Smuts to assume direct ministerial responsibility for the reconstructed National Service Department.[59] He accepted Geddes's argument that reorganisation was the only course of action which would encourage public opinion, and particularly the trade unions, to be more favourably disposed towards the military demand for men. To secure some flexibility in the reform of recruiting procedures Milner decided that 'Neville Chamberlain must go'.[60] He also sought to clarify his precise task in correspondence with the Prime Minister, to preclude the possibility of his work being overturned.[61] Lord Riddell noted

Lloyd George's 'Fondness for a grandiose scheme in preference to an attempt to improve existing machinery'.[62] Milner feared the possibility of such an intervention as part of the Prime Minister's continuing bid to frustrate the concentration of military manpower on the Western Front. Milner's committee met on 8 August and it decided that the recruiting organisation should be transferred to the National Service Department.[63]

Milner was already aware that Chamberlain had no intention of remaining in the government if his department was directed to undertake the task of recruiting men for the army. Milner recognised that an impasse had been reached and he forewarned Chamberlain of the likely outcome of his committee meeting. On 7 August, 'M[ilner] began by saying that he had seen Geddes & ascertained that there was no likelihood of co-operation there and he advised me strongly to "get out of it"'.[64] On the following day Milner's committee met and, accordingly, Chamberlain wrote a forthright letter of resignation to Lloyd George. Chamberlain did not believe that the twin functions of recruiting men for the army and for civilian work could co-exist within one department, which was Lloyd George's original intention in December 1916. He observed that the removal of 'khaki for civilian clothes' by the staff of the Recruiting Department would be recognised as a 'hollow' reform by the public.[65] Even had he remained Chamberlain realised that he was unable to command the full support of the military authorities as the prospect of a successful substitution scheme receded.

Chamberlain's unfortunate experience of ministerial work culminated in an acrimonious departure. Chamberlain attended his last meeting of the War Cabinet on 9 August and afterwards an interview full of recriminations took place with Lloyd George. In his diary account of the event Chamberlain noted that he had told Lloyd George, 'The whole *raison d'être* of my Dept. was that it was to control labour as between Depts & that I could not do if Depts. appealed against me to the Cabinet & Cabinet did not support me.'[66] Chamberlain stated that he was unable to develop the Director's role as an 'arbiter' of manpower because the Cabinet had not assisted the department in distancing itself from the general *mêlée* of competitive inter-departmental relations in Whitehall.

Chamberlain correctly surmised that the creation of an authoritative role in the allocation of manpower had been subverted from the outset. Disputes with well-established departments narrowed the 'broad view' so quickly that a general plan for manpower provision was not developed. Chamberlain made it clear at his final interview that he had a grievance, which provoked Lloyd George to recall the Director's failure to recruit and retain senior advisers. The Prime Minister could not understand why his 'Man for the job' approach so singularly failed to achieve the removal of labour from the restricted trades to work of national importance. The main reason for his failure to come to terms with the débâcle of National Service lay in the fact that the manpower problem had changed out of all recognition since the introduction of the Munitions of War Act in 1915. In particular, the control of manpower had become more closely inter-related with the short term aim of national survival, although the administrative structure had barely altered to accommodate that stark equation. In his conclusion of the meeting with Chamberlain on 9 August Lloyd George did not get much further in his thinking than the Director's inability to 'make good'. He reminded Chamberlain that as far as the conflicting departmental claims were concerned 'Lord Milner has always acted with the most perfect fairness and impartiality'.[67] This view could not be doubted, but the comment revealed Chamberlain's lack of access to the War Cabinet as a whole, and Lloyd George's complete dependence on Milner's handling of the frequent manpower controversies.

Inexplicably, the short communiqué which Chamberlain drafted on his resignation and sent to Lloyd George for his approval never reached the national newspapers. On 10 August Neville Chamberlain finally left his office for a period of political convalescence at Crawley at the house of Godfrey Locker-Lampson, Unionist MP. The letters of commiseration which Chamberlain received from sympathisers within Whitehall tended to identify the enemy of National Service as 'inter-departmental jealousy';[68] for example, the antagonistic attitude of the ministries of Labour and Munitions and the Food Production Department. The main response from the administrative system to the wartime demand for skilled men was the increased compartmentalisation of the supply and allocation of labour.

The former Director of National Service took limited moral compensation from the knowledge that he had accepted the task from his sense of 'patriotic duty' and that only the grave national emergency had persuaded him to undertake the work. On 14 August Chamberlain wrote to his mother,

Although you have not dwelt upon it I see that you have perceived the intense bitterness of a failure which is not my fault but with which I must inevitably be associated. I feel I ought to have a gold stripe as one wounded in the war, but seriously it is only by thinking of those who have had their causes broken by wounds that I can reduce my own misfortune to their proper proportions[69]

At the age of fifty Chamberlain had become a casualty of the expansion of government work in wartime and, more specifically, of the Prime Minister's zeal for administrative innovation and experiment which far from constituted a successful sequel to the Man-Power Distribution Board. Austen Chamberlain later told Lloyd George, 'You treated my brother very badly, and you have never forgiven him'.[70] For his part Neville Chamberlain never forgot or forgave Lloyd George in the following twenty-three years. His ministerial experience provided him with many bitter reflections on the Coalition government, but it also gave Chamberlain the impetus for his return to national politics at the end of the war. By December 1917 his intention to seek nomination for a constituency in Birmingham was clear.[71] His political rehabilitation was greatly accelerated by his speech on 17 December at the meeting of the Birmingham Liberal Unionist Association, of which he was Treasurer, when he forcefully defended his role in the implementation of National Service. Although he intended to re-emerge from municipal politics, Chamberlain appreciated that there was no likelihood that he would be offered, or wish to obtain, ministerial office while Lloyd George remained Prime Minister.

The appointment of Chamberlain's successor was a curious affair which reflected the close relations which the War Office intended to pursue with the new authority for recruiting. Only two names were seriously considered for the post during the first two weeks of August 1917, Edward Shortt and Auckland Geddes. Lord Derby's additional suggestion that Donald Maclean, Liberal MP and member of the Central Tribunal, should be considered for the post was short-lived. Shortt was unacquainted with the detailed procedure on recruiting, but he had chaired, most effectively, the Parliamentary Select Committee on the medical re-examination of discharged men. In November 1915 he had been thanked by Lloyd

George for his work in selecting munition workers which were withdrawn from military units in France. Geddes had won some backing in the government for his articulate opposition to Chamberlain's Tenth Report.

In the complicated 'jockeying' for power, Geddes enjoyed the influential and unqualified support of Derby. However on 6 August, two days before Chamberlain wrote his letter of resignation, Lloyd George offered the post to Shortt, who was anxious to accept ministerial office in the government. Chamberlain remarked that the invitation was made 'on the well known principal always adopted by Ll[oyd] G[eorge] of giving a bone to any dog who shows his teeth'.[72] Lord Derby realised that if Shortt accepted the post Geddes would not be satisfied with a long-term subordinate post at the National Service Department. He therefore suggested that the situation might easily be resolved by a delicate manoeuvre. The Parliamentary Select Committee should be persuaded to recommend the appointment of Geddes 'of its own initiative' for the post.[73] In this characteristic appreciation of the remaining moves before the task was accomplished, Derby revealed that unless the initiative was seen to originate from Shortt's committee, the War Office would be accused of 'humbugging' the people by detaching the Recruiting Department and yet retaining control of the enlistment machinery. Chamberlain observed that Geddes's appointment would 'emphasise my contention that the proposal to hand over recruiting to a *civil* authority is all "eyewash".'[74]

Although Chamberlain's views carried no weight at all in mid-August he had outlined the main issue of contention, for the objective of the War Office was quite transparent. Derby hoped that the provision of men for military service would be the first priority of the new minister. Indeed, after Geddes was appointed Derby told Sir Philip Sassoon, Haig's Private Secretary at GHQ,

I am very glad of this as I am perfectly certain he is the only man who can run the show. He has done marvels and I hope will get us more recruits in the future, though it is very difficult to make brick with as little straw as he will have.[75]

Shortt's position was made untenable by the obvious reluctance of Auckland Geddes to support the appointment of anyone but himself. Shortt had also visited the National Service Department, which occupied the requisitioned St Ermin's Hotel, off Victoria Street, and was dismayed at the scale of resignations which had already taken place. Shortt recognised that it would take him at least four months to understand the recruiting process and, consequently, he declined the offer of office.

On 11 August Auckland Geddes was offered the post, having first discussed with Derby the terms on which he might accept the appointment. Learning from the experience of his predecessor, Auckland Geddes was determined to ensure that his ministerial role was clearly defined from the outset. His letter of 13 August sought to rectify the deficiencies which had afflicted Chamberlain for almost eight months. Geddes specified

That I should be provided with a seat in the House of Commons and that I should be the 'political' head of the Department in a sense similar to that in which my brother is at present the 'political' head of the Admiralty and be responsible for answering for and for defending the Department in Parliament.[76]

As the department was to become a parliamentary office Lord Milner agreed that its title should be changed to 'The Ministry of National Service' and consequently Geddes was designated 'Minister'.

At this early stage the other main prerequisite which Geddes required was the continuation of Milner's Man-Power Committee on a permanent basis. This would enable Auckland Geddes to refer inter-departmental questions to a competent authority which enjoyed the support of the War Cabinet. Milner agreed that his Committee should tackle the problems which the reorganisation of recruiting would give rise to without 'troubling the full Cabinet'.[77] Two important reforms were therefore obtained by the Minister of National Service within one week of his appointment. Auckland Geddes was on the way to securing a parliamentary constituency and the Cabinet committee of Milner, Smuts and Barnes was available to resolve disputes. Both factors represented key elements which were lacking throughout the existence of the National Service Department.

Initially, parliamentary questions on National Service were directed at the Home Secretary, Sir George Cave, until March 1917 when joint Parliamentary Secretaries were appointed to the department. Stephen Walsh and, later, the Liberal Cecil Beck represented the department in the House of Commons.[78] In the Lords, Chamberlain was represented by Lord Peel, a Unionist who had supported Milner's strident opposition to Asquith's premiership. They were frequently troubled by the strength of parliamentary opposition to the department, particularly in relation to Chamberlain's absence from Parliament. His absence led Asquithian Liberal, Labour and Irish Nationalist MPs to associate the development of National Service with the unrestricted expansion of government offices in London.[79] Without a co-ordinating Cabinet manpower committee to support the enrolment campaign the department's significance was further eroded. Instead, disputes were resolved after long delays through the mediation of *ad hoc* negotiations which tended to promote the expediency of short-term agreements.

Auckland Geddes observed these weaknesses in the creation of a civil authority to introduce National Service. His own response to his appointment was to rectify the two complaints which persistently found expression in Chamberlain's letters to his relations in Birmingham during his tenure of office. During the periods of dislocation and disagreement, Geddes was ideally placed to note the problems Chamberlain encountered and he sought to avoid a repetition of them on his appointment as Minister of National Service.

Hailed as a panacea which would sweep away the anomalies of *ad hoc* wartime administration and associate more closely the industrial war effort with the military operations on the Western Front, the National Service Department was one of Lloyd George's least impressive inspirations. Violet Markham, Deputy Director of the Women's Section, wrote in late June, 'I feel that the National Service Department lives on the brink of a chronic volcano and that we may blow up at any time.'[80] In contrast with the fiery existence of the department its end was unspectacular. The only factor which continued to carry an explosive content was the sense of outrage which Chamberlain felt on his early retirement. He composed a tirade on the role of Lloyd George and sent it to Leo Amery:

The failure of National Service is due to several causes but one stands out beyond all the rest – the P.M. Ll[oyd] G[eorge] launched it without ever having thought out or understood what its functions were to be ... He gave me just a fortnight to collect a staff, arrange their administrative functions, make myself acquainted with the outline of one of the most difficult & complicated of problems, settle my relations with other Depts. & invent a scheme ... And presently as things were evidently not going well he turned his back on the whole affair & allowed any Dept to drive a coach & horses through the powers the Cabinet had given us.[81]

Chamberlain concluded that the Prime Minister's failure to understand the complexity of the manpower problem and support his schemes was the most significant factor in his eventual resignation. In fact in his letter to Amery he did not bother to outline the other 'causes'. Certainly Lloyd George failed to define the area of initiative which he had given Chamberlain. As the Prime Minister's frustration grew worse his treatment of Chamberlain deteriorated. On 29 June Cecil Beck replaced Stephen Walsh as Parliamentary Secretary to the National Service Department and Chamberlain first received news of the announcement in the morning papers. Lloyd George regarded the episode as 'a mixture of inadvertence and misunderstanding', caused by the, not untypical, rushed announcement of the appointments.[82] Whether intentional or not, the Prime Minister would not have employed such insensitive methods in the appointment of junior ministers at the Colonial Office or the War Office.

Lloyd George's grandiose expectations of National Service as outlined in his policy statment of 19 December 1916 were completely unrealistic and ultimately damaged the conduct of the war. In June 1917 David Davies, from the Prime Minister's Secretariat, warned Lloyd George that 'the Govnt stock & yours in particular is tumbling down'.[83] However, Chamberlain shared the same high expectations and put forward extraordinary claims at the beginning of the National Service appeal which he fully expected to secure. In particular, Chamberlain expected the enrolment of 500,000 volunteers to take place during an eight week publicity campaign. The general appeal was the most immediate response which could be made to the envisaged scale of the campaign, but in promoting the idea of an 'industrial army' and conveying military overtones, which perturbed his senior advisers, Chamberlain encountered a gathering storm of criticism from the House of Commons, the labour movement and the press.

In December 1916 Austen Chamberlain emphasised his brother's ability to win support from trade unions, although evidence for this facility largely rested on his address of welcome to the TUC as Lord Mayor two months earlier. The labour movement's tacit support for National Service waned as Chamberlain's proposals were identified with the constant demand for men for the army to ensure the expansion of military operations on the Western Front. The uncertain military objectives of the third battle of Ypres and the more forthright criticism of the level of casualities suffered in pursuit of the 'wearing down' strategy, and explained through the vocabulary of attrition, reduced the public's level of commitment to the war effort. This change in the degree of support given to the government was exemplified in the trade union's growing hostility to the concept of National Service. The growing resentment felt towards National Service was fuelled by the fear of encroaching military definitions of discipline into the civilian workplace.[84] Among the opponents of the enrolment campaign the Parliamentary Committee of the TUC was vociferous in its condemnation of this further attempt to develop a mobile reserve of skilled labour.[85] It would have preferred the extension of the Trade Card scheme which gave skilled trade unions greater influence over the government's plans for labour supply.

Throughout his period of office Chamberlain's schemes were haunted by the spectre of industrial compulsion. A clear example of the threat which was therefore posed by the department to the freedom of choice of work was the Restricted Occupations Order which came into force in May 1917. In effect Employment Exchanges could not place men in the 'restricted' occupations unless they remained out of work for six days or became a National Service volunteer.[86] However, agreements were reached in some highly organised trades whereby the provisions of the Order were not enforced in return for a promise to obtain substitution volunteers for the National Service Department. It was widely accepted at St Ermin's that the trades which 'opted out' of the revised Schedule of Restricted Occupations shared the common feature of being sufficiently strongly organised to ensure their exclusion from the Order. Rey, Director of the Employment Department, mischievously cited the most striking case which was 'that of slate quarrying where, owing to the recalcitrance of the North Wales quarrymen, they have been left out of the Order, whereas all other quarrymen are left in! Comment is superfluous'.[87]

The Order became inoperable in any organised trade, but Chamberlain refused to accept that he had treated trade unions most unevenly. The degree of conflict which arose in the employment of men in non-essential trades caused constant irritation during the short existence of the scheme under the auspices of the National Service Department. The controversy which surrounded the inequitable scheme to restrict employment opportunities in the non-war sector of industrial production contributed to the disillusionment of trade unionists which had occurred during the enrolment campaign. This commonly related to the persistent threat that the Prime Minister would seek to be released from pledges previously given against industrial compulsion if there was insufficient voluntary acceptance of government schemes. The potential link between National Service and industrial compulsion was later highlighted as a cause of caution among trade unions by W.C. Anderson, Labour MP: 'That threat [of compulsion], repeated on many platforms, did more than anything else to cause Labour, especially organised Labour, to regard the new development with the utmost suspicion and distrust'.[88] As an 'expert' on manpower Chamberlain was expected to retain a clear understanding of the realistic level of voluntary support which could be expected from the labour movement. Without local machinery, apart from the Trade Committees, the gathering of information proved difficult and senior advisers admitted that the *raison d'être* of the department could not be maintained.

On 24 May Ernest Hiley, part-time Deputy Director, told Chamberlain that he wished to return to his business interests in Birmingham. The *Sunday Times* used the occasion of Hiley's resignation to publish a withering attack on the department before the official announcement was made. The newspaper surmised,

He recognises quite frankly that the department has failed to make good, and is a graveyard for the reputations of those associated with it. Despite the series of secessions and the damaging revelations of its extravagant expenditure, the Palace of Make Believe is, apparently, to continue its existence.[89]

By June 1917 the 'Palace of Make Believe' was universally disparaged. In the same month Henry Page Croft, Unionist MP, provided an interesting insight into the apparent diminution of the status of National Service when he complained to Bonar Law about the termination of his wartime military career:

The public is naturally asking why a man of 35 who has attained the rank of Brigadier-General, is no longer employed and surely, in the light of the fact that not one single criticism can be brought against my military conduct, it is ridiculous that I should be forced to offer to dig potatoes for Neville Chamberlain.[90]

In a similar vein it is to be wondered what work Ezra Pound was offered following his application by letter to Chamberlain for vital war work.[91]

The alienation of the labour movement from the idea of National Service and the ridicule which it attracted stemmed from Chamberlain's failure to give 'concrete shape' to Lloyd George's ambition of mobilising the nation's manpower. The general appeal was vague and failed to attract the men who were most needed. W. C. Anderson observed the irony of a department where the necessity for a big impact led to the avoidance of careful planning. He noted,

It seemed of the very essence of the new scheme that it should look big, dramatic, tremendous – the labour power of the nation directed, controlled from a commandeered hotel. Details were unimportant. It was detail, however, that wrecked the venture.[92]

In particular, the dominant and unresolved problem centred on the division of authority in the enrolment and placement of volunteers, due to the 'indivisibility' of the Employment Exchange machinery.

With Chamberlain's resignation on 8 August, 'the weird chapter of history' connected with the National Service Department came to an abrupt end.[93] On 14 January 1918 some MPs were 'sickened' by Sir Auckland Geddes's tribute to the pioneering work of his predecessor.[94] They recalled Geddes's criticism of Chamberlain's policy recommendations in July 1917. Geddes stated in the House of Commons that Chamberlain was 'due the credit of finally convincing the country of the need of a Ministry to work out the problems of the strategical use of man-power'.[95] It was the hard lessons learnt through Chamberlain's experience, rather than his active espousal of a central manpower authority, which led Geddes to move away from dependence on the harmonious relations of employers and trade unions for the implementation of policy. Geddes's faint praise came too late to ameliorate Chamberlain's damaged political reputation. Even if he eventually entered Parliament, Chamberlain was convinced that he would be unable to dislodge the automatic association of his name with, perhaps, the greatest policy innovation and subsequent failure in the war. His resignation provided the opportunity for the reconstitution of his fragmented department so that it could obtain terms of parity with 'labour-employing' ministries in Whitehall. With Chamberlain's removal, the supervision of the movement of labour between the civil industries and the army entered a more settled period which was characterised by the development of a closer relationship between the formulation of strategic plans and the provision of manpower.

Notes

1   PRO NATS 1/577, Circular letter, Lloyd George to heads of departments, 27 February 1917 & Bonar Law to N. Chamberlain, n.d.

2 PRO NATS 1/577, N. Chamberlain to Bonar Law, 5 March 1917.
3 Addison mss. Box 54, Addison to Lloyd George, 6 March 1917, signed copy.
4 Addison mss. Box 98, Diary, 9 March 1917.
5 Addision mss. Box 54, Transfer of National Service Volunteers, unsigned, n.d. This list was attached to Addison's letter to Milner, 24 April 1917.
6 Addison mss. Box 54, Addison to Milner, 24 April 1917, signed copy.
7 S. Gwynn (ed.), *The Anvil of War. Letters between F. S. Oliver and his brother 1914–1918*, London, 1936, 1 February 1917, p. 169.
8 Milner mss. dep. 88, Milner's diary, 8 April 1917.
9 IWM MPDB 77/66/1, Conclusions of a meeting held on April 24th, 1917, to determine certain questions outstanding between the Ministry of Munitions and the Ministry of National Service, G. M. Young, 24 April 1917.
10 N. Chamberlain mss. NC 18/1/103, N. Chamberlain to Ida Chamberlain, 4 March 1917.
11 *The Times*, 10 March 1917.
12 96 H. C. Deb. 5s, Col. 63.
13 Northcliffe mss. Add. Ms. 62336, Northcliffe to A. Winton Thorpe, 11 March 1917, unsigned copy.
14 N. Chamberlain mss. NC 8/5/2/3, Amery to N. Chamberlain, 8 March 1917.
15 J.M. McEwen, 'Northcliffe and Lloyd George at war, 1914–1919', *Historical Journal*, XXIV, 1981, pp. 658–9.
16 Northcliffe mss. Add. Ms. 62157, Northcliffe to J. T. Davies, 18 February 1917, unsigned copy.
17 N. Chamberlain mss. NC 18/1/102, N. Chamberlain to Ida Chamberlain, 18 February 1917.
18 *The Times*, 1 March 1917.
19 *The Times*, 23 March 1917.
20 Lloyd George mss. F/79/29/4, National Service, Adams, 1 March 1917.
21 Lloyd George mss. F/79/20/2, Memorandum relating to National Service Councils (Decentralisation), 26 March 1917, unsigned.
22 *Loc. cit.*
23 N. Chamberlain mss. NC 15/1(b), Press cuttings, *Glasgow Herald*, 10 February 1917.
24 Violet Markham mss. 4/8, Report of Proceedings at a Meeting of the Women's Section of the National Service Department held at the Royal Albert Hall on 17 March 1917, Speech by Violet Markham. See also Grieves, 'The British Government's political and administrative response to the man-power problem in the First World War', pp. 321–82.
25 N. Chamberlain mss. NC 15/15 vol. 2, Press cuttings, *Morning Post*, 5 March 1917.
26 *The Times*, 24 March 1917.
27 N. Chamberlain mss. NC 8/5/4/18, Parliamentary Committee on Expenditure, Memorandum for Sir Frederick Banbury's Sub-

Committee on the expenses of the [National Service] department, A. Collins, 31 August 1917.

28   PRO CAB 23/2 W.C. 103, 23 March 1917.

29   PRO NATS 1/577, N. Chamberlain to Henderson, 29 March 1917.

30   Lloyd George mss. F/79/20/2, Memorandum relating to National Service Councils (Decentralisation), 26 March 1917, unsigned.

31   PRO NATS 1/577, Mr Hiley's Speech to Substitution officers, n.d.

32   For example, Secretary, Thornton-Cleveleys National Service committee to Director, National Service, 24 April 1917, in UD Th 3/23, Thornton Local Tribunal Letter-book.

33   Addison mss. Box 54, Addison to Milner, 1 April 1917, signed copy.

34   PRO CAB 23/2 W.C. 108, 29 March 1917.

35   These figures were collated from *The Labour Gazette*, XXV, 1917. From June 1917 it was prepared in the Board of Trade, not the Ministry of Labour.

36   Lloyd George mss. F/7/1/6, N. Chamberlain to Lloyd George, 13 May 1917. This letter is incorrectly dated, because it refers to information on substitutes collected up to 6 July and the War Cabinet meeting on 13 July.

37   N. Chamberlain mss. NC 18/1/117, N. Chamberlain to Ida Chamberlain, 23 June 1917.

38   N. Chamberlain mss. NC 8/5/4/12, Tenth Report of the Director-General of National Service to the War Cabinet, N. Chamberlain, 22 June 1917.

39   Bonar Law mss. 82/1/22, Milner to Bonar Law, 28 June 1917.

40   Lloyd George mss. F/79/29/5, The Ministry of National Service, Mr Neville Chamberlain's 10th Report, Harmsworth, 28 June 1917.

41   N. Chamberlain mss. NC 8/5/4/12, Tenth Report, *op. cit.*, N. Chamberlain, 22 June 1917.

42   Lloyd George mss. F/7/1/11, N. Chamberlain to Lloyd George, 19 July 1917.

43   Derby mss. 920DER(17) 27/1, Derby to Lloyd George, 6 July 1917, signed copy.

44   Audenshaw Local Tribunal mss. M138/66, Military Service (Review of Exceptions) Act, 1917, Army Council Instruction No. 640, 19 April 1917. See Appendix 6.

45   Derby mss. 920DER(17) 26/5, Derby to Northcliffe, 19 June 1917, unsigned copy.

46   Quoted in *The Times*, 3 July 1917.

47   Quoted in *The Times*, 4 July 1917.

48   J. M. Winter, 'Military fitness and civilian health in Britain during the First World War', *Journal of Contemporary History*, XV, 1980, pp. 218–9.

49   *Macready, Annals of an Active Life*, I, p. 238.

50   Bonar Law mss. 77/3, Bonar Law to George V, 21 June 1917, unsigned copy; Addison mss. Box 98, Diary, 11 July 1917.

51   *New Statesman*, 18 July 1917.

52   *The Times*, 25 July 1917.

53 Lloyd George mss. F/14/4/59, Derby to Lloyd George, 25 July 1917.
54 N. Chamberlain mss. NC 8/5/2/28, Lloyd George to N. Chamberlain, 20 July 1917.
55 N. Chamberlain mss. NC 18/1/120, N. Chamberlain to Hilda Chamberlain, 22 July 1917.
56 Geddes, *The Forging of a Family*, pp. 303–5; Macready, *Annals of an Active Life*, I, p. 247.
57 PRO CAB 23/3 W.C. 201, 3 August 1917.
58 Quoted in Milner mss. dep 23/1, Thornton's diary, 7 July 1917. See also Smuts's observation in Riddell, *War Diary 1914–1918*, entry for 2 August 1917, p. 261.
59 Milner mss. dep 23/1, Thornton's diary, 4 August 1917. The most informative account of this meeting is in J. Barnes and D. Nicholson (eds.), *The Leopold Amery Diaries*, London, 1980, I, p. 165.
60 Milner mss. dep 23/1, Thornton's diary, 5 August 1917.
61 Lloyd George mss. F/38/2/14, Milner to Lloyd George, 4 August 1917.
62 Riddell, *War Diary*, entry for 13 August 1917, p. 265.
63 PRO CAB 24/22 G.T. 1647, Man-Power Recruiting Proposals, Milner, 8 August 1917.
64 N. Chamberlain mss. NC 8/5/4/17, Diary account, 7–9 August [1917], n.d.
65 Lloyd George mss. F/7/1/13, N. Chamberlain to Lloyd George, 8 August 1917.
66 N. Chamberlain mss. NC 8/5/4/17, Diary account, *op. cit.*
67 N. Chamberlain mss. NC 8/5/2/32, Lloyd George to N. Chamberlain, 10 August 1917.
68 N. Chamberlain mss. NC 8/5/3/2, Beck to N. Chamberlain, 13 August 1917.
69 N. Chamberlain mss. NC 1/20/1/111, N. Chamberlain to Mrs Mary Carnegie, 14 August 1917.
70 Quoted in Amery, *My Political Life*, II, p. 101.
71 N. Chamberlain mss. NC 2/20, Political journal, 17 December 1917. In November 1918 Neville Chamberlain was returned to Parliament for the Ladywood constituency in Birmingham.
72 N. Chamberlain mss. NC 18/1/121, N. Chamberlain to Hilda Chamberlain, 12 August 1917.
73 Lloyd George mss. F/14/4/61, Derby to Lloyd George, 6 August 1917.
74 N. Chamberlain mss. NC 18/1/121, *op. cit.*
75 Derby mss. 920DER(17) 27/3, Derby to Sassoon, 14 August 1917, unsigned copy.
76 Lloyd George mss. F/38/2/16, A. Geddes to Lloyd George, 13 August 1917. Sir Eric Geddes was First Lord of the Admiralty and came to prominence in wartime administration as one of Lloyd George's 'leading hustlers' at the Ministry of Munitions.
77 Lloyd George mss. F/38/2/17, Milner to Lloyd George, 17 August 1917.
78 M. Bentley, *The Liberal Mind 1914–1929*, Cambridge, 1977, pp. 73–5.

79 John Dillon in 90. H.C. Deb. 5s. Col. 1873, 27 February 1917.
80 Violet Markham mss. 4/5, V. Markham to J. Jeffrey, 30 June 1917, unsigned copy.
81 N. Chamberlain mss. NC 7/2/30, N. Chamberlain to Amery, 12 August 1917, unsigned copy.
82 N. Chamberlain mss. NC 8/5/2/25, Lloyd George to N. Chamberlain, 3 July 1917; Lloyd George mss. F/7/1/8, N. Chamberlain to Lloyd George, 29 June 1917.
83 Lloyd George mss. F/83/10/7, D. Davies to Lloyd George, 23 June 1917.
84 E. S. Pankhurst, *The Home Front*, London, 1932, p. 424.
85 Minutes of the Parliamentary Committee of the TUC (Harvester microfilm M 769), 19 April 1917.
86 PRO LAB 2/296/E.D. 30081/70/1917, Restricted Occupations Order, Minute 1, Rey, 6 June 1917.
87 PRO LAB 2/296/E.D. 30081/70/1917, Minute 2, Rey, 6 June 1917.
88 LPCC 24/2/30, *Daily News*, 17 August 1917.
89 N. Chamberlain mss. NC 8/5/2/15, Hiley to N. Chamberlain, 27 May 1917, enclosing a cutting of *The Sunday Times*, of the same day.
90 Bonar Law mss. 81/4/17, Page Croft to Bonar Law, 13 March 1917. See also *Punch*, 20 June 1917, p. 404.
91 Letter displayed at 'Pound's Artists' exhibition, Kettle's Yard Gallery, Cambridge, 1985 and further information provided by Richard Humphreys, Tate Gallery, 8 August 1985.
92 LPCC 24/2/30, *Daily News*, 17 August 1917.
93 Violet Markham mss. 4/5, V. Markham to J. Jeffrey, 30 June 1917, unsigned copy.
94 Quoted in N. Chamberlain mss. NC 1/27/20, A. Chamberlain to N. Chamberlain, 20 January 1918.
95 101 H.C. Deb. 5s. Col. 78.

7
Auckland Geddes and the climate of change
September – December 1917

The consolidation of the Ministry of National Service during September 1917 impressed the same departments which had observed with horror the chaotic conditions of St Ermin's in January 1917. Sir Auckland Geddes occupied the same office accommodation as Chamberlain and Lord Peel and Cecil Beck remained Joint Parliamentary Secretaries, but there any resemblance between the 'Palace of Make Believe' and the reconstituted Ministry of National Service ended. In fact the retention of 'National Service' in the title of the ministry was somewhat of a misnomer. After November 1917 the ministry combined the functions of recruiting for the army and the movement of labour to vital war work. Consequently, the use of the term 'National Service' to describe an appeal for volunteers for various civil 'mobilisation' schemes completely disappeared. In the process the department lost its association with the manipulation of 'volunteer spirit' and the inculcation of 'patriotic good-will' as the necessity of rapid responses to the manpower problems became more urgent, and as it took on the appearance of a 'General Staff' on manpower.

On 12 September 1917 Milner's Man-Power Committee approved Geddes's definition of his department's functions. The tasks included the transfer of labour from non-essential industries to urgent national work, the preparation of lists of Reserved Occupations, the provision of men for the army without detriment to essential public services and the substitution of labour withdrawn from industry for military service.[1] In large measure these tasks were tackled by the National Service Department, but Geddes

ensured that his terms of reference led to the automatic association
of these functions with the clearly defined domain of the Ministry
of National Service. The crucial difference between Chamberlain's
work and the department's outlook after September 1917 was its
power 'To review the whole field of British Man-Power and to be in
a position at all times to lay before the War Cabinet information as
to meaning, in terms of Man-Power and consequent results, of all
departmental proposals put forward to the War Cabinet.'[2] At an
early stage Geddes sought to emphasise the department's potential
usefulness as an advisory office on labour supply to the War
Cabinet.

From this firm foundation Geddes worked to improve the poor
relations which through antipathy and physical remoteness set St
Ermin's apart from more established departments. He regarded the
confidence of Whitehall in his new work as an important priority,
to be secured without delay. Signs of a *rapprochement* between the
Ministry of National Service and the ministries of Labour and of
Munitions took a definite form. Geddes had shared Rey's opposition to Chamberlain's arrival in London in December 1916.[3] Their
frequent meetings in August resulted in Rey's temporary transfer to
the Ministry of National Service as Director of the National
Labour Supply Department. Under this arrangement Geddes was
empowered to issue instructions to the Employment Exchanges on
aspects of manpower supply which came under his department's
jurisdiction.[4] Rey's local officials collated information on current
and prospective demands for labour at the war industries within
each exchange area. This information, which was denied to Chamberlain, was an invaluable source for the preparation at St Ermin's
of periodic reviews of 'the whole field of British Man-Power'. To
smooth relations with the Employment Department, the 1,000
remaining National Service committees were dissolved.[5] Consequently, Rey secured the removal of competing local machinery and
was able to regulate unobstructed 'the demand for and supply of
labour'.[6]

Two weeks after reaching an agreement with the Ministry of
Labour, Geddes secured a further improvement in his department's
prospects through a successful conference with the Ministry of
Munitions. On 17 July Addison was succeeded by Winston
Churchill as Minister of Munitions. He accepted that Geddes's
main task was the unimpeded survey of manpower availability in

Britain. Consequently, on 13 September the two ministers agreed that 'it is essential that new inter-departmental programmes or alterations in existing programmes should pass under his [Geddes's] review'.[7] To facilitate this agreement, Geddes established a National Labour Priority Committee which was representative of all departments which employed civil manpower. This Committee discussed the relative priority of manpower demands. The decisions which were reached on the relative importance of categories of labour were reflected in the Priority List, which was regularly updated and issued to the Employment Exchanges.

In practice, it was extremely difficult to examine manpower allocation within industries. Consequently, Geddes did not control the nation's labour supply, as departments enjoyed considerable latitude in their organisation of war work and complete freedom in the internal movement of labour to priority areas of production.[8] However, the level of co-operation in the allocation of additional labour between departments through the National Labour Priority Committee gradually increased. Geddes took the initiative in the investigation of pools of unemployed labour which could be transferred to essential war work. For example, on 23 October Geddes sent an official to Lancashire to investigate the scale of unemployment among cotton operatives. The industry had diminished in importance after the contracts for the New Armies were completed. The Cotton Control Board supported the recommendation that idle factories should be used for the construction of aeroplanes and the assembling of parts shipped from the United States. The investigation prompted by the Ministry of National Service anticipated 'that a large amount of surplus labour among cotton operatives will be diverted to aeroplane work in their own localities'.[9] This proposal never led to the scale or concentration of aeroplane construction which was located in Glasgow and Southampton, but Sir William Weir, Director-General of Aircraft Production, quickly appreciated the value of this initiative. In Lancashire it precluded the further construction of new factories or the movement of skilled labour.

The close association between St Ermin's and the National Labour Priority Committee was a source of strength to the department. The War Cabinet acknowledged the value of the evidence which the Committee gathered on the state of the labour market, as it did the avoidance of controversies in the appointment of personnel for the department. Apart from Rey's secondment to the National Labour Supply branch, Frederick Macleod joined the Trade and Commercial branch from the defunct Reserved Occupations Committee. In November 1917 Seymour Lloyd became Director of Recruiting but he had originally joined the War Office during the Derby scheme. Colonel Galloway of the Army Medical Service headed the Medical department. Seymour Lloyd and Galloway had both worked closely with Geddes at the War Office. Sandford Fawcett remained at St Ermin's as Secretary, and he was joined by Major Lloyd-Greame, later Sir Philip Cunliffe-Lister and Lord Swinton, who returned to political life after two years on the Western Front.[10] The concentration of this array of administrative talent at St Ermin's provided a remarkable opportunity to manage the work of the Recruiting and Labour Supply branches on the tenet of mutual understanding, through the collaboration of officials whose detailed appreciation of the manpower problem had hitherto been restricted by the compartmentalisation of the war effort. The ministry under Geddes possessed a capacity for the comprehensive reform of policy-making and implementation on manpower should the political will be found. This opportunity had not been available within a single department since the concentration of powers in the office of the Secretary of State for War during the formation of the New Armies.

The recruiting machinery was now discredited and the task most closely associated with Geddes's appointment was its transfer to civil control. During 1917 Macready resented the power of civil departments or 'numerous authorities' to retain men in essential war work. In May 1917, 88,894 men of all categories were recruited, which compared most favourably with 36,543 men who enlisted in October. Despite the introduction of the Military Service (Review of Exceptions) Act, the recruiting returns slumped from July 1917 onwards. By November 1917 the problem of maintaining the British armies in France was so acute that Derby told the War Cabinet that 250,000 category 'A' men were required immediately, and a further 50,000 men each month from December 1917 to June 1918.[11] The recommended intake levels were based on the expectation not only that the Western Front would remain the focus of the Anglo-French war effort, but that the outcome of the Allied offensives would be sufficiently successful to encourage the War Cabinet to endorse the full replacement of the British casualty level. The fact that the government was increasingly persuaded otherwise was not understood by Macready, who shared GHQ's notion of the paramount importance of retaining the offensive on the Western Front.

Macready's anxiety was fuelled by the General Officers commanding the various Home Commands who had long complained that the organisation of the recruiting system within the framework of regimental districts was a source of constant distraction and irritation. During his short sojourn at Eastern Command, which was the principal line of defence against invasion, Lieutenant-General Sir Henry Wilson drew attention to the deplorable state of recruiting in his region. In October 1917 he noted that only 450 men per week, fit for general service, were being recruited in Eastern Command.[12] With this data the War Office placed pressure on the War Cabinet to ensure that recruiting was transferred to civil control at the earliest possible date. The urgent necessity to take action to halt the declining level of recruiting was compounded by the calculation that casualties in October during the Third Battle of Ypres amounted to 76,000 men. In fact this figure understated the problem, because it was calculated by deducting the normal average casualty rate when there was no severe fighting of 35,000 men per month from the total casualties on the Western Front for October 1917 of 4,956 officers and 106,419 other ranks.[13]

In this context reorganisation proceeded apace and by the end of September Deputy Directors of Recruiting were appointed for all ten regions. They were to be responsible for ensuring that the new machinery was functioning quickly as an efficient system.[14] In only one of these appointments did controversy arise. Inevitably, it concerned the arrangements made for Wales, which were always examined most carefully in Downing Street. Geddes was reminded by J. T. Davies that there were one million Welsh speakers whom the department should not ignore by appointing an English speaker as Deputy Director.[15] Lloyd George wanted Geddes to appoint John Rowland, formerly his Private Secretary at the Board of Trade and one of a circle of Welsh civil servants whose association with the Prime Minister developed from the administration of the system of National Health Insurance. Geddes did not follow Lloyd George's advice but appointed the former Liberal MP, Lord Treowen. Geddes's preference for Treowen stemmed from his 'high position' as Lord Lieutenant of Monmouthshire and as a major-

general on the retired list. Geddes preferred established qualifications which were derived from local affiliation. He later extended
his collaboration with the Association of Lieutenants of Counties to
exploit their 'historic connection' with the army.[16]

Shortly before the transfer of recruiting was completed, officers
on the Recruiting Staff of the War Office were seconded to the
department to continue their work. Though this transfer of staff
suggested that old methods of work would continue, it should be
emphasised that men who joined the administrative branches of the
War Office, often from the Civil Service, were awarded the
appropriate temporary commission for the convenience of military
organisation. Consequently, unlike the Medical Boards, the expansion of the recruiting staff in London was achieved without an
influx of regular army officers. Furthermore, the work of recruiting
was passed to a department which was also entrusted with
determining the relative priorities of demand for additional labour
across all aspects of the war effort. On 1 November 'the powers
and duties of the Army Council relating to the recruiting, enlistment, the call up of men of the Reserve Forces individually and
otherwise in relation to the provision of men for the Army' was
transferred to civil control.[17] At the same time an advisory board
was established to promote public confidence in the department's
recruiting work which was an idealised feature of civil control.
Although it only possessed a consultative function, the Recruiting
Advisory Board projected the representation at national level of
'general public interests' in this crucial aspect of the war effort.
Employers, trade unions, local administration and the interests of
Wales and Scotland were represented by the Board.[18] The publicity
material which Geddes circulated to the press indicated his willingness to facilitate the expression of public opinion on manpower
within the operational framework of the ministry. The Board was
eventually dissolved in April 1918, but the limited contribution it
made to the ministry, particularly on industrial and commercial
issues, contributed to the support which Geddes received within
Whitehall during the transfer of recruiting to civil control. This
support was vital if Geddes was to implement successfully the
extraordinary reform of recruiting, amid the uncertainties of
military policy at the beginning of the fourth year of the war.
Macready's hope that the reform would contribute to the renewed
commitment of the government to maintain the British armies in

France was overtaken by the adverse political reaction to the failure to secure a military victory on the Western Front during 1917.

Despite all problems of military manpower supply, 691,415 men enlisted for military service in the first eight months of 1917. Departments faced with the increased demand for war materials required guidance on whether additional contracts should be started at the cost of reducing the level of recruitment for the army. In September 1917 the most important programme to be reviewed was aeroplane production due to the vulnerability of London to 'air flotillas' and the tactical superiority of German aircraft over the Western Front.[19] The War Cabinet appointed a Committee to consider the alternatives of maintaining an 86 squadron force on the Western Front or accepting the Air Board's recommendation for increasing the programme to equip 200 squadrons.[20] The Aerial Operations Committee, as it shortly became known, consisted of General Smuts, Lord Derby, Sir Eric Geddes, Churchill and Lord Cowdray. At its first meeting on 26 September the Committee realised that it could not examine one demand for additional labour without reference to other essential war production programmes. Consequently, Smuts sought to enlarge the Committee's terms of reference 'to settle all questions of priority not only of the present air programme, but of all other munitions programmes'.[21] The War Cabinet agreed to the full review of production programmes on 8 October. The Committee's title was changed to 'War Priorities', and the Minister of National Service joined its deliberations because 'the decisions of the Committee necessarily hang upon the proper allocation of material and man-power'.[22] It was a measure of his importance that Geddes joined the War Priorities Committee. His participation in the review of munitions programmes brought him into the inner sanctum of Cabinet ministers concerned most closely with the efficient use of manpower and materials, at a time when it was increasingly difficult to envisage the continuation of an Allied numerical superiority over the German armies in the field.

The general speculation on the future conduct of the war reinforced the political standing of the Minister of National Service. For example, he informed the War Priorities Committee that considerable orders had been placed with British firms without reference to his ministry. Consequently, he was unable to examine the impact of large foreign contracts on the supply of men for the army. Government agents of Greece, Serbia and the United States had placed contracts with woollen and worsted firms. He observed that the total orders 'are, I believe, of sufficient magnitude to engage the whole man-power of the Yorkshire textile trade, which has hitherto been on short time, and which I have regarded as an available source of supply of men for the Army'.[23] Without Geddes's knowledge, contracts were placed for commodities which were more urgently required elsewhere, or where the labour would contribute more effectively to the war effort by being employed on alternative work. He had also complained that the American government had placed an order for 30,000 tons of steel with the Steel Production Department of the Ministry of Munitions for the construction of hospital huts. Geddes's evaluation of the pool of recruitable labour for 1918 was based on the assumption that British industry would not be called on to supply the American Army with munitions and other goods to any appreciable extent.

Although the steel order was part of a complicated package, which provided Britain with much needed supplies of ship-plates and timber,[24] Lloyd George was impressed by the transformation of St Ermin's from a 'Palace of Make-Believe' to a 'clearing-house' for the allocation of additional labour to important industrial work. The Prime Minister reinforced Geddes's role as the analyst of manpower proposals placed before the War Cabinet and the War Priorities Committee. Accordingly, the Ministry of Munitions was reminded of the importance of submitting new munitions programmes to Geddes for evaluation.[25]

However, progress within the War Priorities Committee was impeded by the absence of a vital piece of information. To cope with the relative importance of war work even within the munition programme, of long-range aeroplanes, mobile heavy artillery, tanks and chemical weapons, the War Priorities Committee needed to know if military victory was expected through a major effort in 1918, or whether provision should be made for the prolongation of the war into 1919.[26] In a sense this question was unanswerable, but it required a response from the War Cabinet and, in particular, an evaluation of the future prospects of the British armies in France. To ascertain the relative importance of artillery output, ship-building materials and aeronautical supplies, and the consequent placement of labour, some indication was needed of the strategic expectations, and the concomitant equipment demands, of the Allied forces for the year ahead. The War Priorities Committee was unable to extend still further its terms of reference, but it did put forward proposals for relieving the labour shortage in essential industries. These were directed at the reassessment of the size of the Home Army and the work of Admiralty dockyards. The War Priorities Committee was important for two reasons. It reinforced Geddes's ministerial position and it prompted the War Cabinet to reconsider the larger issues of the war in relation to the conclusions which were drawn from British military activity on the Western Front in 1917.

The War Priorities Committee only had access to a partial view of the war effort which did not include the conduct of military operations on the Western Front. Haig told Macready in late November 1917 that by 31 March 1918 British infantry units would be 250,000 men or approximately forty per cent below establishment, unless reinforcements were sent to rectify this situation. Haig concluded 'that under such conditions not only will the offensive power of the British armies in France be completely paralysed, but their defensive power will also be curtailed, and they will not be able to hold the same amount of line as heretofore'.[27] The subject of reinforcements dominated the semi-official correspondence which passed between the Commander-in-Chief in France and the Chief of Imperial General Staff from May 1917 until Robertson left the War Office in February 1918. Robertson told Haig as early as 26 May that Lloyd George had informed him, that 'the time had now arrived when we must face the fact that we could not expect to get any large number of men in the future but only scraps'.[28] The reference to 'scraps' was a characteristic exaggeration prevalent among senior staff officers in London and at GHQ in France.

However, the reduction of monthly recruiting returns by fifty per cent during the months June to September led Haig to adopt an extremely critical view of the government's response to the military demand for manpower. Without the capacity to appreciate the importance of increasing the merchant shipbuilding programme, Haig condemned any reduction of the target of 940,000 men for the army in 1917.[29] On 9 August he wrote to Robertson, 'Many thanks for getting a hustle on about "drafts". The country when it discovers what the Govt. has failed to do in this vital matter, will never forgive them!'[30]

Robertson responded to the implications for manpower of the unquestioned concentration of resources on the Western Front by the reduction of British forces in 'side-shows'. The Army Council regarded the subsidiary campaigns as wasteful of manpower and this viewpoint was supported strongly by GHQ in France. In Mesopotamia the replacement of British divisions by Indian units was promoted by the responsibility which General Sir Charles Monro, Commander-in-Chief in India, assumed for the formation of additional battalions.[31] In Egypt the complex command structure had not aided the efficient management of forces on the western border or in the Canal Zone. On his recall General Sir Archibald Murray justifiably told Robertson that his inactivity against Turkish forces in Gaza could be accounted for by the minimal reinforcement of the Egyptian garrison. In a total force of only five complete divisions, an estimated deficiency of 8,000 men in June 1917 had halted the prospect of taking any initiative against the Turkish forces. Murray made it clear that he would not weaken the force piecemeal by carrying out major operations.[32]

The dominance of the 'single front' principle was sustained, partially, by the application of the term 'side-show' which implicitly diminished the significance of all other theatres of war. However, politicians and, eventually, public opinion were less anxious to criticise the government's manpower plans than to understand the continuing operational necessity for the concentration of British manpower in France and Flanders, and the relentlessly high level of 'wastage' on the Western Front. The British attacks on the Western Front in 1917 from Arras to Passchendaele, and the commitment of the War Cabinet to Haig's plans, were maintained by vague accounts which gave the impression that decisive military victory would inevitably follow from continuous offensive activity. GHQ argued, at every opportunity, that these operations were constantly 'wearing down' the twin essences of the German army, namely, its manpower and morale. The capture of Vimy Ridge was secured during the Arras offensive but the proposed new defensive line was not reached. Nevertheless Haig observed on 1 May,

The enemy has already been weakened appreciably but a long time is required to wear down such great numbers of troops composed of fine fighting material and he is still fighting with such energy and determination that the situation is not yet ripe for the decisive blow. Our action must therefore continue for the present to be of a wearing down character until his power of resistance has been further reduced.[33]

On 7 June the Second Army commanded by General Sir Herbert Plumer stormed the Messines Ridge in an impressive, and almost classical, siege operation. Captain Basil Liddell Hart described the attack on Messines as 'the capture of a fortified salient at the minimum cost of lives by the maximum substitution of mind — in preparation – and material – in execution for human bodies'.[34] Haig's plan to exploit this successful operation by the capture of the rest of the ridge and an advance along the Belgian coast assumed that the condition of the German armies had deteriorated sharply since the Battle of the Somme. He emphasised in his evidence to the Cabinet Committee on War Policy in June 1917 that the German army had a severe shortage of manpower. At its seventh meeting 'Sir Douglas Haig said that 12 German officer prisoners had been examined independently, and all admitted that they had been warned that owing to the exhaustion of Germany's man power they must spare their men'.[35] Haig referred repeatedly to the reduced physique of German recruits and the breaking up of infantry battalions to provide drafts. In June he still promised 'results which will make final victory more assured and which may even bring it within reach this year'.[36]

On 31 July the offensive on the Ypres Front recommenced. Contrary to the reports of the Intelligence Department at GHQ, the costly battles around Bixschoote, St Julien, Langemarck and Lens provided no evidence that German reserve divisions even in the vicinity of the British offensive were seriously depleted. Plumer forced German forces to partially withdraw at the battles of Menin Road and Polygon Wood in late September, but Brigadier-General John Charteris, Chief of the Intelligence Department, was entirely mistaken in his prediction that no enemy reserves were 'within immediate reach of the battlefront'.[37] Despite appalling conditions, advances were secured during the Third Battle of Ypres which culminated in the capture of the village of Passchendaele, or rather its site, by the Canadian Corps on 4 November 1917. Again reports from the Second and Fifth armies, the latter commanded by General Sir Hubert Gough, did not suggest that German man-power was being any more drastically denuded than the British divisions which participated in the Flanders offensive. Yet the

Commander in Chief in France and his Chief of Staff persisted in validating their operations on the Ypres front on the sole criterion of the diminution of German manpower.

Haig's guiding principle for his offensive preparations took the form of an idealised three-stage battle on a front where the enemy could not disengage from the attack. He noted, 'the first step must always be to wear down the enemy's powers of resistance until he is so weakened that he will be unable to withstand a decisive blow, then to deliver the decisive blow; and, finally, to reap the fruits of victory'.[38] Kiggell's explanation of the ethos of large scale operations in Flanders was less refined. However, the method he described was essentially the same as that which Haig regularly outlined in his memoranda to the War Cabinet. The Chief of Staff informed Gough, 'We are all agreed that Boche killing is the only way to win. To effect that we want to a) force the Boche to fight and b) force the fight under conditions most favourable to us and least favourable to him.'[39] Kiggell reflected that it was important to convince politicians that decisive victory would be secured on the Western Front. His optimistic reports were reinforced by papers prepared by the Director of Military Operations at the War Office, Major-General Frederick Maurice. He observed that despite the collapse of the Russian war effort and the serious reverse at Caporetto on the Italian front there was no cause for discouragement. His buoyant optimism for the future prospects of the Allied war effort was based on a perplexing analysis of the manpower situation, whose content was scarcely credible:

The German population is about half as great again as ours but their permanent losses are five times as much as *ours*. The strain upon their man-power is infinitely greater than ours and their resources of all kinds are steadily decreasing as ours are increasing with the assistance of Americans.[40]

In the knowledge that the level of 'wastage' had reached 76,000 men per month on the Western Front of October 1917, politicians were increasingly sceptical of the value of anecdotes about the quality of recruits to the German armies. Persistent references to 'Boche-killing' and 'wearing down', which in 1917 replaced the catch-phrase 'breakthrough', compounded the War Cabinet's displeasure at the lack of tangible results from the continuation of the Ypres campaign throughout September and October. By mid-September Bonar Law had lost 'absolutely all hope' of any advantage being gained from the pursuit of Haig's military objectives.[41] Lord Milner was sympathetic to this viewpoint. He shared Bonar Law's reluctance to adopt a position which was antipathetic to 'almost all high military opinion'. Indeed, it was a matter of deep regret to Milner that 'the doubts . . . about the probability of success in the policy of Hammer, Hammer, Hammer on the Western Front, are becoming increasingly strong in my own mind'.[42] Smuts had been unimpressed with the Allied military position in France since April, which was significant as his public *persona* was identified with the subordination of the aspirations of skilled trade unions for a higher standard of living to the constant flow of munitions to the British armies in France.[43] The estrangement of such supportive politicians of the autonomy of GHQ as Bonar Law and Milner was a clear indication of worsening civil–military relations. Their statements fuelled the anger Lloyd George felt as 'trustee of man-power' during the course of the Third Battle of Ypres.[44] Although opportunities in June and again in August were not used to close down the British offensive, the vitriolic content of his *War Memoirs* on the outcome of the Passchendaele campaign was probably an accurate representation of his attitude towards the British high command in late October 1917. He wrote, 'The gigantic casualties of Passschendaele pressed appreciably down the Allied end of the grisly scales. Our military leaders had acquired the habit of prodigality in their expenditure of life.'[45]

The nadir in civil–military relations continued until the introduction of the Military Service Bill in January 1918. The central public feature of the political resentment of the high level of 'wastage' was a spectacular protest by the Prime Minister on the military conduct of the war. At the formal opening of the Inter-Allied War Council in Paris on 12 November Lloyd George took as his theme two sentences: 'We have won great victories. When I look at the appalling casualty lists I sometimes wish it had not been necessary to win so many.'[46] In a foreign capital he criticised the British military commanders for opposing the transfer of six British divisions to the Italian front and resisting closer Allied military co-operation.[47] In the aftermath of the defeat at Caporetto, Lloyd George commented,

It is no use minimising the extent of the disaster. When we advance a kilometre into the enemy lines, snatch a small shattered village out of his cruel grip, capture a few hundreds of his soldiers, we shout with joy. What if we advanced 50 kilometres beyond his lines, captured 200,000 prisoners and 2,000 of his guns. What print would we have for our headlines.[48]

Lloyd George was determined to lay the foundations in Paris of the strategic unity of all fronts through a formally constituted Supreme War

Council. The proposal of 'unity of control' reflected the deep dissatisfaction of the War Cabinet with its inability to determine the use of manpower after its arrival in France. Hitherto, civil control was concentrated in the provision of recruits for the army and the limited expansion of military forces in secondary theatres of war.

In the drive to assert political control over the manpower supply the Secretary of State for War was of little assistance. Lord Derby exercised no operational or administrative control over manpower. As far as the 'Paris Speech' was concerned, Derby wrote to Haig to express his 'entire confidence' in his work.[49] In the political storm which developed in the wake of Lloyd George's speech, the central feature of his attack which highlighted the practical effect of the military control of manpower was ignored. Robertson visited Asquith on 15 November,[50] and Walter Long was urged by Margot Asquith 'to give the lead' and oppose 'that "arch traitor" L[loyd] G[eorge]'.[51] Long did not become the focus of Lloyd George's critics in the government, more on account of his illness than for any other reason. Like H. A. Gwynne at the *Morning Post*, St Loe Strachey used the columns of the *Spectator* to resist the 'insinuation' that the level of casualties should determine the continuation or cessation of military action on the Western Front.[52] It was the defence of Haig's freedom from political interference by Strachey which Lloyd George found so irksome as well as his oft-repeated formula for victory. A typical expression of Strachey's espousal of GHQ's outlook was that the German army should understand that 'we are quite prepared to go on for any number of years hammering away at the line. We have got plenty of food, and you [Germany] are very short, and without making any comparisons of military power we are bound to beat you.'[53]

Strachey and other critics ignored the problem of manpower supply, which was the main reason why Lloyd George adopted a position so critical of GHQ in his speech on 12 November. As far as he was concerned, the offensive which culminated in the capture of Passchendaele merely heightened the realisation that the nation could not afford any more offensives on the scale of 1917. Lloyd George's wrath and polemical language obscured his complaint against the irrelevance of victories won at heavy cost and his public criticism abroad of the British war effort on land was typical of his indirect method of pursuing a desired aim. Nevertheless, Haig avoided the substance of Lloyd George's argument by arriving at two simple conclusions before he had read the full text of the speech. Firstly, it was an 'unpatriotic speech' which 'right thinking people' would ignore. Secondly, Haig resolved to resist attempts to 'make me modify the way in which I carry out my duties here'.[54] Lloyd George's 'Paris Speech' and Haig's continuing emphasis of his urgent demand for more men for France indicated an impasse in civil–military relations which needed to be relieved by a general 'stocktaking' of manpower at the highest level. Before this could commence and the Minister of National Service was called on to review manpower prospects for 1918, GHQ suffered a military setback which further illuminated the schism in civil–military relations and the breakdown of the consensus on the importance of ensuring the constant flow of men to the army.

On 20 November 1917, 381 British Tanks advanced on a six mile front at Cambrai in a surprise attack on the German lines. By the early afternoon the tanks had created a penetration of five miles, except around Flesquières, which was not taken until the following day. Open country lay ahead. Liddell Hart wrote of this initial advance,

On November 21st the bells of London rang out in joyous acclaim of a triumphant success that seemed a foretaste of victory, perhaps at no distant date. And Ludendorff, back at the German Supreme Command, was hurriedly preparing emergency instructions for a general retreat.[55]

The value of this successful operation was not lost on Haig. He welcomed the contribution it would make to his rehabilitation after the hollow capture of Passchendaele and imagined that the government had been given a salutary lesson on the centrality of the Western Front to the overall war effort.[56] The wedge driven into the German front with minimal reserves created the conditions for a counterstroke, but attacks on British positions in Bourlon Wood did not affect Haig's optimism at the eventual outcome of the battle. He observed that the expected German counter-attack should 'bring home to our Prime Minister the folly of withdrawing Div[isio]ns from this front to send to Italy – And so as my maxim Diary says for today "A casualty is not always a calamity"!'[57]

On 30 November the German armies launched an infiltrating infantry attack which rendered the British positions in the Masnières-Bourlon salient untenable. Within one week, all the gains of 20 November were evacuated with the exception of the village of Flesquières. In the

German counter-attack approximately 7,000 British troops were posted missing, of which an estimated one-fifth were presumed dead. The implications of this reverse differed according to whether a military or a civil standpoint was adopted on the findings of the enquiry which was established in France to examine the German 'local success'. The commander of the Third Army, General Sir Julian Byng, discounted the local numerical superiority of the enemy forces as the key factor. He found only one reason for the successful counter-attack, which was the lack of training of junior officers, NCOs and men.[58] Consequently, the powers of defence of some new divisions was suspect. Young machine gunners apparently retired too quickly in the face of heavy massed attacks.

Byng's conclusions set the tone of the Court of Enquiry although he was never called to give evidence in person. The Court eventually concluded that the German attack on 30 November was successful as a result of unprepared outpost lines, lack of vigilance by unit commanders, poor visibility, absence of artillery, lack of defence in depth and low morale due to (entirely accurate) rumours among men on sick leave.[59] The Court of Enquiry localised the implications of the reverse at Cambrai to the lines of two corps and, in particular, the sector which was occupied by the Fifty-fifth Division. Haig concluded that 'large inroads had been made into German reserves' and refused to identify the wider repercussions of the defeat.[60] Derby failed to enquire about the Cambrai operations in his private correspondence with Haig. His panacea was exactly the same as that sought by Robertson in the aftermath of Cambrai. More drafts must be sent to the British armies in France. On 11 December Derby told Haig, 'I have not written to you about the Cambrai affair – these things must happen every now and then and the only way we can make them good is to give you men.'[61]

This opinion was not shared by most members of the government, who were aware that Byng had not complained about the shortage of manpower on the section of the line held by the Third Army. Their suspicion about the specific apportioning of blame to junior levels of command without reference to the absence of reserves behind the line was increased by the delay in the release of information on the counter-attack by GHQ.[62] The Battle of Cambrai certainly raised the manpower issue, though not in a form favourable to GHQ. Lloyd George concluded that the main reason for the reverse lay in the wasteful attacks on the Passchendaele

Ridge, which required the concentration of reserves on the Ypres front.[63] In addition, the ability of German high command to move nineteen divisions into the Cambrai area somewhat belied continuing tales of declining German manpower and morale. In no uncertain fashion Lord Northcliffe told Brigadier-General Charteris, Chief of Intelligence, on 11 December, 'I have been informed indirectly that the members of Government consider that you have misled them by exaggerated statements as to decline of German morale and number of German reserves.'[64] The transfer of Charteris to the Transportation branch at GHQ in December 1917 took place because the exaggerated statements of Allied prospects on the Western Front were confounded by the Battle of Cambrai.[65]

The government's interpretation of the events of 30 November was reflected in the replacement of Charteris, for failure occurred at GHQ and not at divisional level. On 20 November British forces had a numerical superiority of nine to five Infantry divisions, but ten days later there were thirteen German and ten British divisions in the same area. The absence of a reserve sufficiently large to exploit the surprise attack worried the government. The failure of the massive Ypres campaign to achieve all its targets contrasted sharply with the ability of the tank raid to reach its limited objectives. In the absence of the final report of the Enquiry, which was not available until 29 January 1918, Lloyd George drew the conclusion that manpower was mismanaged during the opening phase of the attack. The advance had successfully employed the principles of economy of force but was not provided with sufficient reserves for a scheme where they would have been effectively deployed.

The appearance of defensive operations on the British line posed an important question for the War Cabinet. Would drafts despatched to France be subjected to similar operations, where initial success was overtaken by defective defensive arrangements and the subsequent result was a rout? At a time when public anger over the suppression of information about the German counter-attack was at its height, Northcliffe told Sir Philip Sassoon, 'I am pressing the authorities about man-power. In some quarters it is asked, what is the use of sending out men to be "Cambrai-sed", but I am sure that no effort will be spared'.[66] Northcliffe's support for the unrestricted supply of men for military service underwent a *volte-face* in early December. This was reflected in the disquieting tone in which

The Times reported military activities in the aftermath of Cambrai.[67]

The phenomenon of 'Cambrai' jolted the nation's confidence in the British high command. It gave rise to expressions of dissatisfaction with the uncurbed military control of large sections of the nation's manpower and materials. From the secretariat of the War Cabinet, Ormsby-Gore noted the attempt of rank-and-file organisations in the labour movement to manipulate the war situation to secure statements on war aims, compulsory rationing and the eradication of excess profits. He also drew Hankey's attention to the increasing interest in a negotiated end to the war which the publication of Lord Lansdowne's letter in the *Daily Telegraph* on 29 November 1917 generated. Ormsby-Gore concluded,

Military victory not having been won Labour leaders are wondering if it is desirable, even if it is possible after Cambrai. The idea that the British army in France after being encouraged to believe in great results from last autumn's offensive is now to go on the defensive, is getting generally known and produces a new outlook.'[68]

The Battle of Cambrai highlighted the absence of any military advantage from the estimated figure of 822,000 killed, wounded and missing men on the Western Front in 1917.[69] Despite the introduction of compulsory military service the level of recruiting was still related to the extent of enthusiasm for active participation in the war. Geddes urged that 'The feeling that the war is passing to a happier phase would I believe do more to ease recruiting than anything else.'[70] A 'happier phase' could only be promoted by two factors. Firstly, military success and, secondly, the certain knowledge that victory was attainable without the repetition of the scale and limitless capacity for 'wastage' without 'profit' of the Third Battle of Ypres. Instead, Cambrai showed that the nation could no longer afford to unquestioningly provide drafts to meet GHQ's manpower demands. Cambrai was the catalyst of the War Cabinet's belated realisation of the implications of acute manpower shortage; in particular, of appreciating that labour distribution was so important that the most appropriate forum for its discussion was at the highest policy-making level.

At the War Cabinet on 3 December 1917 Derby demanded to know when the armies in France could expect substantial reinforcement. At the same meeting Sir Auckland Geddes submitted a memorandum which indicated how close the nation was to the limit of its manpower.[71] Of the 3,600,000 men of military age in civil life, Geddes calculated that only 100,000 men were in category 'A' and between eighteen and twenty-five years of age. He noted that older men in category 'A' were nearly all engaged in vital war work but that a further 100,000 men in the lower categories were available. The stark reality behind Geddes's presentation of the manpower position was that future quotas of fit men for military service would necessitate the automatic reduction of either the shipbuilding, food-production or munition programmes. The issue of further legislative measures was also raised by Geddes. He warned that it would be required 'if the policy of the "clean cut" was to be adopted in any form, i.e. if men were to be taken in age blocks' for military service as a possible response to the military manpower shortage.[72]

Several days after the German counter-attack at Cambrai, Geddes's statistical details placed the twin issues of additional labour for civil industries and for military service firmly at the top of the War Cabinet's agenda. On 6 December it decided to appoint a committee on manpower, but unlike other initiatives Lloyd George decided that it should consist entirely of War Cabinet members. With Lloyd George as chairman the committee comprised Lord Curzon, George Barnes, General Smuts and Sir Edward Carson.[73] Instead of travelling to Berne in pursuit of Austrian peace proposals, Hankey was appointed Secretary of the Committee and 'condemned to weeks of concentration on the dreariest and most controversial aspect of our war effort'.[74] Representatives of departments presented evidence and contributed to the committee's discussions. For example, at the first meeting on 10 December Derby, Lieutenant-General Sir George Macdonogh, Director of Military Intelligence, Sir Auckland Geddes and Lloyd-Greame presented evidence to the Committee. As a measure of Geddes's importance as a source of information and 'expert' on manpower he attended all the six main meetings of the Cabinet Committee on Man-Power.

As a basis for enquiry Hankey was required to produce an instant 'history' of the government's manpower plans since the outbreak of war. He charted the competitive relations between the military authorities and civil departments in the context of unprecedented demands on the nation's resources of manpower and materials, arguing that,

The result is that the economic position has become a threatening one, which it is generally recognised must be taken into most serious consideration if we are to maintain our staying power and the *moral* of the nation.

Unfortunately, just at the moment when our economic resources require careful nursing, the military situation has become more menacing than it has been since the early days of the War.[75]

Hankey reinforced the basic message behind Geddes's memoranda on manpower over the preceding two months, by noting that the government faced the task of resolving an actual crisis in the supply of labour, rather than one which was prospective or imagined. He concluded, 'The problem that confronts the Committee therefore is to avert a military catastrophe equally fatal to the cause of the Allies.'[76]

For most War Cabinet members this wide-ranging review of the supply and allocation of manpower was the first occasion they were given access to sufficient information to formulate a comprehensive policy on this aspect of the war. Prior to examining the distribution of men of military age who remained in civil life, the Cabinet Committee needed to ascertain the shortage of men, future prospects and the level of casualties in the British armies in France. On 10 December the Adjutant-General told the Committee that the main manpower deficits were 100,000 infantrymen, 41,000 artillerymen and 40,000 men for the Flying Corps. To fill these shortages and cover 'liabilities' on the Western Front, Macready calculated that 1,304,000 men were required for military service in 1918.[77] Although this figure included men who would be 'combed out' of the Home Army, this grand total was not one which Lloyd George wished to accept as the basis for obtaining further quotas, as it would decimate all essential war output.

Lloyd George highlighted Haig's preparations for further offensives in 1918, despite the arrival of German divisions in France from the Eastern Front, as evidence that the Allied armies would retain a numerical superiority on the Western Front in the first three months of 1918. This opinion was fuelled by vague reports which implied that with German casualties for 1917 reaching approximately one million, enemy *moral* was quite broken.[78] Although GHQ suddenly became pessimistic about prospects after Cambrai, Lloyd George found 'alarmist' reports difficult to reconcile with the information that in a comparison of rifle strength there were 400,000 more Allied men than there were Germans on the Western Front.[79]

Under the Prime Minister's direction the Cabinet Committee made a rigorous examination of 'wastage' levels on the Western Front. He was determined to reduce the military demand for manpower. Belatedly trying to secure civil control, the Prime Minister perceived that the discussion of casualty figures would have a salutary effect on the Army

Council and GHQ. In particular, that 'wearing down' the enemy was no longer appropriate and that the projections for 'wastage' in 1918 should be revised. The permanent British 'wastage' estimated for 1918 on the Western Front and Italy totalled 583,200 men.[80] Lloyd George urged 'that the Cabinet should not pass a balance-sheet which allowed such an estimate of casualties'.[81] The explanation which Geddes gave of 'wastage' calculations had not been provided in such a clear way at any stage in the war. 'Wastage' was a euphemism for men killed, wounded and missing as a result of military action. Geddes explained that in 1917 there was an average temporary 'wastage' of 71,000 men per month, which represented the total withdrawal of soldiers from units. Of this figure twenty per cent were taken to hospitals or casualty stations in the theatre of war and they returned to their units, usually within one month and rarely later than three months. A further twenty per cent represented the number of men killed and missing on the front each month. The remaining sixty per cent referred to men whose wounds required them to return to Britain. Of the total number who travelled to Britain for medical attention, sixty per cent recovered within twelve months, and were fit enough to return to France, although they did not return to front-line units if they were no longer category 'A' men.[82] Consequently, the military authorities estimated that 'permanent wastage', comprising men killed, missing and the larger proportion of soldiers returning to hospitals in Britain, amounted to an average of 52,000 men per month. This figure corresponded very closely to Macready's estimate that between 1 January and 30 November 1917 the total 'permanent wastage' was 574,000 men.[83]

These figures were available to the War Cabinet at a time when Lansdowne's letter, which expressed concern with the level of casualties, was having a profound impression on public opinion. Quite spontaneously, Lansdowne committees were created to promote the discussion of peace proposals.[84] In this context, the painful realisation of the magnitude of British casualty levels and the knowledge that only 160,000 American troops would arrive in France by the end of 1917, led Lloyd George to embark on a project which ultimately made no contribution to the formulation of manpower plans for 1918. Encouraged by the myth of the effective distribution and control of military manpower in the French army, Lloyd George sent for 'Pétain's Patent Plan for Avoiding Losses'.[85]

He realised that casualties could be reduced by a period of 'active defensive' operations. He wanted a formula to minimise casualties and he had observed that while the offensive in Flanders ground to a standstill, the French army had captured fortified German positions at Malmaison on 23 October. Forced to abandon large scale offensives by the demoralisation of the French Army, Marshal Pétain's operations were largely 'opportunist' counter-attacks, characterised by the concentration of artillery for a sudden attack on a limited objective.[86]

On 18 December Major-General Vicomte de la Panouse and Colonel Dufieux gave an exposition on French military activity in 1917 to the Cabinet Committee on Man-Power. Most of Lloyd George's delusions were shattered, with the exception of the value of increasing the proportion of artillery to infantry battalions in each division. Colonel Dufieux refused to accept that the Battle of La Malmaison should be emulated because a series of similar engagements were less costly in manpower than a single battle of the Somme 'type'. The French level of 'permanent wastage' in late 1917 was 40,000 men per month.[87] This lower level was due to the shorter duration of French limited operations than the Ypres campaign which, moreover, had reduced attacks on the French lines by the scale of activity in Flanders. 'General Pétain's method' may have conserved French manpower, but it had hardly contributed to the overall safety of the Allied lines. Hankey was irritated by the attempted comparison of British and French casualty levels because comparable figures were not available and the statistical exercise had a dubious value.[88] The search for an 'ideal' form of military operation briefly distracted the Committee from its task of defining the guidelines for the allocation of manpower in 1918. However, the rude awakening of the War Cabinet to the statistics of the military war effort in 1917 did lead eventually to the introduction of an element of accountability in the reinforcement of the British armies in France.

The actual level of provision of men for military service depended on the importance which was attached to shipbuilding, aeroplane construction and the general munitions programme. Geddes had received labour demands for these programmes which totalled 400,000 men and 100,000 women. During the Flanders offensive Lloyd George was in no doubt that the acceleration of shipbuilding was so important that it should have first claim on manpower. Later Lloyd George observed,

Shipping meant victory or defeat. It would not be possible to make use of the vast man-power resources of America without shipping, and to maintain the war-weary people of this country in good heart by food supplies and other essential imports, without concentrating all our energies upon shipping.[89]

The successful 'protection' of skilled men in Admiralty dockyards was a source of long-standing annoyance in the War Office. Derby was convinced that the process of dilution had been carried out very patchily by the Admiralty.[90]

Within the commonly agreed priority which shipbuilding enjoyed, the Admiralty had given 'first call' on the labour supply to its own work. In private shipbuilding yards 169,000 of the 300,000 workforce were employed on constructing warships and auxiliary naval craft and 50,000 men worked on the hulls of merchant ships, but in the remaining category of ship repair a substantial proportion were employed on naval work. In addition, most of the naval dockyard staff of 57,000 men worked on the repair of warships. The Shipyard Labour Department manpower demand for 1918 totalled 80,000 including an immediate demand for 12,000 skilled men. This requirement could only be met by the removal of men from munition works or the army. The movement of coal miners into shipyards was taking place where such a 'drift' was feasible. For example, Fifeshire coal-miners worked in the Clyde shipyards, but this was no general palliative for the shortage of labour in shipyards.

The Navy Controller, Sir Alan Anderson, explained to the Cabinet Committee that the principle of 'Naval ships first' did not mean that the shipyards were full of half-built capital ships.[91] The battle-cruiser Hood was the only warship of this size which was being constructed. The naval shipbuilding programme consisted almost totally of submarines and ships suitable for the newly-instituted convoy system. Anderson's claim that naval work was as important as merchant shipbuilding was reinforced by the quota of 100,000 men for the navy, including 50,000 category 'A' men, which was guaranteed in advance of the provision of men for the army. Anderson resisted the military viewpoint that the navy should accept a reduction in resources on the premise that it was little more than a cross-channel transport service. The Admiralty was supported in its defence of a sustained level of manpower allocation by the former First Sea Lord, Admiral Fisher. In a vigorous and typically pugnacious message he noted, 'Of this manpower crisis now on – every species of shipworkman should be returned and the thousands already damnably taken to France should be returned.'[92]

Lloyd George decided that shipyards should not be regarded as a source of military manpower and that Geddes should provide the additional labour required by the shipbuilding industry in 1918. This decision made Churchill extremely unhappy. Forty per cent of labour controlled by the Ministry of Munitions was employed on Admiralty work and Geddes was unable to offer any prospect of satisfying Churchill's immediate labour requirement of 37,000 skilled men. However, Geddes was able to initiate measures which secured the expansion of tank and aeroplane construction by the rationing and licensing of industries, especially firms on construction work. This 'gigantic shuffle' of industrial manpower which affected 700,000 men became a major feature of the department's co-ordination of the labour supply in 1918.

Through the extension of his powers under the Defence of the Realm Act, Geddes undertook to close or restrict non-essential industries by rationing raw materials and licensing businesses and transport facilities. For example, Geddes was empowered to curtail non-essential manufacturing capacity when it was in the proven interests of vital war production in adjoining or nearby workshops. Consequently, the use of labour to produce gun-metal cigarette cases was halted in favour of aeroplane construction in Sheffield. He also noted that, 'The War Office had given out contracts to firms who could not possibly undertake the work without enlarging their scope, and who even poached agricultural labour off the land for their purposes.'[93] In the construction industry 20,000 firms jostled for government contracts. To curb the fluidity of the building market and the proliferation of small building sub-contractors, Geddes was given administrative powers which enabled him to regulate the availability of work in this industry. The building trade became available as a 'pool' of labour for the reinforcement of war work far more successfully than through the self-regulatory proposals which Neville Chamberlain had earlier urged the industry to adopt. These powers to limit the employment of labour in selected non-essential trades complemented Geddes's ability to periodically revise the Schedule of Protected Occupations in order to release men for the army.

Geddes's work was supported by the main thrust of the Cabinet Committee's interests which highlighted the safeguarding of civilian manpower to develop the Allied war effort, as the loss of Russian manpower would be compensated for by the arrival of American divisions in France during 1918. The military demand for 600,000 recruits from civil industries was ignored through the expedient of assuming that no offensive activity would take place on the Western Front. Its discussions represented a determined bid to limit the level of reinforcement which the British armies could expect in 1918. The draft report was written by Hankey from the minutes of the Committee's meetings.[94] It was last discussed by the War Cabinet on 22 January 1918 and never formally revised. However, the draft report embodied the fullest discussion of manpower at the highest level of government since the outbreak of war. The results of this concentrated discussion provided the framework of political and administrative action on manpower in 1918.

The demand for labour for shipbuilding and recruits for manning new naval craft was to be met in full and regarded as the first priority on the supply of manpower. Next in order of priority the Committee identified the manufacture of aeroplanes and tanks. The army was therefore regarded by the War Cabinet as having third claim on the nation's labour supply. Geddes's review of the distribution of men under military control led to three recommendations from the War Cabinet which were aimed at securing the more efficient use of men in khaki. The recommendations concerned the size of the Home Army, the divisional structure of the armies in France and the obsolescent employment of cavalry. In the first quarter of 1918 these features became significant elements of the government's response to the German spring offensive, and they came to fruition as the Allied armies came under considerable pressure on the Western Front.

Following the Grand Fleet's assumption of greater responsibility for the protection of Britain from invasion, the number of divisions retained for home defence was reduced from eight to four.[95] This released 40,000 lower category men for employment in France. The maintenence of a large Home Army had few supporters and the War Cabinet effectively removed the discretionary powers of the War Office on the size of land forces in Britain. This method of reinforcing the British armies in France, particularly for work in the rearward areas, marked the beginning of the breakdown of the different roles which were ascribed for operational purposes to 'A' and lower category men.

To alleviate the shortage of infantry the Cabinet Committee proposed that the number of battalions should be reduced from twelve to nine per division. This measure would enable depleted battalions to be disbanded and the men transferred as drafts to battalions which were to be retained. For almost a year GHQ was aware that this step would eventually have to be taken.[96] Haig's opposition to its implementation was undermined by Lloyd George's discussions with his 'unofficial military adviser', Lieutenant-General Sir Henry Wilson.[97] In November 1917 he was appointed to the semi-independent and highly controversial post of British Military Representative at the Supreme War Council. When asked for his opinion on the proposed reform, he replied on 23 December that if 'our man-power conditions make it necessary either to abolish Divisions or change from 12 to 9 then I would not hesitate for a minute but would change to 9'.[98] The British high command's lack of enthusiasm for this upheaval was reflected in the fact that the Fifth Army, in particular, had not completed this reorganisation by the end of February 1918.[99]

The Committee also identified an extravagant level of manpower provision in the mounted arm. Five Cavalry divisions were partially engaged after the initial tank advance at Cambrai, with predictably little success. Haig's defence of their role in June 1917 had ensured the survival of 188 cavalry squadrons in France. Robertson was no longer willing to support their maintenance, as the more efficient use of manpower in the forward areas, on Lines of Communication and at the Base depots was required of GHQ.

The Cabinet Committee on Man-Power indicated clearly that the reinforcement of infantry battalions and artillery batteries would be substantially achieved by the more effective management of the Home Army of 471,000 men,[100] and the British armies in France which in early January 1918 totalled 1,949,000 men.[101] It concluded that the military control of manpower by the Commander-in-Chief, Home Forces and the Adjutant-General's branch at GHQ was insufficiently rigorous to warrant a large increase in the numerical strength of the army. Consequently, it opposed any alteration in the upper military age or the extension of compulsory military service to Ireland.

Finally, the Committee sanctioned Geddes's view that 150,000 men could be recruited from civil life, instead of the 600,000 men demanded by the military authorities. As the stringent operation of regulations to reduce the employment of men in less essential trades would not provide men in sufficient quantities, Lloyd George accepted that legislation was necessary. The government needed to be released from 'pledges' which restricted the government's access to labour in 'protected' industries, some of which were less essential in 1918 than they were during the rapid expansion of the New Armies in 1915. The amendment of existing legislation on Military Service was also required to complement the revision of the Schedule of Protected Occupations, which ensured the continuing withdrawal of fit men from work which could be performed by women or men over military age.

These inter-dependent policy decisions were achieved by the concentrated discussion of military and civil manpower in the War Cabinet. Its members had responded to a climate of change when prospects for military success were sufficiently remote for the War Cabinet to decide that the allocation of manpower should not be left to the mercies of departmental rivalry and intrigue in Whitehall. In the aftermath of the Cambrai reverse, Lloyd George's 'Paris Speech' and the transfer of Charteris reflected a climate where the strategy of 'wearing down' the German army could no longer be tolerated. Indeed in December 1917 a manpower crisis was identified and, for the first time, the War Cabinet became actively involved in relating manpower provision to priority areas of the war effort. During the proceedings of the Cabinet Committee on Man-Power Geddes consolidated his role as the adviser on man-power to the War Cabinet. With the transfer of recruiting to civil control and the concentration of expertise at St Ermin's, the Ministry of National Service was supported fully by the Cabinet in its task of 'discriminating' between the claims of 'Trade, Trench and Bench'. Unlike his predecessor, Geddes participated in determining quotas of men for military service in relation to maintaining essential war production.

The Ministry of National Service was not an integrated labour supply department, because the rate of progress of dilution and the internal mobility of skilled labour in shipyards and factories were controlled by the Admiralty and the Ministry of Munitions. Similarly, the department was not a 'Ministry of Man-Power' because the regulation of wages, hours of work and conditions of employment were vested in the Ministry of Labour, Home Office and the welfare agencies of the 'employing' departments. However, the Food Production Department, Timber Controller and Air Board were utterly dependent on St Ermin's for the supply of additional labour and its success as a 'clearing house' lay in the efficiency of its regional organisation. The Ministry of National Service became 'the War Cabinet's General Staff on Man Power', even if the phrase was unfortunate.[102] The dual existence of the Cabinet Committee on Man-Power and the Ministry of National Service in December 1917 and early January 1918 marked the apogee of manpower planning in Britain during the First World War. Most notably, this combination implemented a policy of downgrading the military priority for men in the light of high British casualty levels on the Western Front in 1917. As a result, drastically reduced expectations of manpower supply were imposed on Haig and the General Staff in France in relation to merchant ship, aeroplane and tank construction.

Notes

1 PRO NATS 1/338, Minutes of National Service Council, 12 September 1917, Appendix A.
2 PRO CAB 23/4 W.C. 231, Appendix C, Functions of the Ministry of National Service, 12 September 1917.
3 Geddes, *The Forging of a Family*, p. 308.
4 PRO CAB 23/4 W.C. 231, Appendix A, Agreement between the Ministry of National Service and the Ministry of Labour, 12 September 1917.
5 PRO NATS 1/338, Minutes of National Service Council, 7 September 1917.
6 PRO MUN 5/23/247 2/3, Scheme of Distribution of Functions between the National Service Department and the Employment Department of the Ministry of Labour. This statement was approved by Milner on 31 August 1917.
7 PRO MUN 5/23/247 2/1, Agreement between the Ministry of Munitions and the Ministry of National Service, 13 September 1917.
8 PRO MUN 5/23/247 2/4, Memo. on the Ministry of National Service and the Control of Labour, Churchill and A. Geddes, 29 November 1917.
9 PRO NATS 1/338, Minutes of National Service Council, 27 November 1917.
10 Lord Swinton, *I Remember*, London, 1948, p. 154, & *Sixty years of Power*, London, 1966, p. 44; J. A. Cross, *Lord Swinton*, Oxford, 1982, pp. 9–14.
11 Robertson mss. I/11/12/1, Memorandum for the War Cabinet, Derby, 28 November 1917. See Appendix 5.
12 PRO NATS 1/876, Wilson to Brade, 27 October 1917. See also C. E. Callwell, *Field-Marshal Sir Henry Wilson. His Life and Diaries*, London, 1927, II, p. 13.

13 PRO CAB W.C. 263, 2 November 1917.
14 National Service Instruction No. 2 of 1917, Cd. 8833, 15 November 1917.
15 Lloyd George mss. F/17/5/1, J. T. Davies to A. Geddes, 15 September 1917.
16 PRO NATS 1/859, A. Geddes to Duke of Bedford, 11 September 1917, signed copy.
17 PRO NATS 1/859, Press Communiqué, [1 November 1917].
18 For the membership of the Recruiting Advisory Board see the papers on its establishment in PRO NATS 1/859.
19 Liddell Hart, *History of the First World War*, pp. 356–7.
20 PRO CAB 23/4 W.C. 237, 21 September 1917.
21 PRO CAB 23/4 W.C. 246, 8 October 1917.
22 PRO CAB 24/31 G.T. 2585, War Priorities Committee, Smuts, 12 November 1917.
23 PRO CAB 24/31 G.T. 2533, The Acceptance of Foreign Contracts in relation to Man-Power, A. Geddes, 7 November 1917.
24 PRO CAB 24/31 G.T. 2578, Ministry of Munitions and American Steel, Churchill, 9 November 1917.
25 PRO MUN 5/23/247 2/2, Hankey to H. H. Piggott, Secretary to the Ministry of Munitions, 14 December 1917.
26 PRO CAB 24/31 G.T. 2510, Minutes of the War Priorities Committee, 10 October 1917.
27 Lloyd George mss. F/44/3/33, Haig to Brade, n.d. This note was attached to Macready's letter on manpower to Robertson, 27 November 1917.
28 Robertson mss. I/23/27, Robertson to Haig, 26 May 1917, signed copy.
29 C. E. Fayle, *The War and the Shipping Industry*, London, 1927, pp. 246–7.
30 Robertson mss. I/23/46, Haig to Robertson, 9 August 1917.
31 Robertson mss. I/32/59, Robertson to Monro, 31 May 1917, signed copy.
32 Murray – Robertson mss. Add. Ms. 52462, Murray to Robertson, 12 June 1917.
33 Derby mss. 920 DER(17) 27/5, The Present Situation and Future Plans, Haig, 1 May 1917.
34 Liddell Hart, *History of the First World War*, p. 324.
35 PRO CAB 27/6, Cabinet Committee on War Policy, 19 June 1917.
36 Kiggell mss. II/11/2, D. Haig's memo., 22 June 1917.
37 Quoted in Liddell Hart, *History of the First World War*, p. 334.
38 Derby mss. 920 DER(17) 27/5, The Present Situation and Future Plans, Haig, 1 May 1917.
39 Kiggell mss. V/III, Kiggell to Gough, 7 August 1917, signed copy.
40 Lloyd George mss. F/44/3/40, Maurice to J. T. Davies, 18 December 1917.
41 Bonar Law mss. 84/6/127, Bonar Law to Lloyd George, 18 September 1917, unsigned copy.

42   Milner mss. dep. 354, Milner to Curzon, 17 October 1917, signed copy.
43   *General Smuts's Message to South Wales*, New York, 1918, p. 14. See also the report of his visit to South Wales on 29 October 1917 in W. K. Hancock and J. van der Poel, *Selections from the Smuts Papers*, Cambridge, 1966, III, p. 566.
44   Lloyd George, *War Memoirs*, IV, p. 2163.
45   *Ibid.*, IV, 2242.
46   Lloyd George, *The Great Crusade*, London, 1918, p. 155. See also *The Times*, 13 December 1917; Lord Hankey, *The Supreme Command, 1914–1918*, London, 1961, II, pp. 725–7.
47   PRO CAB 24/31 G.T. 2572, Haig to Robertson, 31 October 1917; J. Terraine, *Douglas Haig: The Educated Soldier*, London, 1963, pp. 382–3.
48   Lloyd George mss. F/234, Enclosure to written draft of 'Paris Speech'.
49   Haig mss. No. 119, Diary, Vol. 22, Derby to Haig, 14 November 1917.
50   Hankey, *The Supreme Command*, II, p. 728.
51   Long mss. Add. Ms. 62422, Hewins to Long, 14 November 1917.
52   *Spectator*, 17 November 1917.
53   Strachey mss. S/8/1/4, Strachey to Haig, 6 December 1917, unsigned copy.
54   Haig mss. No. 148, Haig to Lady Haig, 14 November 1917.
55   Liddell Hart, *History of the First World War*, p. 337.
56   Haig mss. No. 148, Haig to Lady Haig, 24 November 1917; C. a C. Repington, *The First World War 1914–1918*, London, 1920, II, p. 140.
57   Haig mss. No. 148, Haig to Lady Haig, 30 November 1917.
58   PRO WO 158/52, Information on Third Army, Major-General Sir John Davidson, Director of Military Operations at GHQ, 18 December 1917.
59   PRO WO 158/53, Cambrai Enquiry File No. 1, Causes of German Success, General G. H. Fowler, 17 January 1918.
60   PRO WO 158/54, Cambrai Enquiry File No. 2, Appendix A, Report summarizing the operations between 20 November and 7 December 1917, Haig, 23 December 1917.
61   Derby mss. 920 DER(17) 27/2, Derby to Haig, 11 December 1917, unsigned copy.
62   PRO WO 158/52, Telegram, Robertson to Haig, 17 December 1917.
63   Lloyd George, *War Memoirs*, IV, p. 2258.
64   Northcliffe mss. Add. Ms. 62159, Northcliffe to Charteris, 11 December 1917, unsigned copy.
65   Derby mss. 920 DER(17) 27/3, Haig to Derby, 10 December 1917; Terraine, *Douglas Haig*, pp. 382–3.
66   Northcliffe mss. Add. Ms. 62190, Northcliffe to Sassoon, 13 December 1917, unsigned copy.
67   *The Times*, 12 December 1917.
68   Lloyd George mss. F/23/2/1, The Labour Situation, Ormsby-Gore, 1 January 1918.

69　This figure included casualties in the Dominion forces. PRO CAB 27/14 M.P.C. 19, Cabinet Committee on Man-Power, 17 December 1917.

70　PRO CAB 27/8 G.T. 2295, Recruiting Position. The Problem and Prospects, A. Geddes, 13 October 1917.

71　PRO CAB 24/4 G. 174, Memorandum on Man-Power, A. Geddes, 15 November 1917. See Appendix 3.

72　PRO CAB 27/14 M.P.C. 19, Cabinet Committee on Man-Power, 17 December, 1917.

73　Sir Edward Carson was a member of the War Cabinet from July 1917 to January 1918. George Barnes, Minister of Pensions, joined the War Cabinet in August 1917 after Henderson was forced to resign from the government. General Smuts, South African Minister of Defence, became a permanent member in June 1917.

74　Hankey, *The Supreme Command*, II, p. 737.

75　PRO CAB 27/14 M.P.C. 2, Cabinet Committee on Man-Power, Hankey, 8 December 1917.

76　*Loc. cit.*

77　PRO CAB 27/14, Minutes of the Man-Power Committee, 10 December 1917.

78　PRO CAB 27/14, Minutes of the Man Power-Committee, 11 December 1917.

79　PRO CAB 23/4 W.C. 295, 10 December 1917.

80　PRO CAB 27/14 M.P.C. 27, Estimated Wastage for 1918, Hankey, 27 December 1917.

81　PRO CAB 27/14, M.P.C. 19, Cabinet Committee on Man-Power, 17 December 1917.

82　*Loc. cit.*

83　PRO CAB 27/14, Minutes of the Man-Power Committee, 10 December 1917.

84　K. Robbins, *The Abolition of War*, Cardiff, 1976, pp. 149–51.

85　Clive mss. II/4, Diary, 16 December 1917. Lieutenant-General Sir Sydney Clive was head of the British mission at Grand Quartier Général from January 1915 to September 1918.

86　PRO CAB 27/14 M.P.C. 24, Note on Attacks with a Limited Objective, French General Staff, 16 December 1917.

87　PRO CAB 27/14 M.P.C. 23, Notes of Anglo-French discussion, 18 December 1917.

88　Lloyd George mss. F/23/1/36, Hankey to Lloyd George, 24 December 1917.

89　PRO CAB 27/14, Minutes of the Man-Power Committee, 11 December 1917.

90　Lloyd George mss. F/14/4/78, Derby to Lloyd George, 24 November 1917.

91　Fayle, *The War and the Shipping Industry*, p. 245.

92　Lloyd George mss. F/23/2/2, Enclosure in Hankey to Lloyd George, 3 January 1918.

93　PRO CAB 27/14, Minutes of the Man-Power Committee, 11 December 1917.

94   Hankey mss. HNKY 4/9, Curzon to Hankey, 21 December 1917;
     Lloyd George mss. F/23/1/30, Cabinet Committee on Man-Power,
     Notes for a Report, Hankey, December 1917.
95   PRO CAB 27/14 M.P.C. 19, Cabinet Committee on Man-Power, 17
     December 1917.
96   Robertson mss. I/23/5, Robertson to Haig, 13 February 1917, signed
     copy.
97   PRO CAB 27/8 W.P. 61, The Present State of the War, the future
     prospects and future action to be taken, Wilson, 20 October 1917;
     Note in regard to Sir Henry Wilson, Hankey, quoted in S. Roskill,
     Hankey. Man of Secrets, London, 1970, I, pp. 459–60.
98   Lloyd George mss. F/47/7/5, Wilson to Lloyd George, 23 December
     1917.
99   Terraine, *Douglas Haig*, pp. 393–4; Gough, *Soldiering On*, p. 154.
100 PRO CAB 27/14, Minutes of the Man-Power Committee, 10
     December 1917.
101 Milner mss. dep.144, Strength of Total Forces in France, 5 January
     1918.
102 PRO NATS I/270, Labour Supply, document 24A, unsigned, n.d.

8
Manpower, the German spring offensive and after
January–November 1918

At the beginning of 1918 the nation's resource of manpower was organised more comprehensively than at any previous stage in the war. With the Ministry of National Service as the 'General Staff on Man-Power', the War Cabinet directed the British response to the German spring offensive. Although the importance of the 'continental commitment' was reasserted, a fine balance was secured between sending drafts overseas and maintaining shipbuilding, coal and food production. In this process Geddes was not a 'Controller of Man-Power', but he played a pivotal role in extinguishing some of the uncertainties of policy which had mounted in the first three years of the war. As the German advance on the Western Front ground to a halt, the remaining pools of labour in essential war industries were more vigorously protected. After August 1918 Geddes's remaining task was to ensure that GHQ realised that if the British army suffered heavy casualties while breaching the Hindenburg Line, there would not be another to replace it.

As a result of the War Cabinet's agreement to raise 450,000 additional men for the military, naval and air services, of which 150,000 men would be for the army, Lloyd George warned Parliament on 20 December 1917 that the schedules which provided protection from military service were to be revised.[1] It was not expected that the engineering trade unions would be enamoured of fresh steps to increase the supply of men for the army. In accordance with previous pledges Geddes explained the manpower situation to trade union leaders at a general conference on 3 January 1918. In the following fortnight group conferences were held to explain the impact which the government's proposals would have on each industry. The ASE refused to participate in the meetings of the engineering group. It was hostile to the recruitment of skilled men before the withdrawal of all dilutees from industry. Lloyd George's major speech on war aims to trade unionists on 5 January was directed, specifically, towards winning their support for the continuation of the war effort. His further appearance at the final conference on 18 January was intended to show that the negotiations conducted by Geddes had the unwavering support of the War Cabinet.[2]

Despite the serious opposition which the proposals encountered at workshop level,[3] Geddes introduced the Military Service Bill when the House of Commons reassembled on 14 January 1918.[4] The first of two clauses was designed to simplify the administration of the enlistment procedure. It reduced the time lapse between the issue of the 'calling-up' notice and the recruit's arrival at the regimental depot, by abolishing the allowance of two months' grace on the withdrawal of certificates of exemption. The second clause gave Geddes power to cancel certificates of exemption which were granted on occupational grounds. This met the Cabinet Committee's aim of clarifying the priority areas of war production. Geddes explained,

We require a system of recruitment based on occupation, conditioned by age, and if you will, marital state . . . Under it, if we obtain the powers for which we now ask, we shall be able to proceed with recruiting on an easily understood system of clear cuts by age, by occupation.[5]

This system did not envisage the adoption of the comprehensive principle of 'youngest first'. However, it was the government's intention to reinforce the armies in France by recruiting the youngest men available from industries which were not so essential that there was an embargo on the removal of men as, for example, in the construction of hulls or the repair of merchant ships.

Sir Auckland Geddes's speech provided the House of Commons with the most comprehensive review of the allocation of manpower for civil and military purposes since the outbreak of war. The parliamentary performance of the new Unionist MP for Basingstoke was admired by Lloyd George and Bonar Law.[6] Geddes was congratulated later by Herbert Samuel on his 'conciliatory method' which was 'responsible in a large degree for the smooth and speedy passage of this measure on to the Statute Book'.[7] The Bill received the Royal Assent on 6 February 1918. However, the Cabinet Committee on Man-Power had clearly concluded that shipbuilding and aeroplane construction were of greater priority than the reinforcement of the British armies in France. Consequently, no immediate use was made of the statutory provision to withdraw exemptions based on occupational grounds.[8] The increase in the rate of recruiting was due entirely to the revised Schedule of Protected Occupations which came into force on 1 February 1918. Gradually, the government introduced a partial 'clean cut' as the minimum age of exemption was raised to twenty-three in most scheduled or 'protected' occupations. For non-scheduled trades there was a variety of age limits below which men were recruited for general service, which was fixed at the maximum military age in the least essential occupations.

The Military Service (No. 1) Act 1918 and the Revised Schedule of Protected Occupations provided the framework for the government's policy response to the German attack in March 1918, complemented by the further release of men from Home Defence. In the quiescent conditions on the Western Front during the months December 1917 to February 1918, the government was ill-disposed to ensure the return of the British armies in France to their full war establishment. Nevertheless, the level of recruiting rose in the first two months of 1918, but this upturn did little to meet the original demand for 600,000 men from civilian life in 1918.[9]

On 21 March 1918 German infantry advanced under the cover of a creeping barrage in an infiltrating attack on the British line between Arras and La Fère. Supported by low flying aeroplanes, they advanced on a battlefield which was shrouded in fog and littered with the debris of war. It was a stark reminder of two years of 'attrition' campaigns fought over the same ground. The forward zones of the Third Army, commanded by Byng, in the north, and the Fifth Army under Gough, were rapidly occupied. Hindered by a complicated communication system which was a shattered monument to the rigidity of trench mentality, isolated British units and fragments of divisions either retreated in disorder, or maintained indefensible positions. In the absence of information Gough ordered the Fifth Army to make a general retirement to the line of the Somme, and the Péronne bridgehead fell intact to the German forces. The advance took place on a forty-three mile front and with the exception of the line at Arras, the German divisions recorded exceptional success in the capture of villages, prisoners and heavy guns in the initial phase.[10] On 27 March a penetration of nearly forty miles was achieved when Montdidier was captured twenty miles south-west of Amiens. Ludendorff saw laid out before him the prospect of vanquishing the enemy by large scale troop movements from the south and the simultaneous defeat of the British armies on the Belgian coast.

On 28 March Ludendorff reinforced the attack on Arras which had failed to overcome the elastic defence line astride the ridge. This attack was abandoned and the advance on Amiens was resumed. However, the time which had lapsed since the initial advance enabled Allied reinforcements to flow through the railway junction at Amiens to replace the surviving elements of the original British line. On 9 April the second phase of Ludendorff's offensive began on a twelve mile front in the Lens-Ypres sector with the initial objective of occupying the railway centre of Hazebrouck. Again, the German attack almost reached its objective. Plumer took charge of the defence of Hazebrouck. He was able to halt the German advance by effecting an unopposed withdrawal from the Ypres salient to shorten the line. The 'institutional' consolidation of Anglo-French military co-operation was secured at the Doullens Conference on 26 March when Marshal Foch was charged with the 'co-ordination' of the Allied armies. This agreement led to the reinforcement of vulnerable parts of the British line by French divisions. After a costly assault on Scherpenberg the German attacks on the heights of Flanders were halted and the Battle of the Lys was finally abandoned by Ludendorff on 29 April.

From 21 March until the end of April the British armies in France were forced onto a prolonged defensive for which their tactical plans and offensive mentality made them ill-prepared. The German high command had embarked on a determined bid to defeat the Allied armies to forestall the despatch of American armies to France.[11] With only five American divisions in France, the key factor in the reinforcement of the Allied military position on the Western Front was the immediate despatch of drafts to the British armies in France. On 25 March Derby told the War Cabinet that steps had already been taken by the military authorities as a preliminary response to the disintegration of the Fifth Army; 106,000 men, of whom nine-tenths were infantry, were available for immediate transfer from the Home Forces, including base and convalescent depots, and 88,000 men on leave were also recalled to their units. With the addition of 18,000 men available as drafts, the number of men transferred to France in the four weeks after the German attack totalled 212,000. Derby shed some light on the methods which were used to achieve this level of transfer of men to France. The preliminary military response to the crisis caused resentment and he told Bonar Law,

We are breaking every pledge; we are sending out men with 5 and 6 wound stripes; we are sending out boys of 18½ although we promised that we would not send them out under 19; and, to add to all this, we are sending these men out without draft leave. This is giving us a great deal of trouble, and in one or two places there have been nasty scenes, men not turning out on parade, etc.[12]

Derby's figure of 18,000 men available as drafts included boys who were not yet 18½ years of age and men who were not fit for overseas service, in addition to the men whose convalescence was interrupted by orders to return to France.[13]

From Cabinet colleagues Derby sought support for his demand that civil departments must provide the men to replace the losses. Walter Long, Secretary of State for the Colonies, continued to uphold the 'large army first' stance which he had adopted in December 1914 and persistently upheld oblivious of the impact of the submarine campaign and 'Passchendaele' on the supply of manpower. He told W. A. S. Hewins, his Under-Secretary of State, 'We are trying to do too much. Every decently fit man should be sent to France save few required for Home Defence. None sh[ou]ld be in our fields etc. . . . Our men are magnificent, but are we backing them??'[14] In late March Churchill was sent to France by Lloyd George to survey the whole military situation. His support for the despatch of large numbers of men to France was tempered by his vested interest in retaining skilled men in munition works. Consequently, he looked to the Home Army to provide the men. He told Lloyd George on 31 March,

Our armies require strengthening by every conceivable means. I wonder if there are any spare brigades of Home Defence troops. In the M[achine] G[un] schools there are a great many officers and men. You ought to scrub your whole Military organisation, and the Navy also, in order to diminish the enemy's superiority.[15]

The withdrawal of men from the Home Army took place on the initiative of the War Office. However, the War Cabinet quickly appreciated the gravity of the military situation in spite of its general unwillingness to restore the British armies in France to their full war establishment. During the period 21–30 March the War Cabinet co-ordinated the response to the military manpower shortage without hesitation. Lloyd George concentrated all discussion and policy-making on the impact of the German advance within the War Cabinet. For two weeks the manpower issue was the only aspect of the war effort which it discussed in detail. Preliminary conclusions on the short-term response to news of the German advance on Amiens were reached on 25 March. Apart from the recall of men on leave and in convalescent depots and the despatch of boys of 18½ years, discussion concentrated on the reduction in size of the Home Army. The Army Council was more unhappy about this debate than about the social repercussions of the other methods of transfer.

It was proposed that the remaining four divisions should be reduced from 43,000 to 10,000 men, which would entail their virtual disappearance with the exception of the permanent cadre. In addition, the seven mixed brigades in the vital Eastern Command was reduced from 30,000 to 18,000 men, which meant the abandonment of Lord French's coastal system of defence.[16] Despite the Army Council's reluctance, Derby took this step as a further response to the crisis in France and his view was upheld by the War Cabinet. On 25 March the War Cabinet also approved the expansion in the examining capacity of the National Service Medical Boards and the relaxation of the eyesight test, the removal of 2,000 men from the garrison in Ireland, the transfer of conscientious objectors to France to augment the labour battalions and the liability of ministers of religion for military service. Despite the legal nullity of the Anglo-Russian Convention on Military Service, the War Cabinet supported the recruitment of Russians resident in Britain for labour work.[17] The rapidity with which these controversial decisions were reached was a testimony to the War Cabinet's assertion of responsibility for the distribution of manpower.[18]

Churchill had promoted the shift in the focus of manpower supply after his tour of the British line in France, not least in the suggestion that naval manpower should be used for military purposes. However, the emergency in the supply of men did not bring close co-operation between the War Office and its implacable rival, the Admiralty. On 25 March Sir Auckland Geddes's proposal that the recruitment of general service ratings should cease immediately was approved, except for a limited supply of skilled ratings.[19] At the same time Sir Eric Geddes, First Lord of the

Admiralty, was asked whether the navy could loan Royal Marines for service in France. Churchill regarded the Admiralty use of manpower as 'luxurious', though his complaints concerned the 'protection' of dockyard labour from recruitment, rather than the inference that warships were overmanned. The question of naval personnel was raised at three meetings of the War Cabinet. On 31 March Sir Eric Geddes indignantly replied,

The impression left upon the Admiralty representatives upon each occasion was that the tone of the discussion became one of complaint against the Navy for not being prepared to 'help the Army' and of not being prepared to 'thin the line' when the Army had to thin theirs.[20]

There were 8,690 marines in France and the War Cabinet wanted to add to their number by reducing the number of marines which served afloat. Most of the 18,970 marines afloat were on ships in the Grand Fleet. Fully briefed by the First and Second Sea Lords on the role of marine gunners in turret batteries, Sir Eric Geddes explained to the War Cabinet the principle of 'rapidity of overwhelming fire at the earliest possible moment' in the high speed engagement of modern fleets. With the exception of the release of onshore marines from coast defence, the Admiralty did not 'thin the line' to release men for the army.

The inter-departmental rivalry, even between military and naval authorities, was a hindrance which the War Cabinet and the Ministry of National Service strove to overcome. Its adverse effects were not countered until after the basic foundations were laid of a long term response to the German spring offensive. The temporary embargo on the recruitment of naval ratings was followed by the 'stream-lining' of the Travelling Medical Boards to enable the system to deal with 90,000 examinations per week, and the reduction in the notice of 'calling up' from fourteen to seven days.

As the extent of the worst military manpower crisis since the outbreak of war became clear, the initial response was acknowledged as insufficient by the War Cabinet. Within one week of the launch of the German attack, Macready provided the War Cabinet with an estimate of the number of men which were required to maintain the forces in the field.[21] As a result of the casualty level for the period 21–30 March of 122,000 men and the projection of 'wastage' at 20,000 men per day during the heavy fighting, Macready provided a quite definite 'balance sheet' of manpower 'assets' and 'liabilities'.[22] Macready concluded that 282,200 men would have to be found by the government from civilian life to meet the total 'liabilities' of 505,000 men up to 31 July 1918, which included the assumption of four months' heavy fighting at a temporary 'wastage' level of 84,000 men per month.[23] The remainder of the total deficit would be provided by new drafts of men becoming available during the months April to July and the short term element of the temporary 'wastage' level which comprised sick and wounded men becoming fit for service in France. These calculations ignored the needs of the major 'side-shows' of Palestine and Salonika. Even without their reinforcement, Macready warned that if the existing arrangements were not supplemented by July there would only be sufficient infantry in the army to maintain twenty-five divisions in France. To avoid affecting munitions output, Sir Auckland Geddes realised that sufficient men could only be located by raising the upper military age and extending compulsory military service to Ireland. It was with much trepidation that the War Cabinet requested the Minister of National Service to draft a two clause Military Service Bill.

Geddes's estimates of the impact of this short Bill were quite clear. If the upper limit for military service was raised from the existing effective level of forty-three to forty-five years, 150,000 men would become liable for recruitment of whom 50,000 would be available for military service under the arrangements for release and substitution.[24] The extension of the age limit to fifty years would provide 250,000 and 60,000 men respectively. If military compulsion was extended to Ireland 150,000 men could be recruited for general service. Geddes's draft Bill of 26 March proposed that the lower age limit for military service should be lowered from eighteen to seventeen years and the upper age limit should be raised to fifty-five years.[25] He recommended these drastic changes in the context of the War Cabinet's doubtful political will to enforce compulsion in Ireland. Geddes also proposed that the tribunal system should be abolished. Instead, advisory committees under the chairmanship of Lord Lieutentants should be formed to consider the order of priority in which men were conscripted, rather than the examination of applications of exemption from military service.

On the same day Barnes wrote a hasty note on the proposed Bill to the Prime Minister. He said, 'I hope you won't commit yourself to it. Seventeen is too low and fifty-five is too high.'[26] There was considerable criticism of the plan to lower the minimum age, which was heightened by the political awareness of the deep hostility to the transfer, without formal notice or draft leave, of boys under nineteen years of age to the Western Front. The scale of opposition which the draft Bill could expect to encounter if it included the abolition of the tribunal system and the cancellation of existing certificates of exemption led to an intense flurry of memoranda writing which highlighted the autocratic and centralising features of the proposals. For Robert Munro, Secretary of State for Scotland, 'the substitution of a bureaucratic for a democratic system is manifestly undesirable, unless indeed it be unavoidable'.[27] Like Long, Munro believed that local tribunals offered public opinion a 'sense of security' where dissatisfaction could be expressed and safely channelled without detriment to the war effort.[28] The exemption procedure had depended on local participation since 1915 on a semi-representative basis and the withdrawal of certificates was expected to cause 'serious labour unrest and stoppages of work'.[29] Although industrial militancy had dramatically declined during the German spring offensive, the introduction of a more stringent form of appeals procedure in place of the locally-administered 'democratic' system would have been counter-productive.[30]

With the circulation of critical memoranda, Geddes was pushed on the defensive where he gained the support of Colonel Repington, Military Correspondent of the *Morning Post*. Repington had access to the statistical information on manpower which was produced in the Adjutant-General's office and he also made successful 'advances' to the Ministry of National Service to obtain data.[31] Geddes was warned by Lloyd George to resist Repington's demands for information, without realising how close his relations were with the General Staff.[32] Earlier in the year Repington had embarked on a mission of publicising the 'manpower muddle' in a campaign which he consciously developed on the scale of his treatment of the 'shells scandal' in *The Times* in 1915.[33] Geddes was commended for his work in Repington's articles and they enjoyed good relations during the debate on the Military Service Bill. Geddes participated in the 'mobilisation' of the web of Unionist organisations and luncheon clubs for one main reason – to provide informed Unionist opinion with surveys of the manpower situation on an unofficial basis, to ensure that pressure was brought to bear on the War Cabinet to increase the flow of men for military service in France.

Unlike his neutralist standpoint as an 'expert' in the meetings of the Cabinet Committee on Man-Power, Geddes was politically committed to the legislative extension of military service. For this reason he was anxious about the capacity of the War Cabinet to hesitate and change course. Lloyd George's caution incensed Unionist MPs associated with the pre-eminence of the 'single front' principle. His concern was based on, firstly, the expectation of industrial unrest and, secondly, a belief that the parliamentary opposition could mount an effective challenge to the government's plans on manpower. In the latter area Lloyd George's fears were exaggerated, but he remained concerned about the electoral support which Asquith might gain if he opposed the conscription of men for military service in the forty to fifty years' age range.[34] The strength of feeling against the practical implications of the Military Service Bill were not to be under-rated or, as Geddes did, ignored. An indication of the government's declining capability to mobilise the few remaining sources of manpower could be gauged in the correspondence of two pillars of the Asquithian Liberal establishment. Lord Buckmaster told Lord Harcourt,

The introduction of this Man-Power Bill has caused more acute discontent than any measure since the commencement of the War. The reason is obvious. It will embrace nearly all the effective and active men in our productive industries and in business circles, and, at the same time, threaten us with a confusion in Ireland of which no one can see the conclusion or extent. Self interest, genuine political feeling, coupled with profound anxiety as to our present position, and distrust of the Government combine together to produce a more intense feeling of resentment than I have hitherto witnessed.[35]

It was with some trepidation that Lloyd George embarked on a course of political action to relieve the military position in France, believing that his premiership was vulnerable.

Sir Auckland Geddes agreed to the retention of local tribunals on 5 April. The War Cabinet then considered the proposition from H. E. Duke, Chief Secretary for Ireland, that the introduction of compulsory military service in Ireland without Home Rule would bring minimum results.[36] The issue of military conscription in Ireland was inextricably linked to prospects for a measure of self-government.[37] Anti-recruiting campaigns increasingly rendered the attractive aim of 150,000 Irish recruits for English and Scottish regiments unattainable without the employment of coercion, including the reinforcement of garrisons in Ireland. Following the failure of the Irish Convention, if only narrowly, to sustain its much vaunted inter-party co-operation to the stage of formulating an agreed measure of self-government,[38] Duke was a persuasive advocate of the *status quo*. In addition, his warnings on the low morale of the Dublin constabulary, the Sinn Fein agitation, the lack of a complete register of men eligible for military service and the intimidating environment for local tribunals, were factors hardly conducive to the coercion of Irish manpower. Conscription in Ireland could only proceed with extraordinary military contingency plans and at enormous political and social cost.

During the summer months Lord French,[39] as Lord-Lieutenant of Ireland, and Lord Midleton[40] argued that the extension of military conscription to Ireland had a vital part to play in the reinforcement of the British armies in France. For ministers concerned with the 'temper of labour' and the output of vital war commodities, the suggestion of securing 150,000 Irish recruits was at best a blunder and at worst the potential mainspring of a further rebellion. Irish civil labour was a significant source of supply for large munition centres such as the Gretna works. Similarly, Irish agricultural produce was vital as the increase in cultivated acreage in Britain failed to reach the expected level in 1918. The moderating influence of two figures who had studied nationalist opinion played an important part in the decision to postpone the conscription of Irish manpower. Firstly, Bryan Mahon, Commander-in-Chief Forces in Ireland, who was aware that the best reason for applying the 'Derby scheme' was that it would delay the implementation of the second clause of the Military Service (No. 2) Act, 1918.[41] Secondly, the blunt reminder from James O'Connor, Attorney-General for Ireland, that conscription 'would weld into an active and I may say virulent opposition to Government or to any attempts at settlement, all Irish Nationalists, including the Bishops and Priests of my Church. It would create an animosity that fifty years would not dissipate.'[42]

Irish Nationalist MPs gave vent to their anger on 9–10 April when the First and Second Readings of the Bill were debated in the House of Commons. Consequently, the contents of the Bill which were implemented were not subjected to detailed scrutiny. Lloyd George introduced this measure to the chamber, which reflected the fact that its contents were determined largely by the War Cabinet sitting in semi-permanent session. The Prime Minister stated that Orders were to be issued to cancel 'all occupational exemptions by age blocks in specified occupations. That is the clean cut.'[43] Section two of the Military Service (No. 1) Act, had remained unused, but proclamations were issued on 20 April to withdraw exemption from men under twenty-three years of age who were fit for general service. All munition workers who were medically classified category 'A' or grade 1 had their exemption certificates withdrawn, with the exception of men whose trades were listed in the Revised Schedule of Protected Occupations. Under the Schedule which had come into force on 1 February 1918 the number of men released each week by the Ministry of Munitions rose from 3,700 in the third week in March to 9,000 men in the second week in April.[44]

This response to the crisis in France was made on the principle that it was not merely necessary to obtain men for military service but to recruit them quickly. The Military Service (No. 2) Act was designed to meet the projected sharp increase in the temporary 'wastage' level in April and to postpone the disestablishment of up to five divisions. This legislation bore a direct relationship to the British casualties on the Western Front which escalated to 349,119 men between 21 March and 9 June. The upper military age was raised to fifty years and in certain specified occupations, such as the medical profession, to fifty-five years. The Act also provided for the close regulation of appeal tribunals, the limiting of rights of appeal and the standardisation of grounds for exemption from military service. Lastly, the Act provided Geddes with the power to extend the 'clean cut' to age groups above twenty-three years in the eventuality of a 'national emergency'. Briefly, St Ermin's was closely associated with the military demand for men as rapid strides were made towards the release of men from munition works by the development of the 'clean cut' policy on an occupation modified by age basis. The War Cabinet accepted that for as long as the crisis in France existed, the maintenance of the 'continental commitment' pushed the conclusions of the Cabinet Committee on Man-Power into temporary abeyance. An exceptional situation temporarily overrode civil demands for labour. As Geddes concluded during the Second Reading of the Bill on 10 April, 'There is, I believe, no possibility of any sort or kind of maintaining the British Armies which have been built up in these years of War except by adopting these proposals which are now before the House.'[45] The cost of the constant search for more men for France was the further reform of the administration of the supply and allocation of manpower which was not to be attained during 1918. However, the centralised response of legislation and proclamations through the instrumentality of the Ministry of National Service met the demands of the 'single front' strategy during the difficult months of April and May 1918.

Interdepartmental strife remained a problem which Geddes reconsidered during the aftermath of the German offensive. On 28 April he told Lloyd George that the departments were 'all fishing in the same pool' for manpower. Furthermore, it was

quite impossible to separate labour supply from recruiting & any attempt to do it will lead to chaos. I am more convinced than ever that we have got to have a Man Power Ministry responsible for all man power questions and that no other department must be allowed to touch the question of labour supply.[46]

This note was not a manifesto for administrative innovation. Geddes knew that the creation of a 'Controller of Man-Power' or a 'Ministry of Man-Power' was not politically feasible as the separate jurisdiction of segments of the 'pool' of labour guaranteed departmental 'independence' on the internal management of manpower. Geddes's preference for the 'amalgamation' of the labour controling Departments arose from the sheer frustration of his department's relations with the Admiralty.[47] The proliferation of independent labour supply authorities was an institutional obstruction to the fluidity of labour. Several departments at the Admiralty supervised its labour requirements,[48] and the economical use of skilled labour in shipyards and dockyards would hardly be carried out by production departments which were notorious for barely introducing dilution. The Ministry of National Service had no effective control over dilution in the Admiralty. In Sheffield the separate administration of different policies had led to the introduction of women on the production of heavy artillery guns in munition factories but the continuing employment of men in naval gun-shops in the same city. The poor rate of dilution in Admiralty establishments and factories which fulfilled naval contracts was resented by munition officials. They noticed that labour which was displaced by dilution and substitution in munition firms found a 'safe haven' in Admiralty work and was not therefore available for the army.[49] Churchill could not be assured that men released by the Ministry of Munitions for shipbuilding would be economically used in properly diluted shipyards and marine engineering shops. The threefold division of labour control represented by the Shipyard Labour Department, Director of Dockyards and Director of Works exacerbated the problem of establishing the actual demand for skilled manpower in the Admiralty.[50]

In mid-April Sir Eric Geddes approved the creation of a Labour Priority branch at the Admiralty following pressure to reform its management structure from the Ministry of National Service. However, the water-tight 'labour-employing' departments of state 'fishing in the same pool' showed no signs of submitting to the centralisation of the manpower supply. The Shipbuilding Employers Federation and the Federation of British Industries proposed that St Ermin's should exercise the central function of labour control. They argued that the ministry was appropriate because it had local machinery, its existence was for war duration only, and it occupied a pivotal position from which it could 'weigh' the military and industrial demands for manpower.[51] However, in April the Ministry of National Service was less well placed to supply and allocate labour for all war purposes because the labour movement regarded its primary function as the recruitment of men for the army. In the rearrangement of labour priorities which followed the German advance on the Western Front, Geddes retained his advisory role to the War Cabinet. The function of the Ministry of National Service as a 'clearing house' for additional labour was less relevant in a period when manpower allocation was strongly determined by the requirements of the 'single front' strategy. In view of the conflicting viewpoints, discussion on the feasibility of one labour supply authority was remitted to the War Priorities Committee. On 24 May the Committee, under Smuts's chairmanship, appointed a Permanent Labour Sub-Committee 'to work out departmentally action in accordance with unified policy'.[52]

At an early stage it was apparent that this co-ordinating machinery's contribution to the war effort would not be commensurate with the time expended in the discussion of the deleterious effect of the rivalry of the three labour supply departments. Indeed, the War Priorities Committee had not played a significant role in the creation of government policy since October 1917. In addition, the Army Council was unwilling to submit to further enquiries concerning its labour control from any interventionist authority. In response to the suggested reduction in the size of the military administrative staff in France to provide more men for the front line, Macready noted, 'It would be much better if till the end of the war the Army may be left to those who know something about it and not be interfered with by those who do not.'[53] The Ministry of

National Service was at no time a *de facto* Ministry of Man-Power. It was unable to secure powers which would have enabled its local officials to investigate the use of industrial labour by the Admiralty, Ministry of Munitions and the War Office Contracts Department. However, as the main instrument of government policy on man-power, the Ministry of National Service was a central feature of the 'effective prosecution of the war' in 1918. It assumed with considerable efficiency the onerous role of the 'recruiting office' of the army. By May 1918 the Ministry of National Service repre-sented the culmination of a series of *ad hoc* responses to the problem of achieving an equitable supply of manpower for the pursuit of total war.

The government's response to the German attacks on the British line dominated all other aspects of the war effort. At the end of May 1918 there was a growing sense of release from the manpower question and a belief that the war situation in France was unlikely to worsen. Hankey recorded on 30 May,

To give a comprehensive précis would be an immense task, as the subject was discussed by the full War Cabinet on no less than 82 occasions since the beginning of March 1917, as well as by three Cabinet Committees and there are scores of long Memoranda dealing with every phase of the question.[54]

Similarly the passage of the Military Service (No. 2) Act during the heat of battle later gave cause for reflection. In all other respects Lord Sydenham was a firm protagonist of the military requirement for men. Indeed, he was considered for the post of Under Secretary of State for War in April 1918.[55] However, he was remarkably sensitive to the antagonism of skilled trade unions to the further 'combing out' of men from munition factories. Sydenham told Henry Page Croft that the government

are blamed for not introducing the Military Service Bill earlier; but is it clear that they could have passed it before the German attack had begun & the danger was apparent? . . . What you & I realized could not be brought home to the Trade Unions until the great attack took place. I do not think that the Govt. did its best to explain the situation; but I am not clear that the most impassioned speeches would have produced the necessary effect.[56]

Lloyd George also drew attention to the 'psychological' impossi-bility of prior legislation of drastic proportions, 'to which organised labour would have refused to submit but for the spectacular urgency of the situation'.[57] The 'urgency' continued, although in a less heightened form.

A growing feature of the supply of military manpower was the use of category 'Bi' men for front line service. They were described by Henry Wilson who, in February 1918, replaced Robertson as Chief of Imperial General Staff, as 'nearly "A" men'. To reconstitute divisions which were at cadre strength the reduction of the Home Forces continued apace during May 1918. The nucleus of the four Home Service divisions were kept in Britain, but the remainder of the seven mixed brigades from the Eastern Command and all the independent Cyclist battalions were placed under orders for France.[58] Despite the reduction of the level of enlistment from 80,000 to 20,000 men per month by August 1918 Geddes continued to play a pivotal role through his efficient management of the complex 'clean cut' schemes. From 21 March to 13 July 1918 a total of 351,824 men were sent as drafts to France.[59] This figure included 114,709 'Ai' men for infantry battalions, 40,693 artillery-men and 16,066 men for the Machine-Gun Corps.

Yet the Adjutant-General continued to complain that there was a shortage of infantry drafts. This outlook was the legacy of a time when it was taken for granted by the Army Council and GHQ that drafts would automatically be sent to France so that the force could be returned to full war establishment after a period of heavy fighting. Homage to the principle of 'superiority of numbers' was a fearful commitment, which Clausewitz had shown to be effective only in relation to the element of surprise and the assembly of forces in space and time.[60] With Derby's appointment as British Ambassador to France in April 1918 his successor, Lord Milner, brought a greater sense of detachment to the office of Secretary of State for War.

By 20 July 1918 the interval in the exploitation of German military success and the maintenance of an indented front dominated by three great wedges had depleted Ludendorff's reserves. Following the defeat of his attack on Reims he was forced to abandon the offensive in Flanders. Simultaneously the Allied front was being strengthened by the arrival of 100,000 American troops per month from April 1918 onwards. By July 1918 the main-tenance of the British line was directly responsible for the reduction of aeroplane engine output by fifty-five per cent and tank output by fifty per cent of the programmes agreed by the Cabinet Committee on Man-Power. The War Office was made well aware that in order to re-establish the civil priority areas of the war effort, a reduction of the size of the British army would take place until the new class of recruits was available in October.

Despite the prospect of a reduced force in France, Milner was satisfied that sufficient recruits had been provided in conditions which Geddes later described as 'almost open resistance to the administration of the Military Service Acts'.[61] In the context of severe industrial unrest, Geddes's work for the War Office was not inconsiderable. Before the opening of the Allied offensive Milner told Sir Henry Thornton,

we are scraping up men from every possible quarter & putting a much larger number of trained men into the field than we thought possible even a few weeks ago. I can now promise that we can reconstitute broken divisions immediately to such an extent that the total number of our divisions shall once more be at least equal to what it was at the opening of the battle in March.[62]

On 14 June exemption was withdrawn from men on Admiralty and munition work who were nineteeen and twenty years of age, except in the limited number of trades in which protection from military service was provided at this age.[63] This decision marked the full extent of the periodic modification of the level of industrial manpower by the 'clean cut' and the revision of the Schedule of Protected Occupations. From July onwards the rate of release of skilled men from munition factories rapidly decreased. Each week in June 28,000 men were released from munition work but by September this rate had dwindled to 3,000 men each week. At the end of a full discussion on the manpower question on 19 July, the War Cabinet concluded that the severe strain on industry should not be prolonged by continuing to sustain the military demand for men. Geddes was asked to renew his work on adjudicating the demands for additional labour.

With this War Cabinet decision the priority areas of January 1918 were reasserted and no more category 'A' men were withdrawn by quota release procedures from vital war industries. In the remaining months of 1918 coal production had a higher priority than military recruitment and Geddes urged the War Office to commence the 'combing-out' of coal-miners from the British armies in France.[64] The War Cabinet was also persuaded to resist further military demands for manpower by the slump in the merchant ship construction rate. The target of 250,000 gross tons per month was not attained in the first seven months of 1918. In August 1918 only 124,675 tons were produced. The revised estimate of the construction of 1,545,000 tons of shipping compared most unfavourably with the expected loss of 2,570,000 gross tons of shipping for the year.[65] As in January 1918 the War Cabinet decided that the military war effort could not be continued without regard to industrial supply.

From August until the end of the war Sir Auckland Geddes undertook the task of maintaining an equitable distribution of manpower, which was no less important during the breach of the Hindenburg Line than it was during the defence of Amiens. During the Allied offensive Geddes provided recruits in two ways. Firstly, the special quotas from the remaining 'pools' of labour. They totalled 237,000 men and in August the agricultural quota of 25,000 men was largely untouched. These men were located by county agricultural executive committees which were reorganised by the Board of Agriculture to reduce the resistance of the 'rural interest' to the recruitment of men from the land. Secondly, men were only obtained from civilian life on the principle that requirements for manpower below category 'A' or grade 1 were provided from the Home Defence forces. Consequently, the reduction of the Home Army was carried a stage further during the summer months.[66] Inevitably, military operations were affected by the impossibility of despatching further category 'A' men to France. Brigadier-General Crozier's cavalier memoir provided an insight into the military costs of warfare characterised by high casualty levels over four years. He received an order from GHQ which he was to read to his brigade. Crozier was horrified for 'It promises the 'B' men they will not be put into offensive action! "Is not", I ask, "a local counter-attack offensive action?" . . . I put the order in my pocket and say nothing – for the time being.'[67]

The withdrawal of men from munition factories on the basis of occupation conditioned by age and the transfer of category 'B' men from the Home Army were the main methods of supplying drafts to the Western Front which Geddes supervised in the last four months of the war. At the same time, the War Cabinet ensured that GHQ understood that no additional measures would be introduced to obtain men for the army. Wilson informed Haig of this fact repeatedly. During the attacks on the Hindenberg Line Wilson pleaded with Haig to avoid the risk of 'wastage' rates comparable to 'the unfruitful pouring out of life'[68] during the Third Battle of Ypres.[69] In October 1918 on the road to victory the General Staff in France was fully aware that the path of frontal assault and the vocabulary of attrition was no longer countenanced by the War Cabinet, civil departments, trade unions and men of military age who remained in vital war work.

Notes

1   Lloyd George mss. F/234, Report of Cabinet conclusions, Speech notes, 20 December 1917; 100 H.C. Deb. 5s. Cols. 2216–7, 20 December 1917.
2   Lloyd George mss. F/17/5/8, A. Geddes to Lloyd George, 16 January 1918.
3   *History of the Ministry of Munitions, (H.M.M.),* VI, Part 2, pp. 44–6; Hinton, *The First Shop Stewards' Movement*, pp. 256–62; Wrigley, *David Lloyd George and the British Labour Movement*, pp. 224–5.
4   This occasion was used to refute the suggestion that the army was being 'starved' of men. Geddes, *The Forging of a Family*, p. 317.
5   101 H.C. Deb. 5s. Col. 73, 14 January 1918.
6   Bonar Law mss. 84/6/30, J. Davidson to G. Younger, 22 October 1917.
7   101 H.C. Deb. 5s. Col. 1241, 24 January 1918.
8   *H.M.M.*, VI, Part 2, p. 41.
9   PRO CAB 24/46 G.T. 4021, Maintenance of the Forces, A. Geddes, 24 March 1918.
10 Liddell Hart, *History of the First World War*, p. 370. See also Terraine, *Douglas Haig*, pp. 414–24, and J. Charteris, *At G.H.Q.*, pp. 293–8.
11 E. Ludendorff, *My War Memories 1914–1918*, London, 1919, II, pp. 418–9.
12 Bonar Law mss. 83/1/26, Derby to Bonar Law, 31 March 1918.
13 Lloyd George mss. F/23/2/26, Macready to Hankey, 12 April 1918.
14 Hewins mss. 68/6, Long to Hewins, 3 April 1918.
15 Lloyd George mss. F/8/2/13, Churchill to Lloyd George, 31 March 1918.
16 PRO CAB 24/46 G.T. 4030, Troops available for Home Defence, French, 25 March 1918.
17 PRO WO 32/4774, Minute to Lord Derby, Brade, 11 February 1918.
18 PRO CAB 23/5 W.C. 372, 25 March 1918.
19 PRO CAB 24/46 G.T. 4021, Maintenance of the Forces, A. Geddes, 24 March 1918.
20 PRO CAB 24/46 G.T. 4092, Royal Marines from the Navy, E. Geddes, 31 March 1918.
21 Milner mss. dep. 144, The Number of Men of all arms necessary to maintain the forces in the field, Macready, 28 March 1918. From this note the Army Council produced a resume of the military position. See PRO WO 32/9557, Memorandum by the Army Council indicating the number of men of all arms necessary to maintain the forces in the field, 29 March 1918.

22 PRO CAB 23/5 W.C. 379, 1 April 1918.
23 'Balance Sheet', 28 March 1918, attached to PRO WO 32/9557, Memorandum by the Army Council, op.cit, 29 March 1918. See Appendix 4.
24 The upper military age was forty-one years but in practice forty-three years after the upward revision of the Schedule of Protected Occupations, PRO CAB 24/46 G.T. 4036, Amendment of Military Service Acts, A. Geddes, 26 March 1918.
25 Loc. cit. Compare with Lloyd George mss. F/17/5/14, Rough draft of proposed Bill, A. Geddes to Lloyd George, 25 March 1918.
26 Lloyd George mss. F/4/2/26, Barnes to Lloyd George, 26 March 1918.
27 PRO CAB 24/46 G.T. 4055, Amendment of the Military Service Acts, R. Munro, 28 March 1918.
28 PRO CAB 24/24, Tribunals and Medical Boards, Long, 23 August 1917.
29 PRO CAB 24/46 G.T. 4059, Proposed Military Service Bill, A. H. Stanley, President of the Board of Trade, 28 March 1918.
30 Ministry of Labour, The Labour Gazette, XXVI, May 1918; Hinton, The First Shop Stewards' Movement, p. 266.
31 Gwynne mss. 21, Repington to Gwynne, 20 January 1918.
32 Lloyd George mss. F/17/5/16, Lloyd George to A. Geddes, 22 April 1918, unsigned copy.
33 Gwynne mss. 21, Repington to Gwynne, 19 January 1918. See also B. H. Liddell Hart, Memoirs, London, 1965, I, pp. 72–4.
34 Lloyd George mss. F/30/2/31, Lloyd George to Bonar Law, 10 April 1918, unsigned copy.
35 Harcourt mss. dep. 448, Buckmaster to Harcourt, 12 April 1918.
36 PRO CAB 24/47 G.T. 4133, Compulsory Service in Ireland, H. E. Duke, 4 April 1918.
37 A. J. Ward, 'Lloyd George and the 1918 Irish conscription crisis', Historical Journal, XVII, 1974, pp. 108–27; D.G. Boyce, 'British opinion, Ireland and the war, 1916–1918', Historical Journal, XVII, 1974, pp. 586–91.
38 R. B. McDowell, The Irish Convention, London, 1970, pp. 186–91.
39 French mss. Box 75/46/11, French to Lloyd George, 19 May 1918, signed copy.
40 Midleton mss. PRO 30/67/38, Memorandum with regard to the Viceroyalty of Ireland, Midleton, May 1918.
41 For the 'gradualist' approach see PRO WO 32/9556, Note on the Application of the Derby Scheme of Recruiting to Ireland in the light of the experience gained of its working in Great Britain, n.d. [April 1918], unsigned.
42 PRO CAB 24/47 G.T. 4129, Conscription in Ireland, J. O'Connor, 2 April 1918.
43 104 H.C. Deb. 5s. Col. 1353, 9 April 1918.
44 H.M.M., VI, Part 2, pp. 49–50.
45 104 H.C. Deb. 5s. Col. 1592, 10 April 1918.
46 Lloyd George mss. F/17/5/18, A. Geddes to Lloyd George, 28 April 1918.

47 PRO NATS 1/270, Labour Supply and Regulation, A. Geddes, 21 May 1918.
48 PRO NATS 1/270, Memorandum on the difficulties in connection with labour supply and on the changes proposed, Rey, 7 April 1918.
49 PRO NATS 1/270, Memorandum on Admiralty proposals re. their Labour Dept., Stephenson Kent, 13 April 1918.
50 Fayle, *The War and the Shipping Industry*, p. 247.
51 PRO NATS 1/270, R. T. Nugent, Director of the Federation of British Industries, to Lloyd George, 23 March 1918, and Lloyd-Greame to A. Anderson, 13 April 1918.
52 PRO NATS 1/270, Minute, Note on discussion with Smuts's Committee, 24 May 1918.
53 PRO WO 32/9554, Minute, Macready, 12 July 1918.
54 PRO WO 32/9554, G.T. 4679A, Notes on Man-Power, Hankey, 30 May 1918.
55 Roskill, *Hankey*, I, p. 530.
56 Croft mss. CRFT 1/19 SY/1/1–2, Sydenham to Page Croft, 1 May 1918.
57 Lloyd George, *War Memoirs*, V, p. 2651.
58 PRO CAB 24/51 G.T. 4598, Note, Wilson, 18 May 1918.
59 Benson mss. A4/8/2, Drafts despatched to France from 21 March to 13 July 1918, unsigned, 16 July 1918.
60 C. Clausewitz, *On War*, Harmondsworth, 1968, p. 265.
61 PRO WO 32/9954, Extract from War Cabinet 449, 19 July 1918.
62 Milner mss. dep. 19, Milner to Thornton, 14 June 1918, signed copy.
63 *H.M.M.*, VI, Part 2, p. 53. See also Wrigley, *David Lloyd George and the British Labour Movement*, p. 228.
64 G. D. H. Cole, *Labour in the Coal-Mining Industry*, London, 1923, p. 59.
65 Lloyd George mss. F/87/1/5, Harmsworth to Lloyd George, 20 September 1918; Fayle, *The War and the Shipping Industry*, p. 254.
66 PRO CAB 24/54 G.T. 4876, The Man-Power Situation, 1917–1918, A. Geddes, 17 June 1918.
67 F. P. Crozier, *A Brass Hat in No Man's Land*, Bath, 1968, p. 216. See Appendix 6.
68 PRO CAB 24/54 G.T. 4876, *op. cit.*, 17 June 1918.
69 Terraine, *Douglas Haig*, p. 463; R. Blake (ed.), *The Private Papers of Douglas Haig 1914–1919*, London, 1952, pp. 326–30; Callwell, *Field-Marshal Sir Henry Wilson*, II, pp. 124–9; Hankey, *The Supreme Command*, II, pp. 848–51.

Conclusion : the dilemmas of manpower control

Towards the end of the expansion of military forces through the creation of Lord Kitchener's New Armies the notion of manpower entered the vocabulary of British political life. In August 1915 concern about the control and allocation of manpower was first expressed in the Cabinet as ardent compulsionists became uneasy about the conduct of the war. They were convinced that the demand for an army of seventy divisions was feasible, provided an efficient system of selection of men for military service was employed without delay.[1] The proponents of the immediate fulfilment of military demands for men closely identified the search for a systematic approach to the supply of manpower with the development of a large continental army. The introduction of the National Register placed the discussion of the supply of men for military and industrial purposes on a reliable statistical basis, as it provided detailed inform- ation on the availability of men of military age in civilian life. It facilitated an increased military demand for men because, much to the consternation of the Board of Trade, the theoretical availability of 1,550,000 men of military age was interpreted by the War Office as the required level of recruitment for 1916.[2] This statement was the first of a series of grossly inflated manpower demands which the Army Council submitted to successive governments during the war. Furthermore, conscription was assured by the simple device of making unrealistic demands of the 'Derby scheme'. The failure of the scheme of attestation to produce 35,000 men per week for the army during October to December 1915 ensured the introduction of compulsory military service.

Even so, recruitment did not meet the expectations of the military authorities in 1916. The failure of the Military Service Acts of 1916 to fulfil the demands of the Adjutant-General arose from three factors which the War Office failed to appreciate. Firstly, the complex patterns of labour demand for essential war industries increasingly threatened the 'large army first' principle. Secondly, the newly established tribunal system was unable to cope with the quantity of cases which required attention and considerable delays ensued in the administration of the exemption procedure. Thirdly, British high command imposed an unacceptably high level of 'wastage' on the government's manpower plans. GHQ remained dissatisfied with the recruiting returns, whereas it should have expressed some satisfaction that over 1,100,000 men enlisted in the first full year of compulsory military service, despite the many administrative problems.

The annoyance of the General Staff in France with the level of recruitment originated from the misapprehension that its demand for men was the only claim on the nation's supply of manpower which was worthy of consideration. As it sought to replace the casualties of the Somme offensive, GHQ faced competition for manpower from vital war industries where the basic aim was to retain skilled men and 'protect' them from marauding recruiting officers. The War Office and Ministry of Munitions were rival 'labour-employing' departments and for different reasons and with separate objectives in view they sought the appointment of a central board to determine the allocation and economic utilisation of manpower. Under the chairmanship of Austen Chamberlain, the Man-Power Distribution Board marked a departure from the previous Asquithian practice of *ad hoc* responses to specific aspects of the labour supply problem, which was epitomised by the brief existence of the Lansdowne committee.[3] As a remarkable innovation the Board offered the prospect of a central authority which would curb the major departments' autonomous control of labour. However, under the direction of politicians unacquainted with the complexity of manpower utilisation in armament workshops, shipyards and foundries, the Board foundered. Before its recommendations on dilution, protected occupations and industrial enlistment were discussed the Board was weakened substantially by industrial unrest in Sheffield and other munition centres. Shortly afterwards, the Man-Power Distribution Board was eclipsed by the demise of Asquith's government.

Before its fall, the so-called 'Wait and See' government accepted, in principle, the introduction of compulsory national service.

Robertson greeted this news with jubilation. It was the prospect of opposition to this scheme within the Cabinet which played such a significant part in Lloyd George's rise to the premiership. This under-rated factor in the political crisis of December 1916 was a crucial example of the inherent problems of conducting war policy through a Cabinet of twenty-three members. Ironically, the decision to accept compulsory National Service was arrived at without delay, as a logical outcome of the findings of the Man-Power Distribution Board. Lloyd George's acceptance of this principle provided the main element of continuity of the Coalition governments on the subject of manpower. In fact the discussion of National Service during Asquith's final weeks as Prime Minister, captured Lloyd George's imagination. His commitment to this advanced form of labour control, with few ideas as to how it might be organised, was to have a disastrous impact on the new government's early attempt to attain the 'efficient prosecution of the war'. The appointment of Neville Chamberlain reflected the general perplexity as to what form National Service should take.

The Prime Minister embodied the new efficiency of the 'Do it now' government.[4] To prove the correctness of this image National Service was promoted as a concrete response to the high expectations which were raised by Lloyd George's speech on war policy on 19 December 1916. During January 1917 the War Cabinet was reminded by Arthur Henderson of the extent of hostility among engineering trade unions to 'industrial conscription'.[5] Political constraints led to the rejection of Chamberlain's wide-ranging schemes to redirect labour to 'work of national importance' and, instead, his complete dependence on voluntarism. Compulsion became a 'threat' and the scheme of voluntary enrolment hopelessly failed to meet the expectation of the complete fluidity of labour. The National Service 'Stage Army' was of little more value to the war effort than the availability of cavalry divisions on the Western Front. The disappointment with the scheme's failure was all the more acute because the vocabulary of military organisation was employed in the local appeals for volunteers. Chamberlain persistently referred to 'industrial armies' as if Britain could be described as the rearward area of the front line. The central paradox of the voluntary appeal was the promotion of military formations as ideal forms of organisation, which could be applied to munition and shipbuilding industries in the third year of the war.

In reality, Chamberlain was utterly dependent on the manipulation of patriotic goodwill at a time when war weariness was the dominant response to the continuation of the conflict.

The National Service Department was not the success which has generally been judged of Lloyd George's framework of 'new ministries'. It became a byword for the collapse of an administrative structure in wartime which other ministers worked assiduously to avoid in their own spheres of responsibility.[6] Apart from the chaotic conditions at St Ermin's and the damaging effect of inter-departmental rivalry, Chamberlain had some cause for directing his complaints at the Prime Minister. Lloyd George created the department to implement some of the conclusions of the Man-Power Distribution Board and in response to the introduction of an advanced form of civil mobilisation in Germany which was more apparent than real. He was also disinclined to intervene in the search for an equitable balance of manpower for industrial and military purposes.[7] Similarly, apart from Lord Milner, the War Cabinet resisted the temptation to concern itself with the distribution of manpower. A picture does not emerge, as it has so often before, of an immediate improvement in Britain's ability to prosecute the war effort on Lloyd George's coming to power.

The failure of National Service led to an acutely unpopular piece of legislation which reflected the bankruptcy of Lloyd George's innovations on the manpower question. The reconstitution of the department followed the investigation of the recruiting machinery and, in particular, the Medical Boards by a Parliamentary Select Committee. It identified a profound sense of antipathy from ex-serviceman's organisations and the labour movement towards the medical re-examination of men, previously rejected or discharged as unfit, under the Military Service (Review of Exceptions) Act. Questions were asked in the House of Commons on the recruitment of 'the blind, the halt and the insane'. Such criticism forced the remarkable reform whereby the responsibility for military recruiting was transferred to civil control. For too long the military authorities at local level had persistently intervened in the sensitive political area of the retention of men for vital war work.[8] Initially, the appointment of Auckland Geddes, former Director of Recruiting, as Minister of National Service suggested that the civil department was too sympathetically staffed with former War Office personnel.[9] However, the transfer of recruiting to civil control was not a charade, but an important reform of the procedures which governed the release of men from war industries for military service.

Geddes occupied a unique political role at the juncture of civil–military relations. He participated in the movement to implement manpower plans in accordance with a defined inter-relationship of military operations and industrial production. Administrative expertise on manpower was concentrated in the Ministry of National Service and Geddes's ministerial position was buttressed by the climate of change which existed in the final months of 1917. In particular, the political will emerged at War Cabinet level to impose civil authority over the generals. The reason for the alteration of civil–military relations in favour of asserting political control over the conduct of the war lay in the focusing of attention on the relentlessly high level of 'wastage' on the Western Front for no clear material gain. Dissatisfaction with the casualty levels of 1917 led to Lloyd George's 'Paris Speech' on 12 November. Later that month, the expectation of a 'break-through' at Cambrai gave way to an unexpectedly strong German counter-attack. This sequence of events led ministers to question the possibility of military victory. Assisted by Geddes, the Cabinet Committee on Man-Power identified priority areas of labour supply. It demoted the importance of reinforcing the British armies in France in favour of shipbuilding, to assist the expansion of the American war effort, and aeroplane and tank output, thereby recognising the impact of technological change on and above the battle-field. Emphasis continues to be placed on the denial of reinforcements for France as if Lloyd George's government was engaged in a plot against its generals.[10] For example, the size of the British armies in France in January 1918 when compared with twelve months before, which formed the centre-piece of the celebrated 'Maurice debate'. This sense of conspiratorial activity is misleading, because it does not acknowledge the political and economic sensitivity of the manpower issue early in 1918. Quite simply the War Cabinet concluded that there were elements of the war effort which were more essential than the over-commitment of manpower on the Western Front. Hankey was not alone in concluding that 'by raising an army beyond the capacity of our man-power to maintain' too great a strain had been placed on essential manufacturing output.[11] Consequently, in 1918, but only then, clear principles of military recruitment were established in relation to priority areas of war production.

The importance of balancing this equation was a major lesson of the war which was noted by Churchill's War Cabinet in the Second World War. Early in 1941 it became committed to the principle that military recruitment should be geared to munitions supply. In September 1940 William Beveridge was appointed chairman of the Manpower Requirements committee and he drew on his experience as a munitions official in 1916. He was involved in the planning of industrial enlistment schemes for the Man-Power Distribution Board and as Lloyd George avoided the adoption of compulsory National Service, Beveridge's career became a casualty of the government's reluctance to mobilise labour.[12] Soon after Asquith's resignation he transferred to the Ministry of Food. In 1940 he was again pressing for the 'total mobilization of the civilian labour market'.[13] He also sought an exact definition of Reserved Occupations and a register of skilled engineers. Though his reports to the Production Council were discussed in full by the representatives of departments involved in war output, Beveridge's plans reminded Ernest Bevin too much of the factors which lay behind industrial unrest during the First World War. As a veteran trade unionist, Ernest Bevin assumed control in May 1940 of a department which combined the functions of managing industrial relations and recruitment.[14] As Minister of Labour and National Service he gained the control of manpower which approximated more closely to Geddes's experience than the nebulous role which Chamberlain had adopted. However, Bevin was not an imperious 'expert' on manpower, but the embodiment of the deep expression of popular consent to the government's manpower plans which Churchill could expect as a result of his appointment. Consequently, through consultative procedures and more circumspect intervention, manpower planning had the appearance of being less coercive and more clearly defined in relation to objectives in 1941 than was the case in 1917. The greater degree of consensus which Bevin sought was secured, in large measure, as a result of the lessons which were drawn from the experience of manpower 'co-ordinating authorities' in the First World War.

Until 1918 the implementation of the British government's manpower plans usually depended on *ad hoc* responses which provided, temporarily, weak manpower authorities. The development of 'zones' of departmental interest and expertise in the employment of labour precluded the concentrated control of manpower in one central department. Consequently, the co-ordination of the nation's labour resources depended on the bi-lateral agreements which were reached between autonomous 'employing' departments on specific aspects of the supply and allocation of manpower.

The totality of the war effort was not apparent, in relation to manpower, during the local implementation of the enrolment campaign for National Service volunteers. The voluntary campaign characterised by public meetings, pulpit messages, door-to-door canvass and propagandist literature was an organisational approach more appropriate to the heady days of September 1914. The 'Treasury Agreement' and the Munitions of War Act of 1915 had not led to a level of industrial organisation which could be described as a nation-in-arms. In 1917 the notion of voluntarism, despite its poor results, was regarded as of greater utility to the process of substitution in vital war work than the introduction of 'industrial compulsion'. It should not therefore be automatically assumed that the relationship between the government, Home Army and civil worker was pervaded by the notion of 'general compulsion' after the introduction of military conscription. There were no 'industrial armies' in Britain during the war.

There certainly were many attempts to organise civilian work along military lines. Unionist publicists supported the 'continental commitment' by urging that Britain should transform itself into a 'base depot'. Men conscripted for military service were employed on civil war work, notably in 'agricultural companies'. In 1915 some experimental units were established to conduct civil work in military formations, including the Liverpool Dock Battalion which was raised by Lord Derby. However, these schemes originated, in part, from the obsession of retaining a large Home defence force in Britain to counter an invasion or a raid-in-depth on the east coast. By 1917 the suggestion that the War Office should intervene further in the organisation of essential war production attracted little support. In fact the inability of the Recruiting Department to ward off criticism of the enlistment machinery led to the transfer of this time-honoured function of the War Office to civil control. The subordination of the military authorities to political control on the manpower issue was enforced during the development of the

Ministry of National Service and extended by the conclusions of the Cabinet Committee on Man-Power.

The importance of the Ministry of National Service was apparent in the government's response to the German spring offensive in March 1918. The expertise of Geddes and his staff enabled the War Cabinet to direct its response to the military manpower shortage through the independent mediation of its 'General Staff'. Consequently, the plans for the reinforcement of the British armies in France achieved a fine balance between the need to despatch drafts overseas and the fundamental importance of maintaining shipbuilding, coal and food production. The plans consisted of a substantial reduction in the size of the Home Army and the further 'combing out' of men from industry by legislation and the revision of the Schedule of Protected Occupations. By a staggered withdrawal of certificates of exemptions in separate occupations and different age groups, the fierce hostility which would have arisen to a comprehensive scheme of 'industrial compulsion' was defused. The flexibility of approach provided by the legislative framework of the Military Service Acts gave the government an effective method of regulating manpower levels in essential war production in 1918.

In the crisis of the Allied withdrawal from hard-won, but barely fortified, positions on the Western Front in April 1918 the uncertainties of three years of discussions on the supply and allocation of manpower were extinguished. A 'new totality' had arisen in an industrialised war effort which was no longer compartmentalised. The War Cabinet recognised that at the planning level the relationship between the condition of the battle-field and the capacity of industrial production could not be disregarded. In this sensitive political area the search for a single central manpower authority was concluded by bringing the labour supply branches into an ordered relationship with the War Cabinet through the co-ordinating executive power of the Ministry of National Service. Even in April 1918 the opposition of civil departments and trade unions to the complete mobilisation of labour ensured that Sir Auckland Geddes did not become the Controller of Manpower and St. Ermin's was not transformed into a *de facto* Ministry of Manpower. Nevertheless, the War Cabinet's distrust of GHQ's capacity to achieve strategic objectives commensurate with the supply of men to the army vastly strengthened Geddes's position as supply of men to the army vastly strengthened Geddes's position as the government's adviser on manpower. Macready's advice was discarded and in the remaining months of the war the supply of men for military service was strictly regulated under political control. The rise of the Ministry of National Service in the final year of the war reflected the War Cabinet's belated realisation that the control of military manpower was too important a matter to be left to the generals.

Notes

1 Earl of Ronaldshay, *The Life of Lord Curzon*, London, 1928, III, pp. 136–7.
2 Robertson, *Soldiers and Statesmen*, I, p. 294.
3 Newton, *Lord Lansdowne*, p. 442.
4 See the cartoon in *Punch*, 20 December 1916, p. 423, which depicted Lloyd George as 'The New Conductor' of the orchestra at the 'Opening of the 1917 Overture'.
5 See Lloyd George mss. F/1/3/19(b)3, Memorandum, Addison, 21 May 1917.
6 Lord Beaverbrook feared that the Ministry of Information might be 'snuffed out of existence as befell Neville Chamberlain'. Bonar Law mss. 83/6/40, Beaverbrook to Lord Reading, draft letter, 22 August 1918.
7 Murray–Robertson mss. Add. Ms. 52462, Robertson to Murray, 13 February 1917.
8 For the 'serious raids' of recruiting officers on agricultural labour see Milner mss. dep. 45, A. Lee to Milner, 1 June 1917.
9 R. Smillie, *My Life for Labour*, London, 1924, pp. 232–3.
10 D. R. Woodward, 'Did Lloyd George starve the British Army of men prior to the German offensive of 21 March 1918?', *Historical Journal*, XXVII, 1984, pp. 241–52, and *Lloyd George and the Generals*, London, 1983, pp. 296–304; Major-General Sir Frederick Maurice in N. Maurice (ed.), *The Maurice Case*, London, 1972, pp. 93–105.
11 Hankey mss. HNKY 4/10, Hankey to Esher, 18 September 1918, unsigned copy.
12 Lord Beveridge, *Power and Influence*, London, 1953, pp. 140–1.
13 J. Harris, *William Beveridge. A Biography*, Oxford, 1977, p. 370.
14 J. M. Lee, *The Churchill Coalition 1940–1945*, London, 1980, p. 33; Bevin to Churchill, 13 May 1940, quoted in A. Bullock, *The Life and Times of Ernest Bevin*, London, 1960, I, p. 653; M. Gowing, 'The organisation of manpower in Britain during the Second World War', *Journal of Contemporary History*, VII, 1972, pp. 151–5.

List of appendices

1 Men available for military service in England and Wales. Estimate made by the Registrar-General's Committee, 6 October 1915

Estimate of the number of men available in England and Wales based on returns covering 90% of the population

---

Men of military age returned in the Register	4,385,000
Men who should be reserved for industrial requirements	2,720,000
Gross total available for military service	1,665,000
Deduct for physically unfit included in above	
[This figure of approximately 15% was derived	251,500
from the experience of the Army Medical Boards]	
Net number available	1,413,000

The Committee advised that the estimate be treated as an upper limit and even so subject to considerations, i.e. that more women be employed in industry and that some services be reduced. The figures given above were strictly limited to men between the ages of 19 and 41 years. In addition to the estimate during any 12 months 320,000 youths normally attain military age, though that number would not be available without deductions.

Source: Beveridge mss., Collection on Food Control, Coll. Misc. 92 vol. 1.

2   General review, man-power position, 12 December 1916

Figures according to latest available returns

Strength of army – overseas Expeditionary Forces, Garrisons, etc.	1,500,000
Strength of army – at home	1,535,000
Category A men *at home*	704,000
less men in category A(iv)	46,000
	658,000

Distributed

In home service units	11,000	
Units earmarked for overseas	95,000	
New units authorised to be formed for overseas	133,500	
Skilled artificers	18,000	
[Total]		258,000
Available for drafts		400,000

Estimated Forces to be maintained in the field during 1917	1,700,000
Of these 800,000 are Infantry and require replacement by newly trained men – that is, exclusive of returned sick and wounded – to the extent of 73% of their strength	584,000
900,000 are arms other than Infantry and require replacement by newly trained men – that is, exclusive of returned sick and wounded – to the extent of 24% of their strength	216,000
Total recruits required category A	800,000
In addition about 140,000 B(i) and C(i) men will be required	140,000
Grand total [required in 1917]	940,000

Balance sheet for British Army for 1917
    [On the assumption that an estimated force of 1,710,000 was to be maintained in the field during 1917].

[Expected] Liabilities

Requirements overseas	210,00•
Estimated wastage	1,500,00•
Total	1,710,00•

[Assumed] assets

In depots in training carried over from 1916	400,00•
Category A recruits 1917 [see previous page]	800,00•
1916 casualties becoming fit for G[eneral] S[ervice]	180,00•
1917 Casualties becoming fit for G[eneral] S[ervice]	300,00•
A(iv) who attain 19 years of age	30,00•
Total	1,710,00•

Source: A. Chamberlain mss.
AC 16/1//24, General Review. Man-Power Position (Great Britain only), D[irector of] R[ecruiting], [Auckland Geddes], 12 December 1916.

3   The civil reservoir of man-power in October 1917

Total males in civil life approximately   8,000,000
Total males of military age in civil life   3,600,000
Total males of 18–25 years in civil life approximately   800,000
Estimated total of males of 18–25 years in civil life fit   270,000
    for category A

Of   270,000   young
men,
    approximately   90,000   in coal mines
                      100,000   in/about shipyards, marine engineering
                                shops, and munition works (including
                                some of most highly skilled men at their
                                trades)
                       70,000   Agriculture, railways, transport trades
    and the remaining   10,000   scattered under various headings and
                                cannot be counted on for the Army to
                                any extent

At the outside 150,000–160,000 of these young men, it is estimated, can be
obtained for the Army and it is estimated it will take 8 months to recruit
them.

Source: PRO CAB 27/8 G.T. 2295, Recruiting Position. The Problem and
Prospects, A. Geddes, 13 October 1917.

4   Projected 'Assets' and 'Liabilities' of all arms for the period 28 March to 31 July 1918

The additional provision of men considered necessary by the Army Council

Assets		Liabilities	
Drafts under orders to 31 March 1918	51,800	New units	52,000
Drafts during April, May, June & July	121,000	Deficiency establishment in France	49,000
Sick and wounded becoming fit in France, 4 months at 12,500 a month	50,000	4 days' casualties at 12,000 a day 28–31 March	48,000
		4 months' heavy fighting on basis of 1917 at 84,000 a month	336,000
Balance deficit July 31	282,000	Reinforcements, other theatres of war, say	20,000
	505,000		505,000

Source: PRO WO 32/9557, 'Balance Sheet' dated 28 March 1918, attached to Memorandum by the Army Council indicating the number of men of all arms necessary to maintain the forces in the field, 29 March 1918.

5 Complete monthly returns of enlistments for the army in the First World War

Enlistments for the Regular Army and Territorial Force from August 1914 to November 1918 in Great Britain and Ireland

1914		1915		1916	
August	298,923	January	156,290	January	65,965
September	462,901	February	87,896	February	98,629
October	136,811	March	113,907	March	129,493
November	169,862	April	119,087	April	106,908
December	117,860	May	135,263	May	125,768
		June	114,679	June	156,386
	1,186,357	July	95,413	July	88,213
		August	95,980	August	111,771
		September	71,617	September	81,195
		October	113,285	October	97,684
		November	121,793	November	76,058
		December	55,152	December	52,005
			1,280,362		1,190,075

1917	Category 'A'	Under 'A'	Total
January	51,131	34,538	85,669
February	75,930	42,911	118,841
March	75,445	44,094	119,539
April	55,857	31,175	87,032
May	56,893	31,601	88,894
June	41,879	39,835	81,714
July	32,267	28,100	60,367
August	28,038	21,321	49,359
September	21,455	15,887	37,342
October	21,150	15,393	36,543
November	17,928	12,895	30,823
December			24,923
			820,646

1918			
January	18,906	16,244	35,150
February	20,402	13,320	33,722
March	20,069	10,128	30,197

April	66,525	11,773	78,298
May	71,113	12,906	84,019
June	72,572	16,378	88,950
July	44,379	14,981	59,360
August	21,016	8,902	29,918
September	15,615	6,935	22,550
October	16,715	7,053	23,768
November	5,018	2,512	7,530
			493,462

Grand total 4,970,902

	Total of population July 1914	Enlistment
England	34,618,346	4,006,158
Wales	2,489,202	272,924
Scotland	4,849,500	557,618
Ireland	4,374,500	134,202
	46,331,548	4,970,902

Source: PRO CAB 25/95, Enlistments for the Regular Army and Territorial Force, August 1914 to November 1918. This table formed part of the collection of statistics which were assembled by the Inter-Allied Committee on Manpower Statistics at the Supreme War Council. This Committee was established in September 1918 but its work was disrupted by disagreement between the British and French Permanent Military Representatives as to precisely what information should be exchanged, and how often, between the Allied military authorities on the subject of manpower. Consequently, the above table was by November 1918 of historical rather than military value.

6   The medical categorisation of military recruits

Categories	Description
A. Fit for general service.	(i) Men actually fit for general service in any theatre of war in all respects, both as regards training, physical and mental qualifications. (ii) Recruits who should be fit for A(i) as soon as trained. (iii)Men who have previously served with an Expeditionary Force who should be fit for A(i) as soon as 'hardened'. (iv) Men under 19 years of age who should be fit for A(i) or A(ii) as soon as they are 19 years of age.
B. Not fit for general service but fit for service in North-West Europe (and in any other theatre of war when specially passed)	(i) In field units and in Garrison units. (ii) In Labour units, or on Garrison Regimental outdoor employment. (iii)On sedentary work as clerks, store-men, batmen, cooks, order-lies, on sanitary duties, etc., or if skilled tradesmen, at their trades.
C. Fit for service at home only	(i) In Garrison or Provisional units. (ii) In Labour units, etc., as in B(ii). (iii)On sedentary work, etc. as in B(iii).
D. Temporarily unfit for service in A, B, or C, but likely to become fit within six months, and mean-while either –	(i) In Command Depots. (ii) In Regimental Depots. (iii)In any unit or depot under or awaiting medical or dental treatment (who on completion of treatment will rejoin their own original category).
E. Unfit for service in A, B or C and not likely to become fit within six months.	Awaiting discharge, re-classification or invalided home from abroad.

Sources: compiled from Milner mss. dep. 144, Monthly Summary of Strength of Expeditionary Forces and of Forces at Home, May 1917; and Milner mss. dep. 145, Summaries of the Weekly Return of the British Army and Dominion Contingents at Home, Returns dated 28 October 1918.

Bibliography

Manuscript sources

1 Departmental records

At the Public Records Office, London:
Cabinet.
Home Office.
Ministry of Labour.
Ministry of Munitions.
Ministry of National Service.
War Office

At the Imperial War Museum, London:
Man-Power Distribution Board (uncatalogued).

2 Private papers

Addison mss. (Bodleian Library, Oxford) (uncatalogued).
Asquith mss. (Bodleian Library, Oxford).
Balfour mss. (British Library, London).
Lt-Col. Sir Reginald Benson mss. (Liddell Hart Archives, King's College, London).
W. H. Beveridge mss.
Beveridge Collection on Munitions.
Beveridge Collection on Food Control (British Library of Political and Economic Science, London).
Bonar Law mss. (House of Lords Record Office, London).
Cave mss. (British Library, London).
Cecil of Chelwood (Lord Robert Cecil) mss. (British Library, London).
Austen Chamberlain mss. (Birmingham University Library).
Neville Chamberlain mss. (Birmingham University Library).
Lt-Gen. Sir Sydney Clive mss. (Liddell Hart Archives, King's College, London).
Croft mss. (Churchill College, Cambridge).
Davidson mss. (House of Lords Record Office, London).
Derby mss. (17th Earl) (Liverpool Central Library).
French mss. (Imperial War Museum, London).
Gwynne mss. (Bodleian Library, Oxford).
Haig mss. (National Library of Scotland, Edinburgh).

Hankey mss. (Churchill College, Cambridge).
Lewis, Viscount Harcourt mss. (Bodleian Library, Oxford).
Hewins mss. (Sheffield University Library).
Lt-Gen. Sir Launcelot Kiggell mss. (Liddell Hart Archives, King's College, London).
Kitchener mss. (Public Record Office, London).
E. M. H. Lloyd mss. (British Library of Political and Economic Science, London).
Lloyd George mss. (House of Lords Record Office, London).
Walter, Viscount Long mss. (British Library, London).
Violet Markham mss. (British Library of Political and Economic Science, London).
Midleton mss. (Public Record Office, London).
Milner mss. (Bodleian Library, Oxford).
Murray–Robertson mss. (British Library, London).
Northcliffe mss. (British Library, London).
Pringle mss. (microfilm) (House of Lords Record Office, London).
C. F. Rey mss. (Rhodes House Library, Oxford).
Robertson mss. (Liddell Hart Archives, King's College, London).
C. P. Scott mss. (Guardian Archives) (Manchester University Library) (uncatalogued).
Frances Stevenson mss. (House of Lords Record Office, London).
St Loe Strachey mss. (House of Lords Record Office, London).
Swinton mss. (Philip Lloyd-Greame) (Churchill College, Cambridge).
Weir mss. (Churchill College, Cambridge).
Wilson mss. (Imperial War Museum, London).

The following microfilm collections were examined:
Diary of Beatrice Webb (Mf685);
Minutes of the National Executive Committee of the Labour Party (Mfx5);
Minutes of the Parliamentary Committee of the Trades Union Congress (M769).

3   *Recruiting and tribunal papers*

Minutes of the Parliamentary Recruiting Committee, 1914–16, Add. Ms. 54192 (British Library, London).
Minutes of the Middlesex County Recruiting Committee, 1915, L/101 (Greater London Record Office).
Letter book of Thornton-Cleveleys Local Tribunal, 1916–18, and National Service Committee, 1917, UD Th3/23 (Lancashire County Record Office).
Alderman J. Kellett mss. (chairman of Audenshaw Local Tribunal, 1916–18), M138/66–7 (Manchester Central Library).
Register of cases at the Kingswinford Local Tribunal, 1916–18, D585/187/1/1–2 and Military Tribunal mss. (case-notes of applicants at Leek Local Tribunal) 1916–18, D.3359 (Staffordshire County Record Office).

Printed Primary Sources

4   *Official publications*

Command papers

Cd. 8149   Report on Recruiting by the Earl of Derby, 1914–16.

Cd. 8168   Report on Recruiting in Ireland, 1914–16.

Cd. 8617   Instructions issued by the Army Council in connection with the Military Service (Review of Exceptions) Act, 1917.

Cd. 8833   National Service Instruction (N.S.I.) No.2 Constitution and Organisation of Regions, Regional Headquarters and Transfer of Recruiting to Civil Control under the Minister of National Service, 15 November 1917.

Cd. 8834   N.S.I. No.3 General Directions for the Guidance of Commissioners, Deputy Commissioners, and Members of Medical Boards.

Cd. 8835   N.S.I. No.6 Instruction re. Grade III, 1 November 1917.

Cd. 8836   N.S.I. No.7 Medical Grades in relation to Exemption.

Cd. 8838   N.S.I. No.13 Medical Grades of the National Service Medical Boards, 17 November 1917.

Cd. 8840   N.S.I. No.16 Medical Grades. Attitude of National Service Representatives before Tribunals, 20 November 1917.

Cd. 9005   The War Cabinet, Report for the year 1917. 1918.

Cmd. 325   The War Cabinet, Report for the year 1918. 1919.

Special Report and Report from the Select Committee on the Military Service (Review of Exceptions) Act 1917, Parliamentary Papers, 1917–18, III (126, 195).

HMSO, Notes on the administration of the group system, War Office, London, 1915.

HMSO, Supplement to Notes on the administration of Group and Class Systems, War Office, London, 1916.

HMSO, Schedule of Protected Occupations for men employed on Admiralty, War Office or Munitions Work, or in Railway Workshops, Ministry of Munitions, London, 1917.

Pamphlets on the substitution of women in industry for enlisted men, Home Office & Board of Trade, London, 2nd ed., 1917.

HMSO, *History of the Ministry of Munitions*, 8 vols., London, 1921–2.

HMSO, *History of the War. Military Operations*, Brig-Gen. J. E. Edmonds (general editor and chief compiler), *Egypt and Palestine*, 2 vols., 1928–30; *France and Belgium*, 13 vols. of text, 1922–48; *The Campaign in Mesopotamia*, 4 vols; 1923–7.

HMSO, *The Labour Gazette*.

HMSO, *Parliamentary Debates*, House of Commons, Fifth Series.

HMSO, *Statistics of the Military Effort of the British Empire during the Great War*, War Office, London, 1922.

5   *Contemporary works*

C. Addison, *The Manufacture of Munitions*, London, 1916.

C. Addison, *British Workshops and the War*, London, 1917.

W. Appleton, *The Worker's Resolve*, London, 1917.

G. D. H. Cole, *Labour in War Time*, London, 1915.
W. Crooks, *The British Workman Defends His Home*, London, 1917.
Lord Curzon, *Germany's Move and Britain's Answer*, London, 1916.
H. A. L. Fisher, *The British Share in the War*, London, 1915.
H. Gosling, *Peace : How to get and keep it*, London, 1917.
Lord Grey, *Twenty-five Years, 1892–1916*, 2 vols., London, 1925.
W. G. Hawtin, *The Law and Practice of Military Conscription under the Military Service Acts*, 2 vols., London, 1917–8.
A. Hope, *Militarism : German and British*, London, 1915.
J. W. Kneeshaw, *Conscription enters the Workshop*, London, 1916.
J. W. Kneeshaw, *How Conscription Works*, London, 1917.
D. Lloyd George, *When the War will End*, London, 1917.
D. Lloyd George, *British War Aims*, London, 1918.
D. Lloyd George, *The Worst is Over*, London, 1918.
D. Lloyd George, *The Great Crusade. Extracts from Speeches delivered during the War*, London, 1918.
F. A. McKenzie, *Through the Hindenburg Line. Crowning Days on the Western Front*, London, 1918.
E. Montagu, *The Means of Victory*, London, 1916.
C. E. Montague, *Disenchantment*, London, reprint, 1924.
H. Quigley, *Passchendaele and the Somme. A Diary of 1917*, London, 1928.
H. Samuel, *The War and Liberty and an Address on Reconstruction*, London, 1917.
J. C. Smuts, *The Coming Victory*, London, 1917.
J. C. Smuts, *General Smuts' Message to South Wales*, New York, 1918.
H. G. Wells, *Mr. Britling Sees it Through*, London, reprint, 1933.
D. Williamson, *Lloyd George. A Man of the People*, New York, 1917.
J. H. Worrall, *The Tribunal Hand-Book*, London, 4th ed., 1917.
J. H. Worrall, *Tribunal Law for Sole Proprietors of Businesses*, London, 1917.

6 *Diaries and memoirs*
C. Addison, *Politics from Within, 1911–1918*, 2 vols; London, 1924.
C. Addison, *Four and a Half Years*, 2 vols., London, 1934.
L. S. Amery, *My Political Life*, vol. 2, London, 1953.
Lord Askwith, *Industrial Problems and Disputes*, London, 1920.
G. N. Barnes, *From Workshop to War Cabinet*, London, 1924.
J. Barnes & D. Nicholson (eds.), *The Leopold Amery Diaries*, vol. 1, London, 1980.
Lord Beveridge, *Power and Influence*, London, 1953.
R. Blake (ed.), *The Private Papers of Douglas Haig 1914–1919*, London, 1952.
M. Bondfield, *A Life's Work*, London, 1949.
Viscount Cecil of Chelwood, *All the Way*, London, 1949.
A. Chamberlain, *Down the Years*, London, 3rd ed., 1935.
Brig-Gen. J. Charteris, *At G.H.Q.*, London, 1931.
A. Clark (ed.), *'A Good Innings'. The Private Papers of Viscount Lee of Fareham*, London, 1974.
Janet E. Courtney, *The Women of My Time*, London, 1934.

Lord Croft, *My Life of Strife*, London, 1948.
Brig-Gen. F. P. Crozier, *A Brass Hat in No Man's Land*, Bath, reprint, 1968.
E. David (ed.), *Inside Asquith's Cabinet. From the Diaries of Charles Hobhouse*, London, 1977.
Lord Ernle, *Whippingham to Westminster. The Reminiscences of Lord Ernle (Rowland Prothero)*, London, 1938.
Oliver, Viscount Esher (ed.), *Journals and Letters of Reginald, Viscount Esher*, vols. 3 & 4, London, 1938.
S. Fay, *The War Office at War*, London, 1937.
A. Fitzroy, *Memoirs*, 2 vols., London, 6th ed., 1925.
Katherine Furse, *Hearts and Pomegranates. The Story of Forty-five Years*, London, 1940.
W. Gallacher, *Revolt on the Clyde*, London, 4th ed., 1978.
A. C. Geddes, *The Forging of a Family*, London, 1952.
H. Gough, *The Fifth Army*, London, 1931.
H. Gough, *Soldiering On*, London, 1954.
R. Graves, *Goodbye to All That*, Harmondsworth, reprint, 1960.
A. Griffith-Boscawen, *Memories*, London, 1925.
S. Gwynn (ed.), *The Anvil of War. Letters between F. S. Oliver and his brother 1914–1918*, London, 1936.
W. K. Hancock and J. van der Poel, *Selections from the Smuts Papers*, vol. 3, Cambridge, 1966.
R. Hart-Davis (ed.), *Siegfried Sassoon Diaries 1915–1918*, London, 1983.
J. Hodge, *Workman's Cottage to Windsor Castle*, London, 1931.
B. H. Liddell Hart, *Memoirs*, 2 vols., London, 1965.
D. Lloyd George, *War Memoirs*, 6 vols., London, 1933–6.
Viscount Long of Wraxall, *Memories*, London, 1923.
E. Ludendorff, *My War Memories 1914–1918*, 2 vols., London, 1919.
M. Macdonagh, *In London during the Great War*, London, 1935.
C. F. N. Macready, *Annals of an Active Life*, 2 vols., London, 1924.
Violet Markham, *Return Passage*, London, 1953.
N. Maurice (ed.), *The Maurice Case. From the Papers of Major-General Sir Frederick Maurice*, London, 1972.
K. Middlemas (ed.), *T. Jones : Whitehall Diary*, vol. 1, London, 1969.
Earl of Midleton, *Records and Reactions 1856–1939*, London, 1939.
W. M. R. Pringle, *Letters from a Politician to His Daughter*, London, 1931.
R. A. S. Redmayne, *Men, Mines and Memories*, London, 1942.
C. à C. Repington, *The First World War, 1914–1918*, London, 1920.
R. Rhodes James, *Memoirs of a Conservative. J. C. C. Davidson's Memoirs and Papers, 1910–37*, London, 1969.
Viscountess Rhondda, *This Was My World*, London, 1933.
Lord Riddell, *War Diary, 1914–1918*, London, 1933.
W. Robertson, *From Private to Field-Marshal*, London, 1921.
W. Robertson, *Soldiers and Statesmen 1914–1918*, 2 vols., London, 1926.
Viscount Samuel, *Memoirs*, London, 1945.
J. Sexton, *Agitator. The life of the dockers' M.P.*, London, 1936.
R. Smillie, *My Life for Labour*, London, 1924.
Lord Swinton, *I Remember*, London, 1948.

Lord Swinton, *Sixty Years of Power*, London, 1966.
Lord Sydenham, *My Working Life*, London, 1927.
S. Tallents, *Man and Boy*, London, 1943.
A. J. P. Taylor (ed.), *My Darling Pussy. The letters of Lloyd George and Frances Stevenson 1913–41*, London, 1975.
A. Temple Patterson (ed.), *The Jellicoe Papers*, vol. 2 (Navy Records Society, vol. 111), London, 1968.
J. H. Thomas, *My Story*, London, 1937.
B. Tillett, *Memories and Reflections*, London, 1931.
H. Wickham Steed, *Through Thirty Years*, 2 vols., London, 1924.
T. Wilson, (ed.), *The Political Diaries of C. P. Scott 1911–1928*, London, 1970.

Printed secondary sources

7   *Biographies*

G. Arthur, *General Sir John Maxwell*, London, 1932.
R. Blake, *The Unknown Prime Minister : the life and times of Andrew Bonar Law*, London, 1955.
V. Bonham-Carter, *Soldier True. The Life and Times of Field-Marshal Sir William Robertson*, London, 1963.
A. Bullock, *The Life and Times of Ernest Bevin*, vol. 1, London, 1960.
J. R. M. Butler, *Lord Lothian*, London, 1960.
Maj-Gen. C. E. Callwell, *Field-Marshal Sir Henry Wilson. His Life and Diaries*, 2 vols., London, 1927.
G. H. Cassar, *Kitchener. Architect of Victory*, London, 1977.
R. S. Churchill, *Lord Derby, 'King of Lancashire'*, London, 1959.
B. Collier, *Brasshat. A biography of Field-Marshal Sir Henry Wilson*, London, 1961.
J. A. Cross, *Lord Swinton*, Oxford, 1982.
D. Dilks, *Neville Chamberlain*, vol. 1, Cambridge, 1984.
Blanche E. C. Dugdale, *Arthur James Balfour*, vol. 2, London, 1936.
D. Dutton, *Austen Chamberlain : Gentleman in Politics*, Bolton, 1985.
D. H. Elletson, *The Chamberlains*, London, 1966.
A. Farrar-Hockley, *Goughie. The Life of General Sir Hubert Gough*, London, 1975.
K. Feiling, *Life of Neville Chamberlain*, London, 1946.
P. Fraser, *Lord Esher : a political biography*, London, 1973.
M. Gilbert, *Winston S. Churchill*, vols. 3 & 4, London, 1971 & 1975.
J. Grigg, *Lloyd George : From Peace to War, 1912–1916*, London, 1985.
D. Gwynn, *The Life of John Redmond*, London, 1932.
M. A. Hamilton, *Arthur Henderson*, London, 1938.
W. K. Hancock, *Smuts. The Sanguine Years 1870–1919*, Cambridge, 1962.
J. Harris, *William Beveridge*, Oxford, 1977.
R. Holmes, *The Little Field-Marshal. Sir John French*, London, 1981.
T. Jones, *Lloyd George*, London, 1951.

S. Koss, *Fleet Street Radical. A. G. Gardiner and the 'Daily News'*, London, 1973.

S. Koss, *Asquith*, London, 1976.

F. S. L. Lyons, *John Dillon : a biography*, London, 1968.

I. Macleod, *Neville Chamberlain*, London, 1961.

P. Magnus, *Kitchener. Portrait of an Imperialist*, Harmondsworth, 1968.

V. R. Markham, *May Tennant. A Portrait*, London, 1949.

S. McKenna, *Reginald McKenna. 1863–1948*, London, 1948.

R. J. Minney, *Viscount Addison. Leader of the Lords*, London, 1958.

H. Montgomery Hyde, *Neville Chamberlain*, London, 1976.

K. & J. Morgan, *Portrait of a Progressive. The Political Career of Christopher, Viscount Addison*, Oxford, 1980.

Lord Newton, *Lord Lansdowne. A Biography*, London, 1929.

T. H. O'Brien, *Milner. Viscount Milner of St. James's and Cape Town*, London, 1979.

F. Owen, *Tempestuous Journey. Lloyd George, his life and times*, London, 1954.

C. Petrie, *The Life and Letters of Rt. Hon. Sir Austen Chamberlain*, 2 vols., London, 1940.

J. Pope-Hennessy, *Lord Crewe (1858–1945). The Likeness of a Liberal*, London, 1955.

L. Raskay, *Neville Chamberlain*, London, 1938.

W. J. Reader, *Architect of Air Power. The Life of the first Viscount Weir of Eastwood 1877–1959*, London, 1968.

R. Rhodes James, *Churchill : A Study in Failure 1900–1939*, Harmondsworth, reprint, 1981.

Viscountess Rhondda, *D. A. Thomas, Viscount Rhondda by His Daughter and others*, London, 1921.

K. Robbins, *Sir Edward Grey. A Biography of Lord Grey of Fallodon*, London, 1971.

W. R. Rock, *Neville Chamberlain*, New York, 1969.

Earl of Ronaldshay, *The Life of Lord Curzon*, 3 vols., London, 1928.

S. Roskill, *Hankey. Man of Secrets*, vol. 1, London, 1970.

S. Salvidge, *Salvidge of Liverpool. Behind the Political Scene 1890–1928*, London, 1934.

J. Schneer, *Ben Tillett. Portrait of a Labour Leader*, London, 1982.

J. A. Spender & C. Asquith, *Life of Herbert Henry Asquith. Lord Oxford and Asquith*, 2 vols., London, 1932.

A. Strachey, *St. Loe Strachey : his life and his paper*, London, 1930.

A. J. P. Taylor, *Beaverbrook*, London, 1972.

H. A. Taylor, *Robert Donald*, London, 1934.

J. Terraine, *Douglas Haig : The Educated Soldier*, London, 1963.

S. D. Waley, *Edwin Montagu*, London, 1964.

J. E. Wrench, *Alfred Lord Milner. The Man of No Illusions*, London, 1958.

A. W. Wright, *G. D. H. Cole and Socialist Democracy*, Oxford, 1979.

8   *Other published works*

R. J. Q. Adams, *Arms and the Wizard. Lloyd George and the Ministry of Munitions 1915–1916*, London, 1978.

S. L. Andrewski, *Military Organisation and Society*, London, 2nd ed., 1968.

R. B. Armeson, *Total Warfare and Compulsory Labour. A Study of the Military–Industrial Complex in Germany during World War 1*, The Hague, 1964.

F. P. Armitage, *Leicester 1914–1918. The War-Time Story of a Midland Town*, Leicester, 1933.

W. Ashworth, *An Economic History of England 1870–1939*, London, 1960.

C. Barnett, *The Swordbearers. Supreme Command in the First World War*, Bloomington, Indiana, 1975.

Lord Beaverbrook, *Men and Power. 1917, 1918*, London, 1958.

J-J. Becker, *The Great War and the French People*, Leamington Spa, 1985.

M. Bentley, *The Liberal Mind, 1914–1929*, Cambridge, 1977.

G. Braybon, *Women workers in the First World War : The British experience*, London, 1981.

K. Burgess, *The Challenge of Labour*, London, 1980.

K. Burk, *Britain, America and the Sinews of War 1914–1918*, London, 1985.

Viscount Camrose, *British Newspapers and their Controllers*, London, 1947.

W. S. Churchill, *The World Crisis*. 6 vols., London, 1923–31.

A. Clark, *The Donkeys*, London, 1961.

P. Clarke, *Liberals and Social Democrats*, Cambridge, 1981.

C. Clausewitz, *On War*, Harmondsworth, reprint, 1968.

A. Clinton, *The trade union rank and file. Trade Councils in Britain, 1900–40*, Manchester, 1977.

G. D. H. Cole, *Labour in the Coal-mining Industry*, London, 1923.

G. D. H. Cole, *Trade Unionism and Munitions*, London, 1923.

C. R. M. F. Cruttwell, *A History of the Great War 1914–1918*, London, reprint, 1982.

G. Dallas & D. Gill, *The Unknown Army. Mutinies in the British Army in World War 1*, London, 1985.

G. Dangerfield, *The Damnable Question. A Study in Anglo-Irish Relations*, London, 1979.

J. Darrocott & B. Loftus, *First World War Posters*, London, 1972.

J. Davies, *The Prime Minister's Secretariat 1916–1920*, Newport, Monmouth, 1951.

N. F. Dixon, *On the Psychology of Military Incompetence*, London, 1979.

J. A. Fairlie, *British War Administration*, New York, 1919.

C. Falls, *The First World War*, London, 1960.

C. E. Fayle, *The War and the Shipping Industry*, London, 1927.

G. D. Feldman, *Army, industry and labour in Germany, 1914–1918*, Princeton, 1966.

M. Ferro, *The Great War 1914–1918*, London, 1973.

S. E. Finer, *The Man on Horseback*, Harmondsworth, 2nd ed., 1976.

D. French, *British Economic and Strategic Planning 1905–1915*, London, 1982.

V. W. Germains, *The Kitchener Armies*, London, 1930.

J. Gooch, *The Plans of War. The General Staff and British Military Strategy c. 1900–1916*, London, 1974.

J. Gooch, *The Prospect of War. Studies in British Defence Policy, 1847–1942*, London, 1981.

H. Gordon, *The War Office*, London, 1935.

J. W. Graham, *Conscription and Conscience*, London, 1922.

P. Guinn, *British Strategy and Politics 1914 to 1918*, Oxford, 1965.

Lord Hankey, *The Supreme Command, 1914–1918*, 2 vols., London, 1961.

G. Hardach, *The First World War 1914–1918*, London, 1977.

J. Hinton, *The First Shop Stewards' Movement*, London, 1973.

A. Horne, *The Price of Glory. Verdun 1916*, Harmondsworth, reprint, 1981.

A. Horne, *The French Army and Politics 1870–1970*, London, 1984.

M. Howard, *The Continental Commitment*, London, 1974.

H. Keatley Moore, *Croydon and the Great War*, Croydon, 1920.

J. Keegan, *The Face of Battle*, Harmondsworth, 1978.

T. C. Kennedy, *The Hound of Conscience*, Fayetteville, Arkansas, 1981.

M. Kitchen, *The Silent Dictatorship*, London, 1976.

J. M. Lee, *The Churchill Coalition 1940–1945*, London, 1980.

E. J. Leed, *No Man's Land. Combat and Identity in World War 1*, Cambridge, 1981.

B. H. Liddell Hart, *History of the First World War*, London, reprint, 1972.

H. Llewellyn Smith, *The Board of Trade*, London, 1928.

E. M. H. Lloyd, *Experiments in State Control at the War Office and the Ministry of Food*, London, 1924.

R. Lowe, *Adjusting to Democracy. The Role of the Ministry of Labour in British Politics 1916–1939*, Oxford, 1986.

L. Macassey, *Labour Politics – False and True*, London, 1922.

J. M. Mackintosh, *The British Cabinet*, London, 1962.

A. Marwick, *The Deluge. British Society and the First World War*, London, 1965.

A. Marwick, *War and Social Change in the twentieth century*, London, 1974.

R. B. McDowell, *The Irish Convention 1917–1918*, London, 1970.

A. Mendelssohn Bartholdy, *The War and German Society*, New Haven, 1937.

K. Middlemas, *Politics in Industrial Society*, London, 1980.

K. O. Morgan, *Rebirth of a Nation. Wales 1880–1980*, Oxford, 1982.

K. Neilson, *Strategy and Supply : The Anglo-Russian Alliance 1914–17*, London, 1984.

W. H. Oakley, *Guildford in the Great War*, Guildford, 1934.

J. M. Osborne, *The Voluntary Recruiting Movement in Britain 1914–1916*, New York, 1982.

E. S. Pankhurst, *The Home Front*, London, 1932.

H. M. D. Parker, *Manpower. A study of War-time Policy and Administration*, London, 1957.

B. Pitt, *1918. The Last Act*, London, 1962.

C. E. Playne, *Britain Holds On 1917, 1918*, London, 1933.

J. Rae, *Conscience and Politics*, London, 1970.

W. J. Reader, *The Weir Group*, London, 1971.

R. A. S. Redmayne, *The British Coal-Mining Industry during the War*, London, 1924.

P. Renouvin, *The Forms of War Government in France*, New Haven, 1927.

K. Robbins, *The Abolition of War. The 'Peace Movement' in Britain, 1914–1919*, Cardiff, 1976.

K. Robbins, *The First World War*, Oxford, 1985.

J. D. Scott, *Vickers*, London, 1962.

W. R. Scott & J. Cunnison, *The Industries of the Clyde Valley during the War*, London, 1924.

P. Stansky (ed.), *The Left and War : The British Labour Party and World War I*, London, 1969.

J. Stevenson, *British Society 1914–45*, Harmondsworth, 1984.

G. F. Stone & C. Wells, *Bristol and the Great War 1914–1919*, Bristol, 1920.

N. Stone, *The Eastern Front 1914–1917*, London, 1975.

A. J. P. Taylor, *English History 1914–1945*, London, 1970.

J. Terraine, *The Western Front 1914–1918*, London, 1964.

J. Terraine, *The First World War 1914–1918*, London, 1984.

J. Turner, *Lloyd George's Secretariat*, Cambridge, 1980.

P. J. Waller, *Democracy and Sectarianism. A political and social history of Liverpool 1868–1939*, Liverpool, 1981.

I. C. Willis, *England's Holy War*, New York, 1928.

J. M. Winter, *Socialism and the Challenge of War*, London, 1974.

H. Wolfe, *Labour Supply and Regulation*, London, 1923.

D. R. Woodward, *Lloyd George and the Generals*, London, 1983.

L. Woodward, *Great Britain and the War of 1914–1918*, London, 1967.

G. Wootton, *The Politics of Influence. British ex-servicemen, Cabinet decisions and cultural change (1917–57)*, London, 1963.

C. J. Wrigley, *David Lloyd George and the British Labour Movement*, Hassocks, 1976.

9   Articles

O. Anderson, 'Early experiences of the man-power problem in an industrial society at war, Great Britain, 1854–56', *Political Science Quarterly*, LXXXII, 1967, pp. 526–45.

I. Beckett, 'The nation in arms 1914–1918', in I. F. W. Beckett & K. Simpson (eds.), *A Nation in Arms. A Social Study of the British Army in the First World War*, Manchester, 1985, pp. 1–35.

D. G. Boyce, 'British opinion, Ireland, and the war, 1916–1918', *Historical Journal*, XVII, 1974, pp. 573–93.

J. A. M. Caldwell, 'The Genesis of the Ministry of Labour', *Public Administration*, XXXVII, 1959, pp. 367–91.

R. Cuff, 'American mobilization for war 1917–45, Political culture vs. Bureaucratic administration', in N.F. Dreisziger (ed), Mobilization for Total War, Waterloo, Ontario, 1981, pp. 73–86.

E. David, 'The Liberal Party divided 1916–1918', *Historical Journal*, XIII, 1970, pp. 509–33.

R. Davidson, 'War-time Labour policy 1914–1916 : a reappraisal', *Journal of Scottish Labour History*, VIII, 1974, pp. 3–20.

P. E. Dewey, 'Agricultural labour supply in England and Wales during the First World War', *Economic History Review*, XXVIII, 1975, pp. 100–12.

P. E. Dewey, 'Military recruiting and the British labour force during the First World War', *Historical Journal*, XXVII, 1984, pp. 199–223.

R. Douglas, 'Voluntary enlistment in the First World War and the work of the Parliamentary Recruiting Committee', *Journal of Modern History*, XLII, 1970, pp. 564–85.

D. Dutton, 'The fall of General Joffre: an episode in the politico-military struggle in wartime Europe', *Journal of Strategic Studies*, I, 1978, pp. 338–51.

D. Englander & J. Osborne, 'Jack, Tommy and Henry Dubb : the armed forces and the working class', *Historical Journal*, XXI, 1978, pp. 593–621.

Lord Ernle, 'The food campaign of 1916–18', *Journal of the Royal Agricultural Society of England*, LXXXII, 1921, pp. 1–48.

E. V. Eves, 'The organisation of Man-Power', *Public Administration*, XX, 1942, pp. 19–27.

G. D. Feldman, 'The political and social foundations of Germany's economic mobilization, 1914–1916', *Armed Forces and Society*, III, 1976, pp. 121–45.

P. Fraser, 'British war policy and the crisis of Liberalism in May 1915', *Journal of Modern History*, LIV, 1982, pp. 1–26.

P. Fraser, 'The British "Shells Scandal" of 1915', *Canadian Journal of History*, XVIII, 1983, pp. 69–86.

D. French, 'The rise and fall of "Business as Usual"', in K. Burk (ed.), *War and the State. The Transformation of British Government, 1914–1919*, London, 1982, pp. 7–31.

J. S. Galbraith, 'British war aims in World War 1 : a commentary on "Statesmanship"', *Journal of Imperial and Commonwealth History*, XIII, 1984, pp. 25–45.

M. Gowing, 'The organisation of manpower in Britain during the Second World War', *Journal of Contemporary History*, VII, 1972, pp. 147–67.

K. R. Grieves, 'The Liverpool Dock Battalion : military intervention in the Mersey Docks, 1915–1918', *Transactions of the Historic Society of Lancashire and Cheshire*, CXXXI, 1982, pp. 139–58.

K. R. Grieves, 'Military tribunal papers : the case of Leek Local Tribunal in the First World War', *Archives*, XVI, 1983, pp. 145–50.

K. R. Grieves, '"Total war"? : the quest for a British manpower policy, 1917–18', *Journal of Strategic Studies*, IX, 1986, pp. 79–95.

J. Grigg, 'Lloyd George and ministerial leadership in the Great War', in P. H. Liddle (ed.), *Home Fires and Foreign Fields. British Social and Military Experience in the First World War*, London, 1985, pp. 1–8.

R. Harrison, 'The War Emergency Workers' National Committee, 1914–1920', in A. Briggs & J. Saville (eds.), *Essays in Labour History*, London, 1971, II, pp. 211–59.

D. Hopkin, 'Domestic censorship in the First World War', *Journal of Contemporary History*, V, 1970, pp. 151–69.

C. Hughes, 'The New Armies', in I. F. W. Beckett & K. Simpson (eds.), *A Nation in Arms*, Manchester, 1985, pp. 99–125.

G. Ince, 'Mobilisation of Man-Power', *Public Administration*, XXIV, 1946, pp. 3–14.

B. H. Liddell Hart, 'The basic truths of Passchendaele', *Journal of Royal United Service Institution*, CIV, 1959, pp. 433–9.

A. D. Lindsay, 'The organisation of labour in the Army in France during the War and its lessons', *Economic Journal*, XXXIV, 1924, pp. 69–82.

P. A. Lockwood, 'Milner's entry into the War Cabinet, December 1916', *Historical Journal*, VII, 1964, pp. 120–34.

P. Lowe, 'The rise to the premiership, 1914–16', in A. J. P. Taylor (ed.), *Lloyd George : Twelve Essays*, London, 1971, pp. 95–133.

R. Lowe, 'The Ministry of Labour, 1916–19 : a "Still, Small Voice"?', in K. Burk (ed.), *War and the State*, London, 1982, pp. 108–34.

J. McDermott, 'Total war and the Merchant State : aspects of British economic warfare against Germany 1914–16', *Canadian Journal of History*, XXI, 1976, pp. 61–76.

J. M. McEwen, 'The struggle for mastery in Britain : Lloyd George versus Asquith, December 1916', *Journal of British Studies*, XVIII, 1978, pp. 131–56.

J. M. McEwen, 'Northcliffe and Lloyd George at war, 1914–1919', *Historical Journal*, XXIV, 1981, pp. 651–72.

J. M. McEwen, 'The National Press during the First World War : ownership and circulation', *Journal of Contemporary History*, XVII, 1982, pp. 459–86.

J. M. McEwen, ' "Brasshats" and the British Press during the First World War', *Canadian Journal of History*, XVIII, 1983, pp. 43–67.

B. McGill, 'Asquith's predicament, 1914–1918', *Journal of Modern History*, XXXIX, 1967, pp. 283–303.

R. I. McKibbin, 'Arthur Henderson as Labour Leader', *International Review of Social History*, XXIII, 1978, pp. 79–101.

K. O. Morgan, 'Lloyd George's Premiership : a study in "Prime Ministerial Government"', *Historical Journal*, XII, 1970, pp. 130–57.

K. Neilson, 'Kitchener : a reputation refurbished?', *Canadian Journal of History*, XV, 1980, pp. 207–27.

E. O'Halpin, 'H. E. Duke and the Irish administration, 1916–18', *Irish Historical Studies*, XXII, 1981, pp. 362–76.

E. Parsons, 'Why the British reduced the flow of America troops to Europe in August–October 1918', *Canadian Journal of History*, XXII, 1977, pp. 173–91.

J. Schneer, 'The war, the state and the workplace : British dockers during 1914–1918', in J. E. Cronin & J. Schneer (eds.), *Social Conflict and the Political Order in Modern Britain*, London, 1982, pp. 96–112.

P. Simkins, 'Kitchener and the expansion of the army', in I. Beckett & J. Gooch (eds.), *Politicians and Defence. Studies in the formulation of British Defence policy 1845–1970*, Manchester, 1981, pp. 87–109.

K. Simpson, 'The British soldier on the Western Front', in P. H. Liddle (ed.), *Home Fires and Foreign Fields*, London, 1985, pp. 135–58.

N. Stone, 'Organising an economy for war : the Russian shell shortage 1914–17', in G. Best & A. Wheatcroft (eds.), *War, Economy and the Military Mind*, London, 1976, pp. 108–19.

J. O. Stubbs, 'Lord Milner and patriotic labour, 1914–1918', *English Historical Review*, LXXXVII, 1972, pp. 717–54.

R. H. Tawney, 'The abolition of economic controls, 1918–21', *Economic History Review*, XIII, 1943, pp. 1–30.

J. Terraine, 'The military structure of the First World War', *Army Quarterly and Defence Journal*, CXV, 1985, pp. 277–86.

T. Travers, 'The hidden army : structural problems in the British Officer Corps, 1900–1918', *Journal of Contemporary History*, XVII, 1982, pp. 523–44.

T. Travers, 'Learning and decision-making on the Western Front, 1915–1916 : the British example', *Canadian Journal of History*, XVIII, 1983, pp. 87–97.

C. Trebilcock, 'War and the failure of industrial mobilisation : 1899 and 1914', in J. M. Winter (ed.), *War and Economic Development*, Cambridge, 1975, pp. 139–64.

J. Turner, 'State purchase of the liquor trade in the First World War', *Historical Journal*, XXIII, 1980, pp. 589–615.

J. Turner, 'Cabinets, committees and secretariats : the higher direction of war', in K. Burk (ed.), *War and the State*, London, 1982, pp. 57–83.

J. A. Turner, 'The formation of Lloyd George's "Garden Suburb" : "Fabian-Like Milnerite Penetration"?', *Historical Journal*, XX, 1977, pp. 165–84.

C. Veitch, ' "Play up! Play up! and Win the War". Football, the Nation and the First World War 1914–1915', *Journal of Contemporary History*, XX, 1985, pp. 363–78.

B. Waites, 'The government of the Home Front and the "Moral Economy" of the working class', in P. H. Liddle (ed.), *Home Fields and Foreign Fires*, London, 1985, pp. 175–93.

A. J. Ward, 'Lloyd George and the 1918 Irish conscription crisis', *Historical Journal*, XVII, 1974, pp. 107–29.

S. White, 'Soviets in Britain : The Leeds Convention of 1917', *International Review of Social History*, XIX, 1974, pp. 165–93.

N. Whiteside, 'Industrial welfare and labour regulation in Britain at the time of the First World War', *International Review of Social History*, XXV, 1980, pp. 307–31.

M. J. Williams, 'Thirty per cent : a study in casualty statistics', *Journal of Royal United Service Institution*, CIX, 1964, pp. 51–5.

J. M. Winter, 'Britain's "Lost Generation" of the First World War', *Population Studies*, XXXI, 1977, pp. 449–66.

J. M. Winter, 'Military fitness and civilian health in Britain during the First World War', *Journal of Contemporary History*, XV, 1980, pp. 211–44.

D. R. Woodward, 'The origins and intent of David Lloyd George's January 5 war aims speech', *The Historian*, XXXIV, 1971, pp. 22–39.

D. R. Woodward, 'Britain's "Brass-Hats" and the question of a compromise peace, 1916–1918', *Military Affairs*, IV, 1971, pp. 63–8.

D. R. Woodward, 'Did Lloyd George starve the British Army of men prior to the German offensive of 21 March 1918?', *Historical Journal*, XXVII, 1984, pp. 241–52.

C. J. Wrigley, 'The Ministry of Munitions : an innovatory department', in K. Burk (ed.), *War and the State*, London, 1982, pp. 32–56.

10   *Theses*

D. W. French, 'Some aspects of social and economic planning for war in Great Britain, c. 1905–15', Ph.D., University of London, 1978.

K. R. Grieves, 'The British Government's political and administrative response to the man-power problem in the First World War', Ph.D., University of Manchester, 1984.

J. F. Martin, 'The Government and the control of the British coal industry 1914–18', M. Phil., University of Loughborough, 1981.

F. W. Perry, 'Manpower and organisational problems in the expansion of the British and Commonwealth Armies during the 2 World Wars', Ph.D., University of London, 1982.

J. O. Stubbs, 'The Conservative Party and the politics of war, 1914–16', D.Phil., University of Oxford, 1973.

M. I. Thomis, 'The Labour Movement in Great Britain and compulsory Military Service, 1914–16', M. A., University of London, 1959.

C. J. Wrigley, 'Lloyd George and the Labour Movement (With Particular Reference to the years 1914–1922)', Ph.D., University of London, 1973.

11   *Newspapers and Journals*

Daily Telegraph.
Manchester Guardian.
New Statesman.
Punch.
Quarterly Review.
The Round Table.
Spectator.
The Times.
Labour Party Cuttings Collection (Manchester University Library).

12   *Works of reference.*

Burke's Peerage.
Constitutional Year Book.
Dictionary of Business Biography.
Dictionary of Labour Biography.
Dictionary of National Biography.
Dictionary of Welsh Biography Down to 1940.
Liberal Year Book.
Who Was Who.

Index